AT FIRST CLICK

SURVIVING CODEPENDENCY

B. F. Christman

Courage is not having the strength to go on;
it is going on when you don't have the strength.
—Theodore Roosevelt

PAGE PUBLISHING, INC.
Conneaut Lake, PA

First originally published by Page Publishing 2021

ISBN 978-1-6624-3913-1 (pbk)
ISBN 978-1-6624-3914-8 (digital)

Printed in the United States of America

CONTENTS

CHAPTER 1

My Story

I had just returned to Texas from visiting my daughter and her family in Louisiana. One night, I accidentally fell in my living room while moving the coffee table in order to vacuum. I was bending over and was struck with a moment of vertigo as well as my knee giving out from under me, which was just enough to cause me to lose my balance and fall with all the weight of my body landing on the knee I had replaced just a few years earlier. Falling to the right meant contusions and bruises up and down the right side of my body. I was lying there on the floor, not only hurting from the pain I had induced upon myself but also a little dazed and unable to move. I had hit the wooden coffee table and the wooden TV stand on the way down. I began assessing the situation immediately to figure out if I would have the strength to get up, or would I need to crawl and hit the panic button on the alarm for an ambulance to come. I knew I was alone in the house, so there was no chance of someone hearing me. After lying there for a while and trying to move my body, I figured out that it seemed like nothing was actually broken or fractured. For a moment, I remembered how my son was always accusing me of self-diagnosing myself accompanied by a pity party. Thinking of that gave me the motivation I needed to suck it up and take action. Eventually, I was able to help myself using the coffee table and TV stand as firm supports to lift me. I didn't call the doctor or 911, nor did I inform my son of my accident since he was out of town. Because it did take me a while to maneuver my body up from the floor, I decided to rest in order to begin healing quickly. I simply went to bed and tried to sleep it off with a little help from Naproxen.

The days that followed proved to me that I was unable to move easily or go anywhere. Since I was alone in the house for the week and my son would be coming back to town on the weekend, I chose to rest in bed and take some muscle relaxers along with Tylenol to deal with the pain. As my strength began to decline, I was not aware of other visual changes happening to my body, even though I seemed to have little or no energy.

My son came home and asked me how long I had been like this. I said, "Do you mean staying in bed? About three days of not moving much," I answered. He proceeded to tell me that I looked terrible and probably needed to go to the emergency room. I said there's nothing that won't wait until Monday and I can go in and see my primary care doctor if I am not better. That night, I happened to look in the mirror and noticed my left cheek was red, hot, and swollen. This concerned both of us, and again he urged me to go to the emergency room. As usual, I had to show my stubborn streak and tell him I had not had much luck with urgent care or emergency rooms (since they always checked me out and sent me right home), so again I said I would wait till the next day (Monday) and see my primary care doctor. That night, I could not sleep because my left ear, and the left side of my face was a little swollen and on fire. It appeared that I was unable to touch my head on my pillow without feeling a lot of discomfort and pain. Not only was I dealing with the right side of my body being bruised, but it seemed as if the consequences from the fall were busy camouflaging what was really going on with the left side of my face. When I awoke, my left ear was swollen over three times its normal size. I had lost complete hearing in the left ear and felt a pain on the left side. Everything was very sensitive to touch. By now my left cheek was completely red, including the left side of my nose. *How did this happen?* I asked myself. *What is going on?*

Due to all the discomfort, I didn't trust my ability to drive to the doctor, even though I was able to schedule an appointment for eleven o'clock that morning. Because I was feeling so ill and weak, I asked a friend to pick me up and take me. I was growing weaker by the moment and used a cane to help steady me. Immediately upon walking into the doctor's office, he looked at me and told me that even though I might not like it, I needed to go to the emergency room to be admitted to the hospital. (Yes, I could hear my son telling me I told you so over and over in my head.) I thought that there was no way I was bad enough to go to the hospital, let alone be admitted to one. When I arrived, they said I had an acute case of cellulitis. Here again was something I knew nothing about. The odd thing was that I had just talked to my sister the night before, and she mentioned that her husband had to be treated for cellulitis on his left knee following a knee replacement surgery. I knew I was growing weaker and weaker and was in severe pain. I was immediately admitted and started receiving three different antibiotics intravenously. Blood tests were taken at regular and consistent intervals to validate the presumed diagnosis. The infectious disease specialist and ENT were called in to examine me as well as the primary care physician. My white blood cell count (WBC) was over twenty-five thousand, so they knew that it was not in the normal range of four to nine thousand. They would have to get that number down. I was so weak and immediately became a risk for falling since my balance was being challenged when I stood up or walked. I had definitely lost complete hearing in my left ear, which they were concerned about becoming permanent. My eardrum was so swollen and inflamed that the doctor could not see inside my ear. My face began to swell more as each hour passed.

The doctors ordered me to stay in bed, and I was not allowed up or out of bed without supervision and assistance. I was even given help to take a shower each day. Blood continued to be taken and evaluated several times each day and night to monitor the progress of the infection. Meanwhile, my face and head continued to swell more each day and become even more sensitive to touch. My eyes were so swollen it became difficult to see out of them. The disease was visibly spreading over my entire face and had moved to the top and back of my head, as well as down the right side of my face. After three days, my son came to see me to bring an overnight bag that I needed. Because it was early in the morning, I was sleeping and did not see him before he returned to work. It was clear to see I was looking like the female version of the Incredible Hulk. The infection that invaded my body was taking over, and the doctors showed concern about it reaching my brain. I had no idea that it had become a life-or-death situation, but I really got to know my doctors very well, especially my primary care physician. Their dedication and attention to my illness was admirable. Finally, after four days and being closely monitored, the infection began to get under control, and the WBC began to decrease in number.

After receiving excellent care and being checked daily by several doctors, I was consulted about being discharged. There was a question of whether I should be convalescing at home, a rehabilitation facility, or an infusion center to receive the required amount of antibiotics intravenously so that the infection would not reoccur. I knew again no one would be at the house, so I was going home to a place with no one to give me assistance. The doctors consulted with one another and decided I would not receive the antibiotics intravenously since I was going to be alone and had no means of transportation to and from the infusion center, so they prescribed three antibiotics (two to be taken orally). One of those antibiotics was eardrops to kill the inner ear infection that accompanied the cellulitis all week. A friend of my son's picked me up at the hospital and went to my storage unit, where all my assistive devices were being stored that I needed immediately. It was clearly evident that my condition had worsened and that I would need the use of a walker. He also went to the pharmacy to fill my prescriptions and got me set up in the house so I could begin recovery, removing all obstacles that might be in the way of moving safely throughout the house using a walker. During my hospital stay, I had become dehydrated and low in potassium. I needed to address this issue also.

During the past few years, I seemed to have developed an addiction to sweet tea from Chick-fil-A and knew that drinking it would be helpful to hydrate my body and help me recover more quickly in order to help move the infection out of my body. So I requested that he attempt to go get me some to last for the week. He honored my request and traveled to the fast-food restaurant to pick up two gallons of tea for me. My appetite had been lost, but I could keep hydrated as long as I had the sweet tea to drink. I did not want a repeat performance of the dehydration occurring, which developed while I was in the hospital.

My daughter-in-law (who was also out of town) arranged for one of her friends to bring soup and something to eat for me. As the week continued, I could feel myself getting weaker instead of better, but the redness, swollenness, and soreness on my face seemed to be improving and actually decreasing in size. I could slightly hear out of my ear again. I was finding it very difficult to use a walker while trying to carry my drinks or food or other necessary items. Even though I had entered the hospital using just a cane, I became dependent upon the walker to get around and prevent falls. I only had to warm food in the microwave and eat it, which seemed like a small feat for most, but a large feat for me since I was using the walker and had difficulty being strong enough to complete the simplest of tasks. My insurance from Humana arranged for ten complete frozen meals to be delivered and offered to provide assistance with transportation if I should ever need it.

A few days later, I tried to wash my clothes and sheets. That meant walking across a 5,000 square foot house to the laundry room, making several trips. This was the straw that broke the camel's back. I knew I had bitten off more than I could chew. My son texted me to see how I was doing and feeling, and for the first time, I let him know I was really having a rough time. I was very short of breath and had difficulty balancing and walking any distance. I had purposely told him (as well as my daughter) I was doing just fine each day when they inquired because I did not want him to cut his trip short or be worried. To be safe, he contacted the friend who brought the soup and asked her to come and assist me. He came home the next day and once again asked how long I had been feeling like this and asked why I had not contacted him sooner.

The next day, he took me to see my primary care doctor, who once again immediately sent me to the emergency room to be admitted. This time, the symptoms were shortness of breath, chest pain, lightheadedness with a cough, tremors and chills, increase in blood pressure and pulse, weakness and fatigue, coupled with confusion and decreased ability to process information. Every specialist you could name was called in to examine me, including pulmonary, cardiology, neurology, internal, infectious disease, ENT, and physical therapists. My condition had deteriorated. The tests showed I had a probable blood clot present, and my WBC was still elevated over seventeen thousand. Antibiotics were administered once again, along with test after test in each of the specialized areas. I seemed to display all the symptoms of a ministroke, but the tests did not validate the findings. The EEG did validate I had experienced a seizure coupled with infection, which was leading to pneumonia. I spent an additional five days in the hospital this time and was told I would be sent home with vitals being monitored twice a week with physical therapy for the next eight weeks. I would need to see each of these specialists in the next few weeks to follow up on my condition. The x-ray of the lung depicted pneumonia and an unspecified organism. The doctor told me I would take another chest x-ray in four weeks to see if the hernia (sac on the lung) would dissipate. Meanwhile, my symptoms were a result of dyspnea and respiratory abnormalities in addition to deconditioning from the previous infection and hospital stay. I was very weak and needed to build up my strength to be able to function normally once again.

To make a long story short, because of the eight weeks of recovery with physical therapy in the home that followed this hospital stay, I found myself needing something meaningful to do during my recovery. Since I was unable to drive or get out of the house except to visit doctors with assistance each week, this state of affairs made me realize that this was an opportunity and a challenge, a time for me to reflect on the last seven decades of my life. It was time to tell my story.

CHAPTER 2

The Beginning

It was not easy growing up in a family with six kids. I remember how I had to schedule a time to use the one bathroom in our house with four bedrooms. My assigned time was at 5:30 a.m. sharp each morning. If I missed it, I had to wait to use the bathroom at school. We lived only a half mile from the school in the town of Arthurdale, West Virginia, a little town developed in 1934 from the efforts of Eleanor Roosevelt and the New Deal when her husband, Franklin Deleanor Roosevelt, was president. Because we lived so close to the school, we were not provided the option of riding a bus. That privilege was reserved for people who lived farther away. We had to walk to school (approximately a half mile), even when the snow was above our waist. Only after we were old enough for high school (grades ten to twelve) were we finally permitted to ride the bus from Arthurdale to Masontown (about three miles away where the local high school was located).

As I look back now, we didn't get sick or ill very often because we were always out in the weather, experiencing it as though it was our own personal playground. We also were proud recipients of perfect attendance awards each year. We weren't protected like the young children of today. By that, I mean we did as much work outside in the winter as we did in the summer. The temperature was never an issue. We learned to play in the rain, sunshine, and snow, cherishing every moment we got. If we didn't, it was our fault, because it was the only way to use up all the energy built up inside of us during the day. I imagine this is how we built up our immune system to fight off illnesses and be able to attend school without fail.

I was born in Morgantown, West Virginia, a college town located near the little suburb I lived in called Canyon. In Canyon, we had no bathroom as we know it today. We had an outhouse that was cleaned out professionally at regular intervals. We took all our baths in a washtub outside the house. We filled it with rainwater many times because indoor plumbing was a luxury to us that was rarely experienced.

My family moved to Arthurdale (a town of one thousand people) when I was four years old. I remember that because the sign on the front of our house displayed the address of BB-4, our house number and road name. And wouldn't you know that my nickname was BB (spelled Bebe)? I got that name shortly after I was born because my sister (one year older) could not pronounce my real name, and she called me Bebe instead. Now that all the years have passed by, I realize she was not really nicknaming me. She was probably saying BeBe (meaning baby). My family granted her the privilege of nick-naming me, and it stuck for the rest of my life. I also know that I could tell what period in my life that my friends came from by what they called me. If I was called Bebe, I knew that they were from the time in my life when I was growing up. If they called me Beverly, it was a time in my life when I was in college or shortly thereafter during my first marriage. If it was Bev, it was after my first divorce. It's kind of neat to stir up all those fond memories and feelings every once in a while. I think that is why writing my story has become so important to me at this time in my life.

When I began this journey and adventure, I was very cautious and guarded. And as I began to share my story, the walls started coming down one cinder block at a time. I think that it might be God's way of telling me that my trials and tribulations, in addition to all the sorrows and trauma experienced in my life, has finally caught up with me. And that the only way I can survive this life I have chosen to live is to confront the consequences of all my actions and begin the healing process by moving forward. That includes learning how to forgive myself and taking action to forgive others and asking for their forgiveness for anything I have done to harm or hurt them in any way. It is also a time to learn from everything I have been through and figuring out where I go from here. God is giving me the opportunity to do just that.

I was very fortunate to find God early in my life. I was even more fortunate to have the parents of my high school boyfriend reach out and touch me and guide me toward the Lord our God. Some people (including family members) believed I was joining a cult, only because they were unable to understand the peace and happiness that completed me once I accepted Jesus.

The twelfth step to any recovery program is having had a spiritual awakening as a result of all the other steps, we try to carry this message to others and to practice these principles in all areas of our lives. This might not make a lot of sense at this time, but once I was able to complete this journey, it would take on a new meaning. I have always been someone who sets goals and does everything possible to achieve them successfully. The trick is to measure success by God's standards and not by mine or anyone else's. At the time, I believed this was all a part of his plan for me.

Growing up in a little town could be wonderful for some people; for others, it could be a curse. I happen to love small towns and also love enjoying the rural setting of a close-knit community. In a small town, you get to know everyone by their first name, and you become friends with them. In a small town, everyone looks out for each other. And when they do, they do it effortlessly and sincerely. And because of that, you end up building character. Character might be something you don't really think is important when you are a small child, but it becomes very important to you when you grow up and are on your own. To this day, if I were to visit Preston County, West Virginia, most of my friends and family would know who you are talking about when you refer to me as Bebe. This was the time when you developed a good work ethic as part of your character, along with honesty and integrity.

During the years that I grew up, you knew you would never have to keep the door locked, and your friends and neighbors could walk right in and feel at home. And to this day, when I visit my neighbor next to where I grew up, I can still walk into that house unannounced with the door wide open and feel just as welcome to do that today as I did over seventy years ago. When you were sick, you knew a friend or neighbor was going to be by to bring you food, to check on your progress or recovery, and to offer any help they could with the chores you needed done. I learned the hard way that the character building I acquired while I was a child ended up laying the foundation for all my goals and dreams, which would greatly affect my future. I guess as a child, I didn't quite appreciate all the groundwork that our parents and community provided for us. We tend to take it for granted, but as an adult, we realize that it was our parents' value system that was assisting and guiding us to build our own foundation for what would lie ahead in our future. Attending school and church in this small town contributed greatly to building that foundation also. This was the place where your lifelong friends were going to come from. This was the place where your work ethic would be tested and formed.

Having three brothers and two sisters made living in this small town even better because you met six times as many people than you would have met if you had been an only child. Having eight people living in one house with one bathroom and four bedrooms turned out to be more than a challenge. I was one of the lucky ones though.

My mom and dad were very strict parents. They expected you to follow their rules and show respect, be honest, and work hard. That definitely meant no talking back to them, which demonstrated an act of respect toward others at the time. Mom had never gotten her driver's license and many times found that when she was alone taking care of the kids, she was at a strong disadvantage when emergencies would occur. One example was when my younger sister fell out of the upstairs window and broke her leg, she had to get our neighbor to take them to the hospital. Following that incident, Mom worked hard to get her license. And after that, she didn't stop at getting her license. She went to night school to take business courses so she could get a good job to help out with all the expenses. She wanted to set a good example for her children that taught us to work for what we believed, and we would be rewarded in the end. No one knew what would lie ahead for each of the six children and what financial restraints would occur.

I joined the 4-H club as soon as I was eligible. Participating in that and Methodist Youth Fellowship at church each week provided me with a great opportunity to grow—so much in fact that I truly wanted to attend my first 4-H camp at age nine. My father was a coal miner. Before that, he spent every week in Ohio working on the Ohio Turnpike and was unable to spend a lot of time with his family. Becoming a coal miner meant that he could be home with his family on a more consistent basis. But that also meant that he worked night shift and we had to be quiet during the day so he could sleep. It meant that he would constantly face the danger of roofs and walls caving in several hundred feet below the ground, which came with the chance that we could lose him at any time. Knowing that he survived World War II and all the hazards he faced at the time made working in a deep coal mine a simple task to fulfill. It was a danger-ous job, and thank goodness that today, more safety regulations have been instituted so that less injuries and accidents will occur compared to those during the years 1950 to 1970. Since there was no possible way my family could afford to send me to camp, I had to find an alternative solution. I just happened to mention it to my neighbor. They wanted to help me but knew my parents would never allow me to accept money from them. They asked me if I would be willing to work for them each Saturday cleaning house. That's where the work ethic came in to play. Neighbors would observe our family working inside and outside of the home all the time. They knew the kind of work we did. I had never taken money for the work I did, but then again, money was never offered to me, not even an allowance. So I jumped at the chance to earn some money. Cleaning house for a dol-lar an hour really appealed to me, as well as painting baseboards and walls when needed. I realized I could earn enough to pay for camp in just a few weekends if I worked hard for it.

That's where I got my start. Using a brush and a can of comet cleanser, each week, you could drive by and witness me being out-side scrubbing the oilcloth seats on all the kitchen chairs. I then began cleaning houses and painting on weekends and babysitting at fifty cents an hour in the evenings. I was only nine years old, but as the years increased, this type of work continued during the summer months when I did not have to go to school. Neighbors and their families reached out to me. I even found myself playing the role of hairstylist for my mom and several of her friends in the neighborhood. I loved being industrious, not to mention earning enough money to buy my own clothes. It became rewarding for me personally. I also loved being with people and always felt important and appreciated when I helped them out. That was good for building my self-esteem. Of course, I had to work around the schedule at my own house, which meant finishing all the chores of washing, ironing, cleaning, and cooking, plus working in the garden and mowing grass. As I look back on it now, I wonder where I got all that energy and endurance from. My older sister was just as industrious as I was. Only being a year older didn't stifle our relationship. She was a terrific role model for me. We shared a room with our other sister, all three of us sleeping in one double bed. We lived in the day when we were required to wash clothes in the washing machine (wringer type), hang them out to dry on the clothesline outside, and then iron each piece, fold it, and put it away. This included pressing every dishrag, dish towel, sheet, and pillowcase, as well as bath towels and undergarments. We would be ironing clothes into the late hours of the night. That is why I found myself doing my homework very early on many mornings after I made use of my daily appointed time in the bathroom before I walked to school. It was a great time to study for a test and review my notes.

Grade school was good because I got along with all my teachers. I loved going to school, and I loved being with children my own age. And let's face it, I loved to learn, whether it was by the books or part of life experiences. There was something magical happening when you were able to form lasting relationships outside the home. I respected and loved all my teachers. I found myself wanting to learn as much as possible, and I would pride myself on building relationships with teachers and other adults in the system. I was even placed in a split classroom when there were not enough teachers or class size was overcrowded. My split classroom contained six fifth-graders in a room full of sixth-grade students. Yes, that meant I was in the same room as my older sister, and both of us were being taught by the same teacher. Maybe that is why I always felt closer to her. I'm not sure, but it seemed like we shared more of the same goals together, understood each other better, and appreciated our special relationship of trusting one another and sharing those special thoughts and secrets. She was a peacemaker, and I just wanted to please others. It wasn't as if I didn't like my younger sister, but somehow we never saw eye to eye, and we were always getting into disagreements or arguments—arguments that usually resulted in me getting injured or hurt. She was different from me in that she spoke her mind and didn't worry what others thought or said about her. Not too many people, as I recall, had the luxury of getting along with her or even demonstrating a difference of opinion without being told about it. She might not have been goal-oriented as I was, but she knew how to make the most out of each day. Did I mention her nickname was Butch?

While I attended junior high and high school, I was given permission to attend all the dances. They were held in the gym of the school, which also served the local elementary school I had attended. I asked my mother to chaperone, which she agreed to do regularly. I was also a cheerleader and took advantage of all the many opportunities to show leadership by joining as many organizations as possible. I seemed to thrive on a busy schedule. The more I was involved, the more I wanted to do. This was such a challenge for me to balance school academics with extracurricular activities and yet never neglect my responsibilities and duties at home. In our free time, we would be imaginative and creative by playing games, building tents, or painting old chicken coups or pigpens when needed and making them into beautiful playhouses for us and our friends. We even hung curtains to make it seem real for us.

School actually passed by quickly. I attended grades one through nine in the same town that I lived in—Arthurdale. We even had a ninth-grade graduation ceremony. After finishing ninth grade, I (along with all my classmates) was bused to Masontown to attend grades ten through twelve. I seemed to always have a boyfriend and enjoyed many of those relationships. In fact, I could almost say I had more boy friends than I did girl friends. In junior high, my boyfriends needed to know how to dance as a prerequisite. I absolutely loved to dance and be active in sports or other activities. That allowed us to share experiences that we both enjoyed together. I loved that kids from other towns could attend my junior high school, so I could broaden my horizons. And to have friends from church who attended school with me added a whole new dimension to my life. Most of them were in a band, however, and I wasn't. They were able to share a different kind of comradery than I did. But it didn't seem to keep us apart. I found myself becoming closer and closer to those that attended both than to those who I did not share the love of God with. And then to have those special friends attend the dances held at the junior high, sharing other things that I loved and did, really helped me develop and form relationships that would last forever.

Even though I did have boyfriends in junior high (whom my parents knew about), my first real date was when I was a freshman (age fourteen). He was a senior who invited me to the spring dance at the high school. We had met at 4-H camp. He picked me up at eight thirty, the dance began at nine, and my father told him to have me home by ten. He actually complied with those orders. It was only thirty years later that I found out my date actually went back to enjoy more of the dance that night. My dad felt that anyone who wanted to date me must earn that privilege. He had them carry twenty buckets of coal from the barn to the house before they could take me out. This proved their worthiness and seriousness of intent. I remember how afraid I was that I might be pregnant because he kissed me. I laugh now because I was so naïve at that age and had so much to learn!

In high school, I found that we tend to not appreciate the experiences we share with our friends enough that the years slip by faster than we want them to, and then before you know it, you are attending college and have moved away from the area. I loved being a cheerleader and involved in all the activities that a high school has to offer, such as Girls Athletic Association, Yearbook, Christian Fellowship, School Newspaper, FHA, National Honor Society, Thespians, just to name a few. My senior year, I became class president. This along with being named Miss Personality at the senior prom that year gave me memories to cherish forever. It felt so good to know I belonged. I'm not sure if I ever had that feeling living in my own home. I guess I felt more like the black sheep in the family. My goals included going to college, and my parents were not too happy about that. Their plans for me included working in a bank in a nearby town, and that meant a paycheck would be coming regularly each month and I would have something to contribute to the family and live on. They somehow could not visualize me being successful in my own right if I attended college; it was as if it was a foreign subject not to be talked about. As I completed my college applications, I felt as though I were sneaking around behind their backs to do something I knew in my heart was right for me.

Because I was goal-oriented, I usually held an office in most organizations. I found that doing this did not help me with my brothers and sisters who liked and almost enjoyed giving me a rough time by bullying me and beating up on me. I was the goody sister who chose to turn the other cheek if they chose to hit the first cheek. I thought spreading a little bit of kindness would help them to discontinue their normal actions of abuse. No matter how many times I talked to my mother and father about it, wanting it to change, my parents never did anything to stop it. It was almost as if they encouraged it instead. They wanted me to build some backbone and learn to deal with my own problems. And if you were to ask my siblings now, they would tell you that I instigated their actions by performing the hand movements from *The Three Stooges* to agitate them. From day one, I was told that I was fat. I hated being told that over and over and made fun of all the time. At the time though, I felt unimportant and not worthy of being treated with respect. I even told myself I deserved what I was getting because I was not perfect or didn't do anything good enough or at least the way they wanted me to do it. They felt that the action I served by turning the other cheek was not only stupid but seemed to egg my brothers and sisters on to do even more needling and picking on me. On the rare occasion that I might strike back, I was punished twice as much, and I learned that striking back never solved anything. I had better results with walking away or continuing to receive the abuse without consequence. My brothers and sisters hated it when I would make the arm gesture mimicking Curly (*The Three Stooges*) each time they would hurt me or bully me. At the time, it was the only defense I could think of and actually thought their actions were just a form of discipline that my parents used to keep their kids under control. I was trying to add laughter to the situation, but they saw it as doing something to irritate them, so I was punished even more. I believed, at the time, that I must have deserved it. But I did not like going to physical education class and wearing shorts, which allowed others to see the red and blue welt marks from being punished with a pussy willow tree branch or belt used by my parents. Life was not a picnic, but my grandmother used to tell me that my parents were simply building character in their children and I was better for it. I received no sympathy there. I came to believe this type of discipline was very normal. It was the other kids who had abnormal lives without this kind of discipline, and I believed that they were the ones who were weird. As I became very close to my neighbors, I was able to see that they never used violence or hitting or spanking to discipline their children. I only witnessed love. My older sister once apologized for calling me fat because she says as she looks back now at the pictures of me in high school, I was actually normal looking with a few curves. I think I was a solid size twelve and was able to trade prom dresses with my best friends so each of us didn't have to buy a new one. Yet my sister, my family, and my friends all made me feel like a blimp, and that is how I saw myself and would continue to see myself as an adult. When I looked in the mirror, whether I'd lost or gained weight, I still saw that image they projected on me back in high school. And it was not an image that was accepted, but ridiculed instead.

I loved learning new things, and I loved going to places I had never been before. I also loved going on dates, especially when they included adventure and discovery. I remember my first love and how great it felt. I happened to fall in love with his parents just as much as I fell in love with him. It was devastating when we both decided to go our separate ways during our first year of college. I cried and cried for many nights because I felt so alone. No one should have to feel that kind of heartache. But as time goes on, you learn how to adjust by putting your time, skills, and actions into something else, which would take your mind off the relationship you thought you would have forever.

It was hard to watch my mom and dad argue. But as much as I hated it, it gave me more motivation to find that special someone in my life who would love me unconditionally and not spend our time together fighting. Maybe that is why I hated losing my first love so much. I always felt good and appreciated when I was with him. Sometimes with Mom and Dad, there were threats and violence. But that is how my mom and dad communicated. The odd part is that all the fights they had, verbal, emotional, and physical, turned out to be a way for them to release a lot of stress and eventually participate in makeup sex. They used to tell us that each child was conceived when they had the makeup sex. I remember one time when mom had nothing on but a slip and her underwear. This was because her dress had been ripped off of her body while they were fighting. I watched my mother take a swing at my father while holding a poker in her hand. She actually missed and then ran out the door into the front yard, which was covered with a couple feet of snow. She also had left with no shoes or boots on her feet. These are memories you can't erase from your mind. Yelling, screaming, and hitting one another without showing any remorse was a common thing to witness in our house. But maybe now I understand why my brothers and sisters treated me the way they did. They were only learning how to treat others by watching their parents who played the part of role models for them. We learned very early that a physical fight would end up with someone being a winner and someone being a loser. I can't recall ever hearing the words "I'm sorry" from either one of them, let alone the words "I love you." I even remember when mom would be screaming at us. The phone would ring, and she would answer it in this sweet, soft, and sexy voice, saying, "Hello" right in the middle of yelling at us kids. I knew that witnessing all of this interaction motivated me even more to make something of myself and find a way to get away from this house of doom and crazy behavior.

One of my best memories I had was when I took a trip with some of my closest friends from church and high school members of the Christian Fellowship Club to Pittsburg, Pennsylvania, to see and hear a well-known evangelist, Kathryn Kuhlman. Up until this moment, I considered myself a Christian and a girl who loved God and put him first in her life. But I was reborn the night I heard Kathryn. That night changed me, and I found my soul and God's love within myself. No one can understand how you feel about God unless that person has accepted God as their savior. Even though I thought I always had an optimistic outlook on life, I realized that night that it was God who was responsible for allowing me to feel good and appreciate everything I had in life and see all the good in that.

My high school counselor was someone I looked up to. She also taught history class. I was so enamored by what she did that my hope and prayer was to become a school counselor someday so that I could help others the way she was helping me. She inspired me. It didn't hurt that I loved her son at the same time. And if that didn't work out, I would always have a special place in my heart for her and her husband. They treated me with respect and made me feel loved always. I felt closer to her than I did my own mother. My mother seemed to be closer to my older sister, and I felt that she simply did not have the time and desire to spend quality time with me. Did that bother me? Of course, it did. I was always looking for signs of approval, and trying to please her did not come easily for me.

The good thing that came from all this was that other support groups of people became very important to me and encouraged me even more to continue my education and follow my dream. I met some lifelong friends while staying in an apartment and working my way through college. I also met friends from all over when I competed in 4-H activities. These friends were never privy to my life at home. They had no idea about what I faced each day. And all I wanted, all I ever hoped and wished for, was any sign of love, a hug, a squeeze, and a kiss, anything that would let me know that someone cared. Mom supported myself and my sisters when we were cheerleaders for our school by driving us to games. Back then, cheerleaders were not allowed to ride on the bus with the football or basketball players. Even though that has changed now, back then, it was the rule we lived by. Any time we achieved something related to sports my parents seemed to be proud.

When I left the house and that little town to go to college, no one congratulated me. I knew when I made honor girl from our high school, sponsored by our local newspaper, my mom was proud. Dad, well, I don't think he really cared too much or even knew about the activities that I was involved in. I had to get a job to make it or impress him in any way. I always wanted them to be proud of me, no matter what I did. But it seemed like it was never good enough. Mom and Dad were not going to pay my tuition. They made that very clear, especially when I turned down the job of working in a local bank after graduation. I even tried to pledge a sorority. When I visited the sorority house and realized there was a financial obligation and also a silent requirement of approved dress, I knew I was in the wrong place. I quietly slipped away in my homemade checked tent dress, one that was definitely not acceptable to wear by sorority sister standards. My older sister was kind enough to let me share an apartment with her during my second year of college, and she paid the entire rent each month. I will never forget both the emotional and financial support she gave me at that time. Tuition for college had to be paid by me. I had worked in the summer at a local hotel cleaning rooms to provide me enough money to pay my tuition my freshman year. Supposedly, Dad made too much working in the coal mines for me to qualify for financial assistance. At least, I was told that, and my parents refused to complete the forms that were needed. One day, I walked into the office for work study applicants. It was fate that at the very same time, the Assistant Athletic Director walked in. He had come to find a qualified applicant to fulfill the position of office assistant for him in his office. When he heard I would not qualify for work study, he volunteered to give me a chance, a chance to prove myself. I received many perks on the job, like good fifty-yard line tickets (which my family seemed to love) and a chance to meet all of the football and basketball players for West Virginia University. We had three years together, and at the end of those three years, I was offered a job working in the athletic department full time. Without that part-time job, without that person believing in me, I would not have been able to complete my college education. But to give up what I had worked for (becoming a public-school teacher/counselor) would have worked against me instead of for me. I will always be grateful for the experience and the opportunity to work in such a prestigious athletic department. What I learned there and from the relationships developed would always be part of memories I cherish. And because of that wonderful opportunity, I was able to pay for the apartment I lived in that I had previously shared with my sister before she got married. If it were not for that one special job, I would not have met the person I fell in love with and eventually married. I lived in that two-bedroom apartment during my entire stay at WVU. If I wasn't working, I was studying. So meeting the boy that lived downstairs was obviously meant to be.

Attending West Virginia University in Morgantown for four years provided me a foundation and a background to face what would lie ahead. I received my bachelor's degree in home economics with a minor in biological science. My special someone lived in the apartment below me, and I became friends with both him and his roommate. We had a lot in common. He was my best friend, and we could spend hours and hours talking with each other. Because of that, it took no time to fall in love, yet neither of us were ready to admit it. In fact, it was even hard for us to admit we were actually dating because we were so caught up in each other's world and wanting to share little bits of our lives. It was very clear early on that our families were quite different from each other. He had only two siblings, and I had five. His were very quiet and cautious; mine were loud and unpredictable. I remember when my dad came to visit and found out I had had a boy in my apartment. He told me I was no longer a daughter of his and I would never receive any money from him to go to college. Believe it or not, this act made me want to succeed even more in whatever I did.

Even though I was very outgoing, it was quite a surprise when I came home and announced my engagement to someone who was quite shy and more of a loner. He was from Charleston, West Virginia, and aspired to become a veterinarian. We planned to get married as soon as I graduated in 1969. I was feeling on top of the world.

CHAPTER 3

Is the First Time Forever?

I woke up feeling both excited and yet anxious at the same time. I looked out the window, and the day was perfect. This is a day I would remember for the rest of my life. I made the wedding gown myself (which took me a few weeks), and I sewed a six-foot train attached to the waist that could be detached during the reception, because I so wanted to have a train like Princess Diane. Watching her wedding on TV inspired me enough to wish hard enough to make that dream come true. I wanted to feel like a princess today. And it was going to happen exactly at 10:30 a.m. in the church I grew up in, the church that made possible my very strong and secure relationship with God, the church that allowed me to forge ahead with forever lasting friendships with high school classmates and their families. This was the same church that rewarded me with pins for perfect attendance in Sunday school for thirteen years straight.

As I gathered everything that I needed to go into my suitcase, I looked around the room and realized that I would never be the same person again when I came back to this house. I would be a married woman the next time I stepped into this room, the bedroom that previously occupied my older brother and later my older sister. The room that I would come back to stay as a married woman. This is the house I grew up in. where I learned how to take care of myself as well as others. Cooking and sewing my own clothes came naturally. And it really helped that I joined the local 4-H Club to heighten my skills as well as high school home economics. This was the place where

I learned what being part of the family was like, for better or for worse (and yes, I had quite of few of those memories), the house that provided me security during my formative years and motivation to change my life for the better when faced with challenges and adversities that would possibly make others give up, but would make me see or fathom what I wanted for myself was even possible.

My dad had never been an active part of my life, so I wasn't sure if he was going to show up to walk me down the aisle or not. This was something new for him. He had two other married daughters (my sisters, of course) but had not assumed that role of walking them down the aisle. My younger sister eloped before her husband-to-be had gone off to Vietnam. My older sister had an intimate little ceremony at the local church in a nearby town with only part of the immediate family attending. I had the honor of being her maid of honor. I loved her for including me in her wedding and providing me a memory I will never forget.

My wedding, on the other hand, had been in the planning stage for months. I was special, or so I thought. I wanted to do everything just right. And that's why I followed the wedding guide found in all the bridal magazines as close as possible. I wanted to marry my best friend and confidant because I loved him and he loved me. I was his first love. And I absolutely fell in love with his family. I even felt closer to his mother than I did my own. She was wonderful. She also played the piano at church, which I loved to listen to. And most of all, she respected me and gave me value. I just needed to finish my student teaching, get my bachelor's degree, and make my dream of becoming a teacher a reality. The only problem was that there was no job available in my certified area of home economics or biological sciences seven to twelve in the town we planned to reside. My husband-to-be needed to stay in that town in order to attend the university there and obtain a master's degree in preparation for entering veterinarian school. He had applied once and was rejected, so he decided to work on his masters and then reapply. I had my interview in nearby Preston County and was immediately offered a job. I had signed the contract. I knew there would be a monthly check given to me at least for the next year. I was going to be a second-grade teacher at the very elementary school I had attended. My neighbor helped tremendously in recommending me for the job. He knew me well and watched me grow up. He knew I was a woman of character and possessed a good work ethic. I was very lucky that he was in charge of personnel and worked in the central office at the local board of education. Someone always told me it was not what you know but who you know to achieve success. I guess that slogan came in handy for me this one time. Even though I didn't have an elementary teaching certificate, I loved children. My degree in home economics provided me the training for early childhood programs. So not only did he arrange for me to be an elementary teacher in the fall, but he also offered me a position as a parent-teacher coordinator/nutritionist for the summer head start program. This meant that I would begin my career in education as soon as I returned from my honeymoon. I was so excited, not to mention that I would begin to receive a paycheck immediately! Life is good.

We needed every bit of salary we could get since my future husband was still a student at West Virginia University and would be there for one more year, not to mention we would have to save money to put him through veterinarian school, and that would be a good investment for us. My life was going to be perfect. I was totally in love. We had a place to live (a lovely one-bedroom apartment located downtown in the upstairs of an elderly woman's house) that cost only sixty-five dollars a month, and I had a job. My husband to be was applying for veterinarian school in Ohio and the plan was for me to work for a few years until he obtained his doctorate degree, and we would live a fabulous life. Luckily, we only had to pay instate tuition since Ohio State had an agreement with West Virginia to accept 120 students, each one not responsible for out of state tuition, but paying instate tuition for four years. Immediately following his graduation from veterinarian school, we would start a family. That was our plan.

Everything was perfect. Nothing could go wrong now. I was his very first love, and he was the love that I longed for. He was Presbyterian, and I was Methodist, but we were both Christians and knew that our marriage was meant to be. Together we made a good team, and together we could accomplish anything.

The wedding was a success and very memorable. Over one hundred people attended and later joined us for a nice brunch reception in the church educational building. When everyone finished eating, some gifts were opened, and then the bride and groom needed to get on the road to reach the honeymoon destination on the Skyline Drive in the beautiful Blue Ridge Mountains of Virginia. With a quick stop off at my house to say goodbye to my family, I accidentally discovered they were planning an additional reception of their own for my side of the family, which included alcohol. Why was that a surprise to me, just because I didn't drink alcohol and had none at the reception? Because no one let me know that everyone was invited over to the house after the wedding. I was pleased that the celebration of two people in love and tying the knot could continue at my homeplace. But that wasn't my concern at the moment. I was on cloud nine because I was officially married to the man that I loved, and we were on our way to seal the relationship and union forever. If my family could continue their celebration and enjoy it, more power to them.

The honeymoon was wonderful. That is, if you cancel out the fact that after we arrived, it was too late for the lodge to serve dinner, and we had our first meal out of vending machines. Did we let that bother us? Of course not. We were both feeling new and ready for us to take the journey of a lifetime, a journey that would define who we were, who we are and who we would be. We both felt good about what we had done with our lives and how we planned to spend our future.

Even though that future meant I would have to work while my new and very intelligent husband went to school, in the long-term. everything would pay off for us. I was very proud to be the bride of a doctor-to-be. Anyone would be. And as each year went by, he worked hard toward his goal of being educated, but he never wavered about how important family and marriage were to him. I admired him for that and found myself falling even more in love with him than I was the day I married him.

Like most plans, some kinks had to be worked out. After getting turned down to veterinarian school the first year, my hubby set up a second interview for the following year. This time, I accompanied him and was privileged to meet those who interviewed him. They felt that because he had a more than stable home life and demonstrated more maturity than in the past, he would definitely be a good candidate for veterinarian school. Obtaining a master's degree did not hurt any of his chances also. Ohio State only accepted 120 students from West Virginia, and he was fortunate enough to be one of them that year.

This meant that I had to go job hunting again, but this time, it would definitely be in my certified area. There we were, one year later, moving to Ohio. Once again, we found a cute little apartment (upstairs over an office building) that we could afford, located about a half hour away from my husband's school. After receiving two or three job offers, there was one that stood out to me. It actually seemed perfect, teaching home economics in a high school out in a rural country area, and I would start July 1. It looked like my dream job, but it meant that we had to speed up our plans. It also meant that I had to drive one hour each way every day. I would be part of a two-teacher team in the department and allowed to focus on my areas of expertise while the other teacher focused on hers. I loved the job, and I loved my coworkers. Once again, God had worked his magic. While hubby lived with my parents during the summer so he could finish his master's degree in West Virginia, I went ahead and moved to Ohio and lived by myself till he could join me. Life was good.

We were a team, and even though we lived on a very small salary that I received for teaching (only five thousand a year), we somehow managed to make our lives very comfortable and livable. We relied on each other, and that was a good feeling to have. During the following summer, we even worked at a school that taught canines to be guides for blind students. Hubby was the teacher, and I acted as cook for the facility. We both enjoyed being part of service dog training. Yes, we struggled at times, but we learned how to live on a shoestring budget. We were so much in love. We were even fortunate enough to make friends with other married couples who attended Ohio State University Veterinarian School. After a year or so, it wasn't long before we realized that I was pregnant with our first child. She was born in 1972 and the most precious-looking baby ever. She was perfect in every way. No one could ask for more. She became a part of our lives and interweaved with us in our unpredictable lifestyle very easily. It was never a chore to have her around. I was able to find a babysitter in the town where I worked so she could remain very close to me if I were needed. When she turned two, it was time for Daddy to graduate and all of us to move again. We chose to make our new home in the state of Almost Heaven, West Virginia, where both of us were born. My mother and brother came to Ohio and picked up our little girl and took her back to West Virginia to watch her so that our move and search for a job could be easier on us.

At the time, it felt pretty good to start a new veterinary business in Elkins, West Virginia. We had researched the whole state of West Virginia and found that Elkins was another rural community but only a few miles away from an interstate, which made traveling easier for those on the road. It was a town of growth and only had one veterinarian, so we decided to begin our lives once again in this very industrious and beautiful town. My husband and I worked hard. We were a team, and it felt good to work together. We had no money saved up and had nothing to our name when we left Columbus, Ohio. However, it seemed like all stars were aligned because one by one, every last detail was executed by a power greater than ours.

When my hubby worked, he had the ability to be kind and passionate about his work. He related well with clients. He loved working with animals, and he loved the process of getting to know residents in the town we lived. The magic appeared when he communicated with others. He never once made you feel as if he were better than you. He was a common man who shared common goals and values. There was mutual respect established immediately, whether it was with his wife, his family, his friends, or his clients. This meant that we found a place where we could capture the happiness that we finally deserved. Our vision of a good life and family was now within reach. And the wonderful church family we discovered did not hurt us either.

We were beginning a new life, one that would shape our entire future. We were part of a new community now.

CHAPTER 4

Trouble in Paradise

Before long, all the stars were aligned, and we found ourselves opening a veterinarian practice in West Virginia, right in the heart of heaven, surrounded by beautiful mountains and landscapes. This time, we were able to rent a house just like the one I grew up in and rent an office space to begin our practice. Eleanor Roosevelt was responsible for developing the town of Arthurdale, West Virginia, as well as East Dailey, West Virginia. So moving to this little town was a little like moving home again. The house was surrounded by a few acres, just like my home in Arthurdale. Eleanor made sure each homesite was made up of three- to five-acre lots. The air was clean, and the valley was welcoming.

We did everything as a couple and a team. I was the receptionist, the bookkeeper, the vet technician as well as the janitor and surgery assistant. He was the doctor and the surgeon. I enjoyed learning so much about the practice, and my husband was truly dedicated and demonstrated a deep passion toward helping all his clients. He even decided to take care of both large and small animals, which turned out to be very good for the community. When we attended church in West Virginia and Ohio, we attended the Methodist Church. This time, we found a wonderful Presbyterian Church, which became a good foundation for our lives and community for us and our family. Once again, life was good.

Borrowing money in a strange town we knew would be difficult and quite a feat for a new graduate from veterinarian school. But as we visited each bank, it became clear to us that getting a loan to start a business was going to be harder than we thought. We wanted them to know that we were here to stay and we would contribute to this small community for years to come in a town we could call our home. Finally, the president of one bank had graduated from Ohio State University, so we were able to develop a connection with one another immediately. He was willing to gamble on a fellow alumnus. That was music to our ears. We had to have a loan to be able to open up a new practice and to purchase all the equipment needed for the practice in order to get it up and running and make it prosperous.

Before the first year was up, we had our second child. I had a difficult pregnancy and had to quit working at the clinic to concentrate on delivering a healthy child. The baby was pressing on my spinal cord and caused me to pass out spontaneously. We had to hire someone to work in my place at the clinic. My little girl learned not to panic when I passed out, and she simply put a pillow under my head and lay down beside me until I came to. She was such a brave little girl at the age of two and such a blessing to us. A few months later, I delivered a little boy who had the energy of a choo-choo train, who warmed up slowly, but once he got started, there was no slowing him down. He loved life, and life loved him. He had such a thirst for knowledge. He even got the nickname of Curious George because he would get into so much trouble all the time. Surprisingly, he got along very well with everyone, and the older he became, the more diverse his topics would be. He was sometimes challenged to talk with adults, and he could carry his weight on any subject. He was easygoing, just like his father, and never carried a grudge. He constantly maintained a healthy relationship with family and friends, including his sister, and she felt it was totally her responsibility to teach him everything she knew. Playing the role of teacher was her main objective, and he didn't seem to mind. I was so proud to be a mother to both of them, but then who wouldn't be? We felt so blessed to have our family and knew that God had totally answered our prayers.

All was well when we bought our first home together and enjoyed spending time in the woods nearby and experiencing the freedom of the countryside. For the first time in our marriage, we planted a garden. Taking care of it was a challenge during the pregnancy, but we made it happen and harvested many vegetables from it, enough to last us all winter. Money was tight the first year of opening the practice, but we were in this for the long haul, so we knew all the hard work and labor would be worth it in the end. When I assisted my husband with night calls from clients, the kids went with us and got to spend time in the waiting room, watching us take care of the emergencies and/or surgeries that would arrive or need to be taken care of in the middle of the night. There was no doubt that God had been very good to all of us. Every day was a gift. It was so clear that God and family came before our career and work.

For a while, everything seemed perfect. We had our love, our first house, two wonderful children (one boy and one girl), and a business that was thriving. I then played the role of hubby's designer of a new veterinarian office that we were purchasing for our family's future. As we designed and started to build our first clinic together, once again, it was a team effort. We decided that it had been in our best interest to hire some help for him so I could spend more time being a mother and supervising the building of the new clinic. It was working out well, and we were both good at collaborating.

Everything was good for us. He had long hours from 7:00 a.m. to 7:00 p.m., but he always took Wednesdays off and made it our family day. We would travel with him the first year to Clarksburg every Wednesday so he could meet his final requirement of practicing with a small animal veterinarian before obtaining his West Virginia state license for independent practice. He also was mentored by a large animal veterinarian located in Elkins as well. We absolutely loved spending time together as a family and made sure our special days always provided a new and wonderful memory for us. Our bond continued to grow, and I felt nothing could break us apart.

I loved being a wife and a mother, and we loved being parents. I don't think there was ever a day that I regretted one ounce of being either one. I was so determined to live a life that not only provided love and nourishment to my inner being, but I loved sharing the passion I had for these roles with those whom I came in contact with.

There were so many times that the children would do something that made my day. They were such happy children, and they certainly loved their mom and dad. It was always nice to put work aside and just be a family in the evening and on weekends.

One day, I was visiting our new office after we completed all renovations, and a client walked in. He smiled as he greeted my husband and said, "Doc, I always get mixed up. Which one of these ladies is your wife?" I turned around and felt kind of stymied by the question but became even more interested in my husband's response. He said, "I guess it's hard to tell since I spend as much time with one as I do with the other." Did I think this threw up a red flag to me? Absolutely not at the time, since I had personally hired our receptionist/assistant. Not to mention that the only reason I hired her was to help out while we prepared the new building to be a clinic that would last a lifetime and provide us a future forever. Yet as I listened to my husband's answer, I did not seem to find the humor in it as everyone else did.

Then on one Saturday afternoon, he never came home, and he never called after working till noon at our veterinary clinic. The kids (who were age two and five at the time) and I had stopped in to see him that morning and volunteered to pick up the mail for him. He basically told us not to do that because he would be going to the mailbox later himself, but we decided to pick it up anyway since the kids always knew that we would make a trip to the donut shop (a special place Daddy liked to stop and eat after finishing office hours on Saturday) if we did. But that particular day, Daddy did not come to the donut shop to join us. He did not come home either, and he did not call. Since this was in the day of no cell phones, after several hours of not hearing from him, I tried calling the office. We had a private line in, which we used only to talk to each other or family. That way, neither of us ever felt a threat of not being able to reach one another if needed. I had no idea that morning would be the last time we would talk to him or see him playing the role of a father and husband. We had no idea that it would be the last time our children saw us together as a family. We had no idea that the receptionist/assistant we hired would eventually become the children's stepmother. We had no idea what was really happening or going on in that mind of his. The truth of the matter was that we hardly ever argued and were always able to talk things out if we disagreed on something.

Trying to track him down and find out what was going on became almost impossible. I finally called his parents later that evening, who lived about four hours away in Charleston, West Virginia, and they told me he was there. Even on that day of remembrance, he chose to tell his parents of his decision before he told us. Explaining the situation to my children was one of the hardest things I ever had to do. Realizing that we were going to be alone, I packed up the kids and got on the road to visit my family. I needed to be around someone who could support me and make me feel like my world was not coming to an end. I needed my children to be loved and feel part of a family till I could emotionally and rationally accept what was happening to us.

Access to all checking, savings, and credit card accounts along with visible cash was taken away from me. In a split second, our life as we knew it had disappeared. We had no access to any funds to buy a loaf of bread or a gallon of milk. Why had I sacrificed nine and one-half years of my life helping him to achieve what I thought was our dream only to have him walk out on me after we were able to make that dream happen? I was totally committed to him, and to this day, I have never gotten an answer to that question. Our pastor made several attempts to bring him in for counseling with me to find a resolution to our problems or at least discover why and how all of this had happened. I was very active in our church as a volunteer and also a member of the bell choir and Sunday school. He was a respected member and supporter of the church, and yet he refused the pastor's request time and time again. That meant he and I had no decent or meaningful conversation or communication with one another after that Saturday. It was beginning to look like our marriage was over, yet being angry with him for walking out on us was never a part of my thinking. I truly believed that he would realize what a mistake he had made and would walk through the door at any moment. Accepting his decision to walk out on us and file for divorce was not only difficult, but it was so foreign to me. I was so emotionally affected that I could not even attend the hearing at the courthouse and was housed in a room nearby. I was told that it was said at the hearing that I would not let him smoke in the house (our son had asthma), nor would he get freshly made meals when he walked through the door at 7:30 p.m. (both children had to be fed much earlier in order to prepare for bed). The same meal I made for the children was later warmed up for him. Yes, these statements were true, but were they worth ending a marriage for? Because he chose not to talk to me after that day, I never knew the real reason our marriage was terminated and probably never will. Yet I believed if the children and I were to go visit his brother in California, that would give him time to rethink everything. It did not happen that way. The employee in question was married. Her husband had called the house several times telling me that she was having an affair with my husband. I didn't believe him, of course, because I trusted my husband and knew he would never betray me. I even shared with him that I was receiving the calls from her husband.

When the divorce papers were delivered and taped to the back door of the house on the day our daughter graduated from kindergarten, not only was it a shock, but it was also a great disappointment. Why couldn't he tell us in person? Why would he leave us without giving us any notice? My kids to this day still remind me, "He didn't leave us, Mommy. He left you." It was true that their statement was technically correct. I can't disagree with them. But that day, my whole life changed. In fact, all our lives changed forever, both theirs and mine.

And yes, I have learned to accept that a better life for all of us had to be in the works, and eventually I would learn to forgive him. But that forgiveness did not come easily or quickly. I found out painstakingly that life does goes on. I learned very quickly that you can't become a victim; you must become a survivor. But at the time, all I could think of was how I must have failed in some way or he would never have left. What was it that I didn't do right to cause this man to walk out on me without a word?

I would be remiss if I didn't take time to share how easily I fell literally to the bottom of the barrel—physically, spiritually, emotionally, and mentally. It had been three months since I was served the papers for divorce. Wednesdays were still family day, and since our youngest child was not in school yet, he continued to see them every Wednesday to spend quality time with them. Our first child spent time with him after school was out on those days, but of course, during summer break, he had them both all day. My mother was kind enough to give us some petty cash to buy groceries till something could be done. Because he did not give us any access to money to live on and had emptied all our bank accounts, I had to do something to make him provide us some funds to maintain a standard of living until the divorce was final. On the advice of my lawyer, I actually kept the kids from seeing him on Wednesdays until he finally agreed with my lawyer that he would give us a couple hundred a month to oversee and fulfill the basic needs of the two children we shared. He would also make house payments until the divorce was final. The very word divorce sent chills through me. I wasn't sure what this meant to my future and to my children's future. To this day, I have never received an answer to tell me why he left us on that Saturday.

One Wednesday, when the kids were visiting their father, I couldn't take the loneliness. The pain of being without the man I adored and loved would not go away. I could not accept the fact that there was no chance of us getting back together and that he and I would never have a civil conversation together ever again. I couldn't take the feeling of not being good enough for him. I couldn't accept the fact that our wedding vows would be broken and that this union we had committed to would not be forever. He was suing for total custody of my two beautiful and wonderful children, the very miracles that the two of us together had put on this earth. He was taking my identity, he was taking my self-worth, and now he wanted to take my children. What did I have to live for? Yes, I was at the lowest point in my life. Why would God let this happen to me? Why would he allow me to feel this much pain?

I started losing weight because I had no appetite. I was constantly crying and spinning my wheels. Acute depression seemed to take over my mind and body. The experience I am about to share will make some of you wonder if what I am telling you is real. But believe me, divine intervention is definitely real.

I found some Percocet pain pills in the medicine cabinet left over from recent knee surgery my husband had during the last year we lived together in the same house. For a delicate moment, I gave up on myself. I gave up on life. I wanted to end the pain I was feeling that was controlling every breath that came from my body. I had already lost over seventy pounds, and I prayed to God to give me the strength to do what he thought I should do and prayed that I was doing the right thing. I believed that the children would be better off without me simply because I could not focus on being a good mother right now. And I could not imagine them living with their father full-time and myself only getting visits with them after having them full-time during the past two years. I couldn't envision how their lives would change forever not having their mother in their lives on a daily basis.

I took that medicine bottle and poured all the pain pills into the palm of my hand. I got a glass of water to wash it down as I threw them all to the back of my throat. I swallowed quickly so that the severe, deep, excruciating pain that encompassed my very soul and being would quickly numb every nerve, joint, and feeling in my body. I wanted to feel nothing. I wanted all the pain that had built up in me for months to go away forever. For a moment, I felt as if I was living back in my parents' house, where no one would give me love or support, where no one seemed to care whether I was alive or dead. As my body started to relax and my mind started to become foggy, I realized I owed it to my husband and my children to tell them goodbye. So I called my husband on the phone (since he was living above the nearby veterinary clinic), and as my words were difficult and slurred, I told him what I had done. To the best of my recollection, he didn't believe me. It was his girlfriend (office receptionist) that convinced him to come and check on me. The next thing I remembered was the image of me floating above the hospital bed in the hospital, looking down on a body that looked like me as I floated in and out of the room. He had obviously checked on me and transported me to the local hospital. I heard my mother say, "Why are you trying to give up and take your life when I am fighting like hell to save mine? Think of your children. They need you. They don't want to be without their mother." My mother had been given a diagnosis of terminal cancer with only six months to live. She had already lived those six months and was working on making it through the next six months. Witnessing my lifeless body following the execution of charcoal ridding the contents of my stomach was not something she had planned on doing that day. But I was grateful to my husband for notifying her of the circumstances so she could be there for me.

These words touched me in a way I never thought could happen. I wasn't doing this to punish my children or my mother. I was doing this to escape the pain. But in that crucial moment of decision-making, did I think of all the pain I might instill upon my children and family once I was gone? Never. All of a sudden, instead of floating above that lifeless body, I chose to go back into it and fight to live. Yes, it was God himself that was giving me strength and courage to do what I had to do. I had to live. God was not done with me yet. To do that I had to want to live enough to bring that body and soul back to life. And with that will to live, that is exactly what happened. I woke up seeing my mother sitting there, my inspiration, my love, my life. I was required to go to therapy for several months, and I was not allowed to have my children back until I proved I was worthy enough and wanted to live and would never, never, never try to take my own life again. I realized that those two bundles of love meant everything to me and what a mistake I had made to ever think of leaving them. No one person is ever worth taking your own life for. I shouldn't have been surprised that my ulterior motive of getting my husband back in my life by him showing me that he cared and would never let anything happen to me never came to fruition. I realized that what I really wanted was not to kill myself, but I wanted my husband back to love me again and make me feel worthy of that love. I thought he would come to the conclusion of wanting to be with all of us as a family again. Instead, it became clear that he did not love me. He chose not to tell me and chose not to be part of my life again. It even seemed like he was not even fazed by the act I had demonstrated, except that he acquired more evidence to award him total custody of the children. That was a hard lesson to learn, but it was a good lesson for me to figure out the love you have for your children can give you the will to live and the will to make their lives even better than they ever were. That was the love I felt for them and the unconditional love I had searched for all my life. It was quite a surprise to me to find I could give it easier than I could ever receive it. I realized that I had come to believe that my husband had chosen and had committed to love me unconditionally, but that belief was false. And my dream was being demolished right in front of my eyes. Could I go on by myself? I didn't have a choice anymore. This, obviously, was part of God's plan for me, and I had to respect just that and do my best to carry out that plan, even if it included never getting another chance to talk to or be with my husband. It was hard giving up that dream of spending the rest of my life with the man I loved. And did I want the receptionist to become the mother of my children instead of me? Absolutely not.

Meanwhile, while helping my mother fight for her life to survive with cancer, I struggled through the divorce proceedings as best I could. Every Wednesday, instead of family day, I let the kids spend that day with their father while I drove to Preston County to take my mother to her chemotherapy and doctor appointments. I did that every week till the doctor decided to hospitalize her six weeks before her death. She lost her battle and went to heaven on November 22. The divorce was finalized on December 11 of the same year. I remember that day as if it were yesterday. I was not emotionally strong enough to go to the hearing. My lawyer represented me while I stayed in another room close by. I was still having trouble accepting the fact that this man I loved and took care of had decided to walk out on me and be with someone else without even once talking to me about it. My heart was broken, and my ego and self-confidence forever bruised.

Needless to say, that was a very hard year for me. Here I was, only thirty years old and going through a divorce I didn't plan on while watching my mother die. But some good did come from it. I was able to spend the last few months with a woman that I really didn't know till that last year of treatment but came to admire. I was able to help her prepare for her upcoming demise and say goodbye in a dignified manner.

My husband proposed to the court that he take one child and I take the other. After being interviewed by the social worker who told me of his wishes, I simply told her that he could have both of them before I would split them up and give him one. I knew they were much too close to ever separate. She told me she could see how much love I had for them.

As a result of this one statement, I was awarded total custody of my two beautiful children. I then got busy looking for a job to support all of us. I actually took a lead from the social worker and applied for a job as restaurant manager of a local retail food store. I had the interview on Friday and was asked at that time if I would consider a different position as training director. I was given the weekend to come up with a bona fide training plan for a grocery manager. That weekend, not only did I visit the library but also called anybody I knew that served in the capacity of a training manager/coordinator and was able to put a plan together. After presenting it to the personnel manager of the chain, I was notified on Monday I would have the job. Step one was now complete: finding reasonable employment to support my family. My ex-husband would be required to pay child support of $350 per child per month until the kids turned eighteen. During that time, we became closer as a threesome than I could ever imagine. Each of us acquired an innate ability to look out for the other. My son was three and my daughter was six by the time the divorce became final. That was pretty young for children to lose their father. And yes, as they told me and I had to keep repeating to myself, they did not lose their father. I lost my husband, my best friend, and my lover, but they did not lose their father. Our lives changed from that day forward.

Together we faced the stages of grief for a while, and we helped each other survive. A tremendous loss was felt by all. I continued going to therapy to help us cope better. One day, I remember getting called by the principal of the elementary school. The kids were standing in line at the water fountain. All of a sudden my six-year-old pushed someone out of the way so she could get her drink first.

My little girl had been the perfect role model of a student up to this point. So this was very abnormal behavior for her. After I took her to counseling, I discovered that she was very angry with me for getting the mail that day and making Daddy mad enough to not come home. Then she drew a picture for the counselor. This picture depicted me and my two children in a plane in the air looking out through the window to a man standing by himself with tears falling from his face. That man was her father. Her perception of our divorce was that I was at fault because I took the kids with me to Disneyland and to visit his brother in California. At the time, I thought that all he needed was time, time to think about what he had done. I had convinced myself that he would come home to us if I was just a little patient. Obviously, denial is a common emotion that thrives in my body. But that didn't happen, and I had to accept it was never going to happen. One, because he refused to talk with me after the one day when he did not return from work to our house, and two, because the children needed someone to blame, so I allowed them to place their anger on my shoulders, and three, I also put that anger on myself.

I felt good that I was able to obtain employment. I guess it showed the judge that I could take care of my family after all. I never wanted to depend on a man again. If he would have offered to pay me back for the years I put him through veterinarian school, I would have accepted his offer because it meant that he valued what I had done for him. But since he offered nothing but a little child support, I placed my self-worth and worth to others once again at the bottom of the totem pole. My new job meant that I had to move out of town and out of state to Maryland, and it also meant that I would be gone on long trips a lot. I was able to choose a beautiful new home, which the children adored, and that was a challenge, being a single parent and all. The builder knew my employer and agreed to financing along with putting up my house in Elkins as collateral. The kids loved their new neighborhood and loved their new school. It took them just a short time to find their very best friends for life living right in our neighborhood. They loved their teachers and babysitters. Each of us would begin our new lives independently yet together, and they would visit their father every other weekend, so they did not have to be without his love or his guidance. That was the agreement stated in the divorce papers. He remained a very important and central figure in their lives, and I would never do anything to discourage that from continuing. We found a wonderful church, which gave us the foundation we needed for keeping God in our lives and pointing us in the right direction. Once again, life was good.

One weekend, the kids did not come home. I literally freaked out. What had happened? And I received no word or communication from their father that they would not be returned at the court designated time of seven o'clock each Sunday. After two hours had passed, I called his home. His new wife answered and told me that he had been called out for an emergency and had no intentions of returning the children since I did not meet him halfway after moving out of state. The thought of not having my children made me question his motives and their safety. Once again, he chose to walk away and not even think to discuss for one minute with me about the situation. He just decided on his own that the children would not be returned. I asked his wife as a mother to another mother if she could please meet me at the halfway point to return my two children. I would be eternally grateful. She agreed to do just that, and my children were returned to me. Their father sued again for custody and continued to sue for custody more than once, but I was always given total custody, thank goodness. He was angry that I had moved out of state and wanted me to pay for it by taking my children away. Thank goodness, the courts did not agree. He never took time to think how he was punishing the children by keeping them away from their mother. They needed stability and structure in their lives. It was hard enough for them to accept and adjust to their parents not being together. To witness an act of noncompliance with the divorce agreement would definitely confuse them.

Going through a divorce is never a good thing or delightful, but when it is necessary, you learn to make the best of it. When you start life over, you are given a unique opportunity to begin again. It's like having a clean slate to start over. No one ever wants to make the same mistake twice. Believing and accepting the fact that your marriage failed is something that no one is proud of. But when children are involved, you can't just think about yourself. You have to think of your children and what you can do to make this whole experience a positive one for them. Children seem to be more resilient than adults. And because of that, we never stop learning from them. They make it so easy to love them and care for them. All they want is love and their basic needs taken care of. It's always a pleasure as a parent as well as a responsibility to be able to provide that for them. But it is even more important to make sure they feel that love you have for them. They used to say the best gift you can give your children is for them to see you happy. Then they will know what happiness is like. I'm not sure I was able to do that for my children, but I do know I put a lot of effort into trying.

CHAPTER 5

The Second Time Around

My life finally started to make sense. Here I was, starting a new career as Director of Manpower Development for a multisight retail grocery store chain that wanted to expand not only in number of stores and locations but in different states as well. I had an awesome boss, and I was given free reign at developing my own department and training staff. I was in my glory and felt so much respect from others, and that didn't hurt the building and development of my self-esteem. It was exactly what I needed to start over again—a sense of value and importance as an individual and contributor to society. Because a complete physical was required by the corporation, I was able to be honest with my new employer about the attempt on my life since the word suicidal was printed across my medical files that transferred when I changed doctors and locations. I was surprised by his reaction but elated about his response. He told me everyone makes mistakes, as long as we learn from them. The downside to that was I was unable to purchase life insurance because of that suicide attempt.

I bought my first new home built from scratch and located in Oakland, Maryland, to start my life again. My two children were with me, and they were happy. If they were happy, I was happy. They loved the neighborhood, they loved their school, and they loved their friends and babysitter. Life was good once again. I turned all my energy into being a good mother and provider for my children. The additional child support of $350 per child assisted in giving them about half of the lifestyle to which they had been accustomed to, and

I wanted them to feel secure, knowing that even though their parents had divorced, they would still have the love they deserved from each of their parents. Even though their father had a yearly salary of six figures or more, I knew that I would never reap the benefits that came along with that. My salary at the new job was $10,000 a year before taxes. That could hardly compare to the earnings of a veterinarian. I also knew that, painfully, I was all on my own. Even though coparenting is an ideal way to bring up children in a home, that would no longer be the case because their father refused to communicate with me on any level. I spent a lot of hours wondering what I had done wrong. But the time came when I had to put my children's lives first and not be concerned so much about what went wrong with my marriage, but be more concerned with my children being able to adapt and accept the change in their lives, knowing that they would continue to be loved no matter what.

Sometimes I worked long hours, but I gave this job everything I had. I needed to prove to myself and to the company I was worth every penny they were paying me. Eventually, I learned to respect myself as an individual again. I vowed that I would never need a man to make me feel whole again. Not to mention I wanted to demonstrate to my two children and others that with the help of God, we could make anything happen for us. It was okay to dream and go after those dreams. We just had to try and, more importantly, have faith.

It took a couple of years before I started feeling comfortable enough that I could even consider going out with friends for a drink or for fun. I wasn't a drinker but felt very comfortable ordering a virgin daiquiri when I was out with others. While I was getting ready to dive into that comfort zone, a friend of mine in Sunday school and I decided to start a new social group called Single Again. We wanted to provide a safe place and environment for singles to meet without a lot of pressure to date and to have support while going through life's struggles and adversities thrown at them spontaneously and without any warning. Our local church provided the meeting place, and everyone was asked to bring a snack to share. We decided to meet once a month. It became a lot of fun, and the membership continued to grow. The group was a success as a great support group for individuals who found themselves living alone again for whatever reason, and we started expanding by planning social events outside the church for all to enjoy at least once a month. Having the support of the church congregation and the community gave more meaning to this adventure.

When I went to the local American Legion to dance and meet others, I was in my element. I had always loved to dance, even when I was a child and especially in junior high and high school. Of course I never had any formal lessons, but it was always a way I could express my freedom and my spirit and love for life. I even had memories of riding the bus to Pittsburg with a bunch of friends to be on the American Bandstand back in the sixties. That was the ultimate experience.

One of the gentlemen that I met dancing asked me out for a date, and I accepted. We dated a few months, and I met his daughters. We got along fine, but I knew that there was no chemistry and we would never be able to take the relationship as far as he wanted. The first time I went to the legion, I met three wonderful guys who were very easy to talk to and dance with. I called them the three musketeers because they were almost like the three stooges, making me laugh and providing company that gave me a comfort zone I appreciated. But even more so, they made me feel safe to go out in public without any strings attached. They promised me if I ever came back, they would always look out for me so that no person there could take advantage of me. I thought that was such a nice gesture and considered taking them up on that offer. Sometimes, I would go back to the legion just to dance but always made sure that I had a girlfriend to accompany me. Eventually, one of those guys stood out to me, and we became very good friends. I actually became good friends with all three of them but seemed to have more chemistry with only one. We both continued to date others as our friendship became more endearing. He was about fifteen years older, but he shared the same passion for dancing as I did, and that felt very good to me. The difference was that he liked to drink alcohol, and I didn't, so I questioned whether this relationship could work or not. We talked on the phone together, and he started attending all the Single Again group activities, even though he lived in another state. Within a few months, we had our first blind date that we shared with another couple, and it didn't take long for our relationship to blossom and turn to love.

Because of that, I had broken things off with another gentleman so that I would only be dating my special guy exclusively and he would only be dating me. During that time, I would see the other guy here and there around town. Then one night, the doorbell rang. My kids were upstairs asleep. It was the guy that I had broken things off with. He was not happy about our breakup and was determined to not accept it. He didn't want to accept that I wanted to be with someone else and told me that the person I had chosen to date exclusively was only using me and had chosen me because I looked like his ex-wife. He thought that would make a difference to me and I would happily go back to him. When that did not happen, he forced himself on me. I could not scream or make a noise because my two young children were sleeping upstairs. But he knew when he was finished that he should leave immediately and I would never see him again. I felt so dirty and violated. I ran upstairs crying and proceeded to take a shower, but the water and soap just wasn't enough to wash off the scum of what had just happened to me. Because there was no protection, I was so worried that I might become impregnated from this act. Yes, I should have gone to the police, but instead, other than telling my best friend, I wrote a letter to the perpetrator and made sure that he understood that he could and would never be part of my life again and that I never wanted to see his face anywhere near me. For that, I would not go to the police. I never heard from him or saw him again.

It took over a month before I could tell my soon-to-be future husband about what happened, who asked me to marry him after five months of dating. I needed to make sure he could be a good father to my children first, and all signs pointing to that happening seemed to follow. But I also did not want to start off my marriage with a lie. When I told him about what happened, he surprised me and broke it off. He felt that no woman could be raped unless she wanted it to happen. That threw me for a loop. It was hard enough to remember and relive that night over and over, but to have the man you loved not believe you was like sticking a knife into my heart. We broke up, and I didn't hear from him for a few weeks.

Remembering how my mother died of cancer during the same year I got divorced sent caution flags to my brain about the same time as my doctor found a lump in my breast. My doctor wanted me to have a double mastectomy. I knew I could not get married if the lump was malignant. Just to be sure, and knowing I would feel better with a second opinion, I called my mother's previous cancer doctor, and he examined me only to say that he could perform a simple lumpectomy, and if not malignant, I would not need a mastectomy of any kind. This turned out to be the news that changed my future. I realized how quickly life can be taken away from you.

When my ex-fiancé learned of my condition, he apologized and came back into my life and supported me one hundred percent. He did not hesitate to ask for my forgiveness for not believing me. At the time, I was feeling as if I had been scarred and was not good enough to become his wife. But he assured me all this would be in the past, and we should only look toward the future. A rape, however, never leaves your memory. No one wants to feel violated. No one asks for something like this to happen. Sometimes triggers, would appear out of the blue, and I would relive that night over and over.

As soon as I recuperated from the surgery, we decided to have a quick and intimate ceremony at the local church where I lived and got married. West Virginia day became our wedding day. My kids were spending the weekend with their dad and had traveled to Charleston, so they were unable to be at the ceremony but would find out upon their return. I phoned them and told them I had a big surprise for them. They thought they were getting a puppy. Little did I know that not including them in the ceremony was not a simple caution flag but instead a gigantic red flag that would predict the entire family's future. When they saw that it was a wedding ring and not a puppy, they displayed many acts of disappointment as well as a little confusion. When I expected them to jump with glee, I got a couple frowns and sighs instead. They did not like being left out of my future plans, which would infinitely affect them also. Their father had remarried a few months before, and they had been an integral part of the ceremony, so I could understand their disappointment.

My job kept me pretty busy, traveling to conferences, visiting new store locations, training future employees, and also building a strong department of qualified trainers. During that first year of marriage when my new husband was needed to take care of the two children while I was off on business trips, red flags seemed to appear on his coping and fathering skills when working with younger children. I knew we had become a blended family. He had three teenagers (all boys), while I had two children still in elementary school. He seemed to get along fine with them when we were dating, but obviously, this was a totally different environment than he had expected to be in. Having fifteen years spanned between us was going to present some different challenges that we had not considered before. Being responsible for them without me in the picture was not what he signed up for or bargained for evidently. My children were very young and felt very secure in their environment while it was just the three of us. Then this person moved in with us and brought three older children to live there also. His children (one by one came to live with us) were teenagers and adults. He had been divorced himself for about three years. He was unable to commit to taking care of younger children when needed for the long-term. When I came back from a long business trip, he moved out with his youngest son and got an apartment in the town in which he was working in West Virginia. His other two sons joined the service, so they were out on their own by this time.

He lived in West Virginia, and I lived in Maryland. We actually separated before we completed our first year of marriage. It seemed as if at any time there was a problem with the boys, he told me only he could handle it, that it was none of my business. (Oops, another red flag!) Yes, I should have paid attention to all the warning signs. But it's so easy to ignore them when you are in love. He was not up to taking care of small children and frankly did not want to. A very thick wall began to develop between him and my children.

For the longest time, I felt that I failed in my first marriage. It took me a long while to figure out that it was the marriage that failed and not me. I certainly didn't want to repeat myself. Yet having someone love my children, treat them with respect, and be a good role model for them was at the top of my list when finding a suitable mate. I believed I had done just that, or I would never have gotten married the second time around. I also questioned how this man I fell in love with could not love my children as his own if they in fact were a part of me.

The next few months were hard, both on me and my children. Because my friend from church, who helped me start the group Single Again, lived across the street from me, we shared the same passion of the role our own children would play in our lives. We decided to share babysitters, and that helped my children feel very secure and happy when I was late getting home from work many times.

In order to spend more time with my children, I decided to leave my job in personnel and renew my teaching certification so I could go back to teaching and have days off the same time that my children did. I quit my job in Maryland to become a school teacher once again in West Virginia. I couldn't find work in Maryland, so I accepted a job in West Virginia, where I could use the one year of experience I had there previously to my advantage in obtaining employment. This meant, however, that I would once again have to travel one hour each way to keep my job. Eventually though, I would run into my husband since I now worked in West Virginia, and we would find ourselves dating once again.

Neither of us had filed for divorce, so as we became more attached to one another, we decided to move to West Virginia, buy a house together, and try to make this marriage work. He felt he was trying to fit into my life in Maryland, and it wasn't working. Working in West Virginia and the two of us buying a house together to start over seemed to give us a better chance of making our marriage work. One night, I went to pick him up from work, and his second eldest son was there. It was obvious he was not acting himself. After his father came out of the building, the son went to pick up a manhole cover, and I could see in my rearview mirror that he had intentions of causing me harm. He tried to throw that manhole cover at me in the car. My husband was able to stop him and make him put the manhole cover back in place where it belonged. Then his son hurriedly grabbed a rock about the size of a cantaloupe, and he started coming toward me. Keep in mind I was sitting in the car in the driver's seat. As I saw him approach, I realized that his intention was not honorable. As he raised his arm with the rock in his hand, I knew he was about to throw it at me. I quickly put on the gas pedal and moved the car several feet ahead to a stoplight. He was running and then threw that rock. I had stopped for a red light, and he took advantage of the situation. I saw the rock reeling toward me. It busted through my rear window, breaking it, and headed toward me. I ducked my head as the rock went into the seat in which I was seated. I hurried and turned left to go to the sheriff's office as soon as possible. As my husband watched the whole thing, I turned left. I remember his son picking up another rock to throw at me. So yes, I did run that red light to get myself to a safe place. I had to believe that he was under the influence of drugs and/or alcohol or he would not have tried this negligent action toward me.

After completing a report at the sheriff's office, I asked them to arrest him for intentional assault. I think my husband was in disbelief that his son could do this to me. He joined me at the sheriff's office, and together we left the courthouse and began to drive to his mother's apartment at the top of the hill to check on her. As we began to ascend up the hill to her place, his son jumped out of the bushes on the way and tried to come toward me again. What had I done to deserve this kind of intentional behavior? I had no idea. After he was arrested and put in jail, we found out that he was under the influence of drugs. Because he saw me driving a new car, he assumed that his father had bought me that new car but refused to give him money for his drugs. He was thinking his father thought more of me that he did of him. He had no idea that I paid for the new car myself while his father and I were separated. He stayed in jail for thirty days and then was released. Because he was drug-free upon his release, I was able to forgive him for his actions. And yes, I had to get that new car repaired without his help or assistance. I don't remember getting an apology from him. But I do know that he knew not what he was doing at that time. I even took him chocolate chip cookies and visited him in jail each week. Apparently, it was the drugs causing his actions that day, not him. What can I say? I have a soft heart.

Because I had obtained a job in public education that gave me holidays and summers off to be with my children, whom I adored, we became a two-salaried household. The house we found was definitely my dream house and had everything I wanted. Most of all, it was located in a town where my father, sister, and brother lived, the town named Arthurdale, where I had grown up. This meant I would have family support for everything. It meant once again I could attend family events because I lived near them instead of hours away. The house itself was big enough to accommodate our blended family and gave us a reason to do what we could to make it work for all of us. Of course, my kids were happy to be near their friends, cousins, grandparents, uncles, and aunts, who treated them like royalty. Once again, life was good.

We lived there ten years, more time than I had ever spent in any one place since I left home to go to college. Eventually, we watched my husband's sons and then my two children all graduate from high school. Even though there was a lot of tension between my husband and the children, not once did I ever think that tension meant that they could ever be harmed or threatened in any way. If I did, I would never allow or agree for all of us living together to continue. But somehow, I knew deep down that those red flags would reappear now and then because my children would feel like they were being treated differently than the three sons my husband had. I also noticed a resentment or jealousy toward my children from my husband anytime they would achieve success, whether it was with report cards or playing sports. Finally, as we experienced one of his sons having drugs in the house, another having too much alcohol (to the point of passing out in a chair or bed urinating by losing complete control of bladder), tension continued to grow as problems escalated. I was naïve enough to think that all his children needed was a little love and everything would be all right. When they abused alcohol and drugs, I tried my best to be a good stepmother. But that was not enough. When I found marijuana and drug paraphernalia in their rooms and in our house, I instituted some rules, which I thought were obviously understood already. The foul language they used to talk to their father was unacceptable, and I finally had to take a stand to inform them if they continued talking to him this way, they would have to leave the premises. I gave them an ultimatum to either stop the behavior at once (drinking, drugs, foul language) or they could not continue to live under our roof. They were all over eighteen when this happened. I could not expose their unhealthy habits and language to my younger children. But when the boys heard the rules, they rebelled, one at a time, until all three moved out of the house. The last straw was when they cussed off their father and showed no signs of remorse. As it turned out, my husband did not agree with my terms of tough love, and once again, we found ourselves separated. Once again, I found myself becoming a single mother. This was hard on me emotionally. When I fall in love, I fall deeply. I believe in the vows taken at the time of marriage before God. It was not easy for me to say goodbye. But with that goodbye, I knew I would not face the same depression I had faced in watching my first love walk away. I knew that this time, I must be strong so that the three of us could move forward.

My husband gave me his word that he would get counseling/therapy before I would even consider taking him back. This was because he threatened to saw the house into before he would allow me and my children to continue living there. He also tried to man-handle me and threw an object at me, breaking the skin and leaving a bruise. During one of these separations, we both had individual counselors who practiced in the same building. I'm not sure why I did it, but one week, I stopped by reception to confirm his appointment during the following week. They informed me that he was not a client of theirs and that he had never received counseling from this firm.

Needless to say, I was very disappointed to find out that I had allowed him back into our lives and he had lied about getting help with his feelings and treatment toward us. The children were not happy that he returned. During this time, I also went back to graduate school to get my master's degree in counseling so that I could receive a larger paycheck and also live out my passion to help others.

My husband continued to insist that he would not help to assist in paying for costs of my biological children living there. He would only support his own biological children. Even though we were living as a family, once again, I felt like a single parent supporting my children. I was completely unaware that the law had changed in 1984 that would change the amount of child support I would receive from my ex-husband. Even though it would have been to my children's advantage to take him back to court, I continued to support them by myself, including the cost of medical insurance and additional monies needed for applying to colleges and other activities. When they were given a chance to charge off to college, that's exactly what they did and moved out of the house forever. Sadly enough, I thought things would get so much better for my husband and me. Because of his belief that it was the presence of my children that caused so many problems in our marriage, I thought we would be on a second honeymoon every day following their leaving and going off to college. I was wrong, however. Things never changed at all, and our relationship continued to be strained.

After receiving my master's degree and accepting a job as a school counselor, I was able to work with elementary, junior high, high school, college, and adult students. After eight years, the unexpected happened. I was riffed from my job as school counselor at the largest and only consolidated high school in the county. What did this mean for me? My husband had been at his job for over thirty years and never knew another since then. It's where he had always worked and never saw a need to change that. I had had many different jobs and thought this one was the one I would retire in. I enjoyed the challenge of being in a new position and challenging myself. I had given education more than eighteen years of my experience. I had taught classes from preschool to college level. But instead, I found myself sending out over fifty applications up and down the East Coast to find a job in my certified area. Before I did that, however, I asked my husband if he would support us if I chose to just be a substitute and not have a contracted job (to just stay in the area until a job with my certification would open up). His answer was a strong and definite no. He said it was not his job to support my children, and he knew both of them were in college, and I was committed to seeing that through. Whoops! Was that another red flag I missed? This is when I knew, without a doubt, that our marriage was not what I thought it should be or wanted it to be. The odd part of all this was that my two children had moved out and were going to college, so why they were any kind of threat to our marriage or financial situation? I don't know. Go figure.

Even though the divorce papers stated that my first husband would take care of the children's medical insurance and provide a college education for them, that did not happen. I had difficulty just collecting the child support due them, let alone what other requirements were listed. After making sure my two children were secure in their college pursuits and making sure what their scholarships would cover and what help I could give them, I accepted a job about two hours away as a school counselor for a K-12 country school. This meant I needed to move, so I found an apartment in the same town I had started over after my first divorce, Oakland, Maryland. I had succeeded in taking care of my family the first time living in this town, so why not go back to this town to start again? My husband said he would not live in Maryland. So he filed for divorce, and we sold the house we shared. He got his own apartment in the town where he still was employed while I found my next dream house. I went ahead and bought it after he decided to give me the equity we earned from our other home once it was sold.

The job was great, and I was very happy. I found new friends and absolutely loved the house I lived in. My favorite part was the huge island in the kitchen/family room with the fireplace and two patio doors leading out to the wraparound deck. It may always be my favorite house I lived in. My kids would visit me when they had days off or holiday vacations. Everything I wanted in life was happening, and without a care or concern, we were a threesome again, just like after the first divorce. There was no stress, just contentment and happiness when my children and their friends visited me in Maryland.

I thought the divorce was final, and because I had signed all the papers, I knew of no reason why I needed to attend the court hearing in West Virginia. To my shock and surprise, my husband decided not to go through with the divorce, even though I thought the hearing was conducted and the divorce was final. When I found out he decided to retire and start dating again, I became very confused. But once again, our love was rekindled, and together, we bought our last dream house together and moved to a city closer to where I was working, Keyser, West Virginia. Life seemed very good once again.

By this time, my children were both out on their own in very good jobs. I had to ask them to ask their father for some financial help in paying for their room during their senior year or they would have to take out a loan. He agreed to help them, and they were able to graduate without being in financial debt. I was so proud of them. My daughter was in the Air Force, and my son was working for an oil company. This arrangement continued for several years, and I ended up traveling to see them as often as I could because many times, they would be stationed out of town and out of the country.

Visiting Hawaii was something I found on my bucket list, and I hoped to accomplish it someday. To have both my children fall in love and plan to get married in Hawaii within the same week became a mother's dream. I was on top of the world. I will never forget that experience. My memory book does not have other memories equal to what I experienced that week. There is something humbling about watching your own two children experience the happiest day of their lives and to witness in person the choices they made for their partners in life. I am the luckiest mother in the world, because I fell in love with these two people my children chose as their partners. I gained a son and a daughter and definitely did not lose the ones I had. I felt very much a part of their life experiences and also felt proud that I played a small part in helping them get to this place in their lives. There is no other joy better than to see your own children find happiness by selecting the person of their dreams to become their other half. A mother's dream is to see both her children happy. I achieved that dream during that trip to Hawaii. I could only wish that I could someday find my true love as I saw each of them do. I was also fortunate enough for my two sisters, best friend, and two nieces to join me on that trip, so it became a nice getaway for all of us. Even though my children had jobs, which kept them away from me most of the time, it gave me an opportunity to travel all over the world to see them. In addition to traveling to countries I had never visited, I also had the opportunity to visit Texas, Washington state, Washington, D.C., Virginia, and many other states in America. My children always helped with expenses and many times provided the transportation for me. Sometimes, it began to feel like our roles of parent and child were being reversed. I didn't mind that at the time because they were being so good to me, and it was a win-win situation. It also kept them from having to visit me in the states where they never felt welcome by my husband.

Learning about the possible existence of a new grandchild from my daughter brought tears of joy to my eyes. I was so happy I could hardly wait to share the news with my husband. In the past, I was lucky if I got to see my children once a year because of where their home base related to their jobs was located. Needless to say, my husband had chosen not to accompany me to Hawaii, just as he had chosen many times to not share family outings or vacations with me the past few years whenever my two children (grown-up or not) were involved. He also chose to share something with me that threw me into complete shock. Was it too much for me to expect him to be as excited as I was that we were expecting another grandchild? Only this time, it would be from one of my biological children instead of his. Was it too much for me to remember how loving and supportive I had been throughout the years as we not only took care of his grandchildren many times, but we also attended their graduations together as well? He proceeded to inform me that no grandchild of mine (meaning me, and keep in mind that we already had four grandchildren and two great-grandchildren through his biological children) would ever step foot in the house that we presently occupied as long as he was alive. For a moment, I wasn't sure if that was a threat or a joke. When he repeated the statement, I knew then it was not a joke.

To make a long story short, I filed for divorce the very next day. I mean, who does that? Who is willing to come between you and your children or grandchildren? My husband was not happy that I made the decision to choose my children over him. The divorce became very nasty and also included a restraining order to keep him away from me after a gun and bullets were found by the police in a random search of the house. So why was I surprised when this man to whom I had been married for twenty-six years told me that if I didn't stay married to him, he would make sure my children were killed, and if he didn't finish the job, his sons would finish it, and I would never find their bodies because they would be buried in parts all over the place in West Virginia woods. The restraining order was only good for six months, and it took all that time for the divorce to become final. We parted ways much sooner than that legally. He was forced to leave our residence until the divorce was final. I was able to enjoy my new grandchild prior to the divorce hearing. I visited Texas, where my daughter lived, and arrived on the day of delivery. I actually spent the first three weeks with my new granddaughter, whom I absolutely adore. There is nothing that can replace the feeling of having your first grandchild, whom you knew you would always be connected to you through blood. Down deep, you knew that nothing could ever take this away from you. Blood is thicker than water. Because it was not present in my last marriage, I lost something very precious to me. I did not like giving up my family as I had known it and loved through marriage. To this day, I'm not even sure that my stepchildren even know why their father and I divorced. But they never asked either, and why would I want to taint their image of their father? But if this was what they wanted, I understood their loyalties to their father and would never try to come between them or stand in their way. I respected their decision to have no more contact with me. This was another fond memory going into the memory book of time.

And then a second miracle appeared. My son and daughter both kept trying for many years to become pregnant and have more children. After experiencing more than one miscarriage, neither of them were successful, until six years later, my daughter was blessed with a set of twins. One boy and one girl were born one minute apart. I now have three grandchildren. Do I regret my actions? Of course not. No one should ever attempt to come between a mother and her children.

Shortly after the divorce was final, I adopted a cute little pomapoo, which gave me the company I needed to live in the house alone. It took some time for me to get past those last eight months, not knowing if you were going to have to give up your home and find a new one or not. I was given that wonderful gift from a dear friend, who happened also to be my neighbor. She reached out to me once I was divorced, and I actually looked forward to coming home each day after work. We went to yard sales, dinner, and gospel sings together. It was exactly the support I needed after living in crisis the past year. My coworkers at the career center, where I worked, were also supportive and provided me serenity when it was needed.

One day, I was driving on a road that provided a shortcut to the downtown area where I lived. I happened to look to my left that day, and there standing in a garage working was my ex-husband. I kept driving, but a little voice inside me told me to turn around and face the fear or demon that lurked around inside of me. I realized that I couldn't go to the grocery store or a Walmart or even a restaurant without fear of being spotted and/or harmed by my ex-husband. He used to tell me he didn't forget nor did he forgive. He only believed in revenge.

So I did just that. I turned the car around, pulled into his driveway, parked the car, and got out. I had been living in fear of being hurt by this man for ten months. How was it ever going to stop if I didn't acquire the courage to face him? This was someone who threatened to kill my children and me. I walked with strong determination and approached him in the garage. He showed a look of extreme surprise to see me. I asked him, "Do you still want to kill me or see me dead? Because if you do, you can do it right here, right now. I am tired of living in fear." His response surprised me. We had had no contact with one another for the past several months, except in court hearings or through our lawyer's communication to one another. Yet our eyes met, and we stared in silence in what seemed like an hour but was only a second or two. He said to me in a soft yet deliberate tone, "I mean no harm to you. Why don't we let bygones be bygones?" I couldn't believe it could be this easy and wondered if I were in a dream or was this real? Did he really just say that? How do I know if I could believe him? But something told me that I could. I had put all this in God's hands, and I wasn't sure what would be the outcome to all of this. I knew if I were to be able to live my own life, I needed to forgive him and move on.

If God can forgive us, I can forgive those who sin against me. And I did just that. Following the silence, our eyes met, and it was as if the last ten months had never happened. Yet here he stood in his home now, something that was very foreign to me. We continued to converse, and the fear that I possessed just minutes before seemed to leave my body and my head as I relaxed and listened to his apology. I knew at that moment he meant every word and that he had regretted his actions in the last ten months. He wanted a different outcome, but it was not to be. He actually seemed surprised that we were actually legally divorced. I also realized at that moment that his pride would never have allowed him to come to me to seek forgiveness or offer an apology. Once again, God was working his magic. If I had not taken the time to turn around and confront him, who knows when or if we would ever speak to one another again?

So I left him that day and felt a great deal of relief. Then one day, at a restaurant where I planned to have dinner, there he was, sitting in a booth by himself. I said hi, and he asked me to join him. He bought my dinner that night, and we put the past in the past where it belonged. Yes, that means I am friends with my ex-husband, and we will always have a special relationship. But to ever be married to him again simply did nor does not seem to be in the cards. I know how important love is, and to receive that love from your children by giving you the miracles of life all over again is something that can never be replaced. My children had informed me that the reason they never came home to visit me was because I was married to him and they did not care for him in any way, shape, or form and could never forgive him for all the abuse he gave me and the way he neglected, threatened, and disrespected them. I also heard this statement from family and friends. So I looked forward to the many visits from them in the future. The odd part is that in the five years that followed the divorce, I never saw my children, family, or friends any more than I had seen them when he lived with me, which seemed unusual if it was more than once a year. The divorce had no effect on whether they chose to visit me in my home or not. Oddly enough,

I was told the same thing from a very special and dear friend from Morgantown. And oddly enough, she never came to visit me once after my divorce. I guess some people look for an excuse not to visit when sometimes they may have never wanted to visit you at all. This action helps you question the real value or quality of your relationship and/or friendship.

Later on, I never realized the strong effect that second marriage had on my daughter. I found out from her that not only had he threatened to attack or hurt her, but he had said to her that he hoped she had an accident on the way home and died so he could piss on her grave. This conversation followed after she delivered me to my home from a visit with my family two hours away. She picked me up because I was ill at the time but wished to visit with my father and family, and my husband would not take me. Because of those harsh words, she has become very bitter inside and resentful toward me. I thought that with the counseling and help I provided for her during her teenage years, she had moved past the perception that I was the one who caused the divorce between her father and myself, and now she was telling me that I was the one who brought this person into her life and forced her to live with him when he hated her guts. It has been over thirty years since she lived in the same house as he did (more years than she was old at the time). And she is as bitter today as she was thirty years ago. She feels that I chose him over her and that the only way to make her feel better would be for me to completely end all contact with him. I actually did that during the divorce, and it did not change how she felt about me. Yet somehow, I know deep inside that only she can deal with her own bitterness and anger. I simply have and will never have any influence on what she decides to do with her life.

You see, he and I have become more than friends. He became genuinely sorry for what he had said and done during our marriage and has apologized over and over and admitted his wrongdoings. I chose to forgive him. Forgiveness will set you free. My daughter happens not to believe in forgiveness and chooses not to forgive me. I pray before I leave this earth that she will find it in her heart to forgive me for anything I have done to hurt her. I also hope she can forgive anyone else who she still holds a grudge toward. I have apologized and prayed and even begged her for forgiveness over and over, but she said it will never happen and that she and I will never have the mother-daughter relationship that we once had. She said she thought she could depend on me and found out that when I did not return to help her out after taking care of her during her pregnancy and weeks after the twins were born, she could never depend on me because I let her down.

The sad thing is that once I divorced my second husband, I really thought that because I was doing what my children wanted, that it would make them happy and they would come visit me more often. That never happened. During the years I was so sick, unable to drive, and unable to work, I needed someone to help me and take care of me. My sisters drove two hours once a month to visit and do what they could. But they had families of their own. It ended up that my second husband, without being asked to do so, stepped forward, feeling badly about how sick and disabled I was, and he volunteered not only to do maintenance duties at the house but to transport me weekly to all my doctor appointments and therapy. From mowing lawns, changing oil filters and snow blowing, to transporting me out of town to see specialists each week, he showed up without complaint. There were many times he had to pick me up at work or at the hospital after I had been admitted. My vertigo condition had literally disabled me. His acts of kindness displayed the unconditional love I had looked for during our marriage but never received. This man had no ulterior motives. He just wanted to help, and it seemed that he wanted nothing in return, just to see me get better. I'm not sure where I would be today without his assistance during that time. I only know that when no one else was there to help me get through a difficult period of illness, he stepped up and asked nothing of me in return. I could not find fault in that.

Today, he continues to call me each and every day to check on me and see how I am doing. For some odd reason, I've come to look forward to his calls. It's kind of ironic, but in reality, he is now showing the unconditional love toward me that I longed for during our marriage of twenty-six years. He has learned his lesson and now realizes that he lost something pretty darn special when he lost me. I will forever be grateful for his kindness and support during this critical time, but I will never forget the reason I divorced him, nor will I forget the ten months of agony that he put me through when the divorce was in process. Once again, my own personal identity was in question, and I had to work hard to find the real me again. I still pray and hope that both my daughter and son can find it in their hearts to forgive me and my second husband someday so that they too will feel the peace and tranquility inside their hearts also.

CHAPTER 6

Betrayal

While going through my second divorce, I built a special relationship with a coworker who prayed with me every morning before I started work each day. Before work each morning, a group of us would gather for devotions in the conference room and share personal stories with one another as well as devotions. We had to arrive early each morning to make sure we did not do this during the hours of a regular work day. Even though the center's nursing instructor was my best friend, I found myself being drawn to a male coworker who used to be a pastor. He became my special confidant and, along with his wife (whom I had worked with, shared the same name as myself, and respected highly at a local elementary school), gave me the key to his house in case I ever needed a safe harbor or became afraid to go home during the length of my divorce proceedings. I trusted him with my life and my most intimate feelings, and each time we were together, a nice sense of peace came over me. He seemed to understand everything I was going through. As I shared the most intimate details of my breakup with him, I noticed he would always take notes and sometimes even review what we had talked about that day. That seemed a little abnormal to me since I knew about his past as a pastoral counselor, but I ignored that behavior, even though it was probably a bright red flag for me. We continued to pray together daily, and I felt honored to have him as a friend. I watched him at work many times as he reached out to the troubled children in his alternative education class setting. He spoke to those children through his heart, and they seemed to respond to that. Yet when I visited his classroom, it was pretty much operated as a boot camp would be. The students stood up at attention each time I entered the room. But somehow, they exhibited an air of respect coupled with an air of fear toward their instructor and others, but mainly toward themselves. I admired this man for his dedicated work with these kids who entered the program due to unacceptable behavior at their home school. Yet I continually observed a very orderly classroom upon entry each time.

It was tough being afraid of the man you had been married to for twenty-six years. Sometimes, fear tends to take over all other emotions in your body, and you find that you become a little irrational in your thoughts and feelings. You tend to allow the fear you have for someone or for a situation be the driving force for all the actions and thoughts you have.

He seemed to understand the fear I was experiencing as well as understanding where I was coming from as I faced uncertainty each day. Every time I received another letter from my husband's lawyer threatening me, I knew that the content information in the letter could only have come from my ex-husband. My new friend and confidant became available to console me, no matter what time of day. He offered me solace and advice so that I would never feel alone in the journey I was taking. He even suggested I talk to a therapist to make sure I was approaching each day with a solution in mind. I took him up on that advice and started seeing a therapist immediately on a weekly basis. I even shared with him that I never wanted to go to the bottom of the barrel again as I had with my first husband. Hurting myself to alleviate the pain would never be an option. I shared a very elevated level of trust with him to even share my personal experiences and life stories from the past. We spent a lot of time discussing my survival tactics and how I could face the future ahead without my love no longer in my life. He told me I could call on him anytime, whether I was at work or at home. He shared his home number and his cell number with me in case I needed to call him at odd hours of the day or night. He prepared a room for me to stay in at his house if I should ever need to use the key, he had given me and gave me instructions as to how to enter his home if it should become necessary after hours. But most of all, he encouraged me to believe in God's help and guidance and know that I would never be alone in my journey. He even assisted me with his pastoral gift of advice and counseling when there were other staff members who needed support and counseling. I looked up to him, just as his students and other staff members did also.

Then one day, everything changed for both of us. My divorce had been finalized for almost two months. I received a phone call from one of my coworkers one day during the summer months while visiting my son in Texas. She informed me that my friend and confidant was being recommended for the position of director of the facility at which I was employed. The previous director of the center had retired and taken a job as president of the local community college. That man had been the best boss I had ever had the pleasure of working with. Going back to my position with a new director in his place filled me with a little apprehension. My coworker was very concerned that this might actually happen and that the alternative education teacher might not be the best choice for the position. She seemed to know more about his previous and personal life than I was ever made aware of and expressed a lot of concern about his tactics for dealing with students and/or staff. I told her I had trusted him with my life. But the recommendation I gave my coworkers was to trust the administrative council. This was the board that governed our facility, and under their leadership and guidance, our career and technical center had become a school of excellence the previous year. With a board like that and one who had always supported the present faculty and staff, I knew and trusted that they would never consider this person for the position unless they had the confidence and reassurance that he could lead us into the twenty-first century. The board was made up of superintendents from three different counties as well as a board of education member from each of those counties. A state department of education representative joined them. Knowing that any decision they made would affect their own counties tremendously assured me that they would indeed make the right decision to hire the best possible person for the job. I had faith in this board and had gained their personal respect for me during the past few years I had worked at the center.

Faculty members continued to call me and share many concerns about him being placed in the new position and concerns about his threatening them and behaving unlike anything I had heard of from a boss. It sounded almost as if he were acting very much like the ex-husband whom I had just divorced. I thought they had to be exaggerating. No one could have changed this much in the four weeks that I had been away from the center that summer.

Because I had to have emergency surgery the week I was supposed to return to school, I had not planned on going into work that day since I was on medical leave. But being the good school counselor I was, I felt it was my responsibility to be the mediator between the director and staff to clear up some misunderstandings in communication. All of us wanted the upcoming school year to be the best that it could be.

Little did I know what was about to unfold. After arriving early at the center, I took the opportunity to have an informal conversation with my confidante while he sat behind his desk in the new position as director of our facility. I informed him of the faculty's concerns and asked if we could have an informal meeting with them to discuss their concerns and end all rumors that were building on staff and out in the community and causing them to be very apprehensive about returning to work that year. He gladly agreed to meet with those concerned in the break room prior to a formal meeting scheduled to begin in one hour. Other faculty members joined me as we discussed informally all our concerns. But something unfolded while we were there. It was clear to me that circumstances had changed, and the man I considered my friend and confidant was sounding like a stranger whom I had just met for the very first time. This really made me apprehensive to continue, so we ended the conversation there and then and decided to table it till after the workshop and meeting planned for nine o'clock that morning.

While we were in a faculty and staff meeting, I witnessed this new director acting hostile and actually harassing our financial coordinator right in front of us. Accusations and references were made that she had not been performing up to her ability and was making every attempt to undermine him. He actually accused her of not having the budget for the following year completed by the deadline he had given her. Earlier, I had met with her, and she confided in me that he had directed her emphatically never to talk to the rest of the staff, and she could not allow them to step into her office to consult with her. She actually exhibited the same fear in her face and voice that I had shown toward my ex-husband just a few months before. This could not be so, I thought. Because this person had served the center for many years, she was always thought of as the glue that held the center together. She was very close to the previous director and his assistant (the dean of student services) and supported them without failing for as long as she had worked there. I also learned that the new director bargained with the administrative council to do the job alone without an assistant or dean of students if they would hire him. This would save them many thousands of dollars on the budget per year. Learning about all of this was the main reason I wanted to talk with him informally and I guess to validate everything I was hearing from others to be a gross misunderstanding.

The financial coordinator was also given orders to not talk to or contact the previous director and his assistant as long as she continued to be employed at the center. The regular secretary had already been relieved of duties; so the financial coordinator was the only employee left to manage budgets, personnel and finances, and any other secretarial and/or accounting duties needed at the time. I couldn't believe my eyes or my ears, and my heart simply wanted to reach out and help her since I was actually a witness to the emotional and physical toll it was having on her body. She was visibly shaking and slurring her words. It was obvious she was having some kind of reaction to all this stress. I thought I must be having a nightmare. I simply could not be witnessing such an outright and deliberate form of verbal and emotional abuse right before my eyes. My new boss was sounding like a dictator as he continued to talk, almost directing angry words and gestures toward this woman as she became severely and physically distressed. This type of action would be alarming if it was done in the privacy of an office, let alone in a conference room in front of the entire faculty and staff. She tried so hard to hold it together; but the attack on her integrity was not only unprofessional, it was unyielding and continued even as I got up and assisted her in leaving the room so I could remove her from the stressful situation. Her breathing had become short and spasmodic, and color was leaving her face. It was clear that she was in distress, and I was concerned about her as tears ran down her face while she was trying hard to defend herself and her position. I had concern about whether she would pass out or have a heart attack. The director ignored what was happening and continued to address the group as if this situation in front of him did not exist. I was able to get her out of the room and the interim secretary called 911 for me. I watched as this dedicated and fellow employee was taken out by ambulance as she tried so hard to respond and/or defend herself with the director but was unable to as her breathing became even more labored as time went on. I tried to grab any personal belongings (including medication and cell phone) and put them into her purse so she would have what she needed if she would have to be admitted to the hospital. I made an effort to contact her family to meet her there. I also felt the strain myself of doing too much to assist her (after having emergency surgery previously that week) and needed to take my scheduled medication as soon as possible. The stress of the entire situation was getting out of control. Other staff members came out to assist me as the interim secretary expressed extreme concern for me. After the gurney was transported to the ambulance, I noticed the new director standing in the doorway behind me. As the ambulance pulled away, I was about to go to my office to get my medication, and the newly appointed director stopped me. He purposely blocked the way to my office, extended his hand and arm, pointing me toward his office, and then insisted that I go to his office with him immediately. I told him that I needed to take my medication, but he told me it would have to wait because he needed to talk with me right away. After witnessing what had just happened to my coworker, I knew that I needed to obey his orders or be guilty of insubordination.

When we arrived in his office, he closed the door behind me and leaned over me as I sat in the chair next to the door. He began to harass me much in the same way I had witnessed him doing to the financial coordinator. He wanted to know why I told the emergency medical technician that the other employee had only been on anxiety medication for the past couple months. At first, I replied, "Because he asked me." He then asked me how I knew that it had only been the last two months. I told him that I saw the date and number of refills on the medicine bottle when I took it off of her desk and put it in her purse to give to her prior to her being escorted by ambulance away from the center. Once again, I also told him that I was in dire need of taking my medication. He continued to ask me the same question over and over as if he did not understand my answer. I then consistently replied to his questions with the comment "I need my medication." As I reflect now, I am thinking that our conversation could be heard by others outside his office door. When I didn't respond with the answers he wanted, he almost badgered me even more. I told him I needed to be released to take my medicine, but it seemed as though he wasn't hearing my request or that he purposely was ignoring it. I still could not understand why he continued to question me with the same question over and over and why he would not accept the answer I gave him. I actually began feeling concern for my well-being and safety. I guess I didn't think about the fact that he had only been director for a couple months and that he was thinking that I thought there was a direct correlation between his being there and her being on anti-anxiety medication for two months. I also think he was worried if someone else would think that it was a direct correlation. It was as if he was accusing me of giving false information to the EMT. Thank goodness and finally, a fellow employee could see through the glass in the door that I needed assistance. The stress from the situation was putting me into a vertigo spell, and my world was spinning out of control. I was getting upset, and the color was draining from my face. My fellow employee opened the door and asked if I needed help, and I replied yes right away. I needed my medication. Against the wishes of the director, the coworker assisted me to get my medication, but not before it was too late. My coworkers thought that I might need to be taken by ambulance also, but I was conscious enough to tell them I did not want the publicity of two employees being taken away by ambulance from the center at the same time. If they could just help me to a chair and retrieve my medication from my office, I could allow some time for me to recover. By now, I was unable to walk or balance myself. I became very dizzy and was not only facing pain and discomfort, but I could feel myself going into a serious vertigo episode. I'm sure the anxiety and stress of the situation contributed to this condition, and of course, he knew that I did have a history of vertigo. Coworkers searched for my medication and were able to give it to me right away. But by this time, I needed additional medication for my vertigo as well as the medication for pain from the surgery. During this time, the director did not ask how I was or what happened or anything. Nor did he inquire about the status of the financial coordinator. Once again, he chose to ignore what was going on right in front of him and seemed to be interested only in his own welfare, not of that of others surrounding him. This was the same man that seemed to appreciate the fact that I came to work and did not stay home on the advice of the doctor. This same man had placed a hernia cushion on my chair at my desk earlier that morning to welcome me back and let me know he appreciated my willingness to attend school that day.

I was immediately taken back to the nurse's station and put in one of the hospital beds in the nursing classroom. With all the additional stress, I was suffering from an anxiety attack as well as a vertigo spell in addition to enduring more pain from sitting too long without lying down. I had planned on staying a few hours to improve communication between the director and the staff, but this had turned into a situation beyond my control. Due to the severity of my condition, the nurse had to call someone to come pick me up since I could no longer drive myself home. The only person she knew to call was my daughter, who could not possibly be there since she lived in Texas. By using the numbers in my personal cell phone, she was able to get ahold of my ex-husband, who volunteered to come get me immediately.

Since the staff was gathered around my bedside and very concerned about me, there was no one in the conference room except the director himself. He then insisted that the entire faculty return to the room to hear his lecture on sexual harassment and told them they could not stay with me. After much objection and being concerned about my welfare, the staff finally agreed, as long as the nurse could stay with me until my ride came. They knew that this was not a normal situation, so they also notified the teachers union representative for guidance and direction in regards to what was taking place at the center. It was clear that the entire staff was beginning to fear for their safety and welfare after witnessing all that had taken place that morning, not to mention they were being ordered and forced to leave two employees in need of help without any type of debriefing or explanation and told they must come to the same conference room where they had witnessed harassment toward those two coworkers without any consequences or action being taken. Absolutely no one could focus on the agenda of the day to be carried out by this new director. The ironic thing was that the very topic he was discussing was being practiced in front of their very eyes, but not being positively resolved or responded to in a satisfactory or acceptable manner. The entire faculty was confused yet filled with questions and concern for the center's future.

As the days continued and my recovery made enough progress for me to return to work, I had no idea upon my return to work what was going to happen next. It was as if I were only working so that I could be used as an example to be punished and/or persecuted for not supporting his actions that day. And he was going to make me pay for what he deemed as my disloyalty to him. The interesting part of this situation was that I found out that this man had written a book called *If Gold Rust, What Will Iron Do?* After careful examination and reading of this book, one could actually trace step by step what this person would do when placed in a role of supervision. It was even discovered that he had been removed from both a principal's position (in the same county) and a teaching position at a local community college (in the same district) for committing acts and duties that were found unacceptable by his powers to be. And yet this man was allowed to practice in a similar position again once these facts were presented to the governing board. I'm not sure how justice can be served if this was allowed to happen. Evidently, unlike me, the governing board of the center was clearly aware of his past and chose to ignore the consequences of placing him in a supervisory position once again. Needless to say, I was very disappointed in the actions of the administrative council at our facility.

The financial coordinator was never able or allowed to return to her job or the center again. He actually convinced the board that it was in their best interest that she no longer be employed at the center and not be permitted to return to her present position. She was immediately relieved of her duties. And even though she rebutted this decision, she was unsuccessful in getting her job back. I knew then that I would be the next victim in line on his agenda, and my life as I knew it would begin to change.

As I continued to come to work each day, I almost forgot what it was like to enjoy my job and carry through with my personal passion for teaching and counseling. I felt uncomfortable any time that he was present or near me. He would sit in a chair among my students, stare at me and take notes, and even try to record the session. Even one of my students shouted out, "Why can't you leave her alone? She's done nothing to you." The stress and tension continued to increase and grow between my director and me. The representative from the teachers' union even contacted him and informed him to not be alone with me again to remove the stress from this tenuous situation. Not only was I continually harassed by him, but I was also punished by an increasing workload. It was as if he was trying to find a way to relieve me of my duties if I didn't perform up to his standards. I also noticed that every meeting he had with me, he would take several notes and always had another staff member/coworker present as a witness to our conversations. I noticed later that he was recording our conversations with a tape recorder without my permission. He also installed cameras and recorders in my classroom so he could collect evidence of my personal conversations and actions with students and/or coworkers as well as the representative from the teachers union. He made sure that the additional duties and deadlines he was imposing upon me were part of a written record that could be used later if he should need evidence against me. I had never been put in this kind of position before. At least that was the vibe

I was getting from him. It was clear that the personal and past relationship the two of us had no longer existed. It was all professional and almost distant as we met face to face. In fact, it was almost like a chess game that we were playing, and each of us waited for the next move to decide what play to execute. What I wasn't prepared for was the amount of fear that I felt when in the director's presence. I admit that some of that fear might have been caused from the experiences I encountered during my divorce proceedings. I was not a stranger to feeling that around the next corner, someone could quickly cause me harm, whether it was in the form of physical, verbal, or emotional abuse. But this was happening in my work situation, not my personal life. It was seeming to me that his actions of revenge had become very personal and that he was looking at what had happened as a form of betrayal. From having many private conversations with the director when he acted as my confidant, he learned the triggers that I would feel to cause me to have anxiety and/or the fear to be in his presence. I was feeling more and more unsafe as the days continued. I couldn't believe that this was the very same man who offered me a safe haven and now was making his goal every day to harass me as much as he could. I felt as if he wanted me to quit my job or make it hard for me to successfully stay in it.

After having another anxiety and vertigo attack one day and taken to the hospital by ambulance, I realized the toll this relationship was taking on my health. The doctor and therapist had both warned me about the effects that additional stress could have on my recovery from vertigo attacks. After being released from the hospital and once again picked up by my ex-husband, I came home that day to find that the director had left a message on my telephone answering machine. He told me that he believed I was unable to work to his satisfaction and I could not return to work unless I agreed to have a twelve-hour psychological evaluation that would prove I was unfit for duty to work. Not only had I been officially suspended of all duties, but I was also being required to travel to the state capital of West Virginia to see a specially assigned clinical psychologist who would decide my fate for the future. This whole episode was beyond belief and such a betrayal from my director, a man who knew intimate details of my past, a man who chose to divulge those details to the administrative board and gave them just enough information to support his action on suspending me for the several months ahead. I was now being punished for something I had done decades ago. It may have only been details that I shared with a friend, but I trusted that friend. He promised to keep me safe. And now he was threatening me and trying to get me fired. This action was going to be as bad as, or even worse than, going through a divorce for me. My career and integrity were being questioned. I had never experienced this kind of activity in my whole life. Now not only were my life and my career being threatened, but I felt as if the future of the students and staff who worked at the center could also be in jeopardy. He communicated to the council that all my actions and medical problems were due to the stress of my recent divorce and had nothing to do with him or his actions toward me.

I found out later that the students had staged a walkout at the center. The day I was taken by ambulance, they felt proved that the center was not safe for them. And when they stated their concerns, the director told them that my being taken by ambulance had nothing to do with him and was all a result of my personal problems in the past. Because he shared my history with one of the superintendents in the county, students were also told that I might be suicidal and unfit for duty to work because of my emotional instability. Meanwhile, he told the board that I was responsible for the walkout and that the only way to control the student body and keep them safe was to remove me from my position. It was as if I was step 2 in his plan to sabotage the center's growth and success. I'm not sure at this time what step 3 was going to be, but the faculty and students and community were about to find out.

So that I wouldn't be alone in facing this, I asked my sister to accompany me and drive to the city with me. It took us about four to five hours. I submitted myself to the evaluation and passed with flying colors. Only after contacting the local teachers union representative and retaining services of a lawyer did I find out the evaluation showed that I only had anxiety and fear for safety when I was in the presence of the director. What he had hoped to prove was that I had become incoherent and suicidal. In addition, he wanted to prove to the board and to the student body that my fears, concerns, actions, and words had nothing to do with him but everything to do with what had happened during the time of my first divorce. He felt that completing this evaluation would give him the evidence he needed to terminate my contract and find me unfit for duty to work. He tried so hard to convince everyone that because I had attempted suicide during my first divorce, I was contemplating doing it again after my second divorce, and the emotional and physical reaction I was having due to his sexual harassment was actually in response to being recently divorced and had nothing to do with his harassment. He shared all this confidential information without my permission to do so. The evaluation also demonstrated no other actions that would label me unfit for duty. Being declared unfit for duty and removed from my position as school counselor/diversified cooperative training instructor was the objective of his actions. But even with all his effort to do so, he was unable to reach success. His retaliation against me for standing up for the financial coordinator when she was being harassed would not cease. He was determined to make me pay for my actions. He kept me from being able to perform my duties for seven and a half months. I was not allowed to even step into the building without his permission. Passing the psychological examination was not enough for him to allow me to return to work. With the help of legal assistance and support from my coworkers and teachers union, I was eventually able to obtain a little justice. My lawyer representative from the teachers union worked it out with his lawyer that I was fit to return to work, but he was to stay away from me unless he had someone present to witness our actions. The betrayal I felt and experienced from this relationship resulted in a class action lawsuit, which, in time, finally removed this individual from his duties, but not before the state department of education and governing board had to take over operation of the career and technical center and place a state monitor in the position of director after declaring the school an unsafe place to attend. This man ordered me to stop giving GED exams and service personnel testing. He also issued an order to all faculty that we could not send any student to the office during our classes for anything. He took away our ability to make phone calls without calling the office and getting permission first. We were not allowed to communicate with previous administration or state department officials. Thank goodness, the state department of education listened to all the calls they received about the center being an institution that was not safe. They responded and did their best to correct the situation.

Make no mistake, the damage had already been done and was irreversible. My ability to trust others had been damaged, and I wasn't sure if I could learn to trust anyone again. It was clear that the damage that was done to faculty and staff at the center was also irreversible. The center would suffer consequences for many years to come and may never be able to get back to being a school of excellence. This particular lawsuit went on for several years. This man was determined to be placed back in his position so he could retaliate and do even more harm to more individuals. Luckily, I was able to retire and move out of the state before he was able to accomplish that. Had it not been for the wonderful coworkers that I kept company with, I may not have survived that ordeal, but my coworkers and staff bonded together and turned into a family. We became a force to be reckoned with. We were fortunate to find a lawyer to represent us that treated the lawsuit as a class action suit. She believed in us and could see the collateral damage that one man could do in a few short months. She had experienced similar behavior once in a workplace, and so she attacked this case with passion and gave it her top priority. She knew that it was not just the faculty and staff being harmed by his actions, but it was also the students and community being harmed. And yet as she worked each and every day to fight our battle, we all watched as the superintendents of the three counties and the administrative board continued to be manipulated by this man as if they were puppets on a string. And that is why when the state board of education had to take over, they also had to take all authority away from the administrative council and functioning governing board as well. Our faculty connected fiercely with one another through crisis and trauma. As a result, together, this body of believers of right and wrong became a strong entity when fighting for survival. I will always feel close to the people I worked with and will always remember that you don't have to go through any adversity alone. Just look around and those who are feeling what you are feeling will offer support, both emotionally and financially. Eventually, we won our case. The financial coordinator ended up working for a neighboring county, and they truly appreciated all the assets she had to offer.

It has been several years since all of this took place, and the gentleman in question is still trying to sue the state department and its entities. The scars of the effects of his actions will remain in our lives forever. It has taken many years of praying for that friend that he too could find peace within. I wasn't sure whether I could find it in my heart to forgive him, but I remembered how God forgave us and set the example for us to follow. So why can't we forgive those who sin against us? It took longer than I would have liked, but with lots of prayers and guidance, I finally was able to reach that point of forgiveness, yet I have not been tested with that by coming face to face with him. I can only hope, with God by my side, I will have the strength to demonstrate my forgiveness in his presence and set the same example to him that God has set for me. To quote Matthew 14:31, it says, "Immediately Jesus reached out his hand and caught him. 'You of little faith,' he said, 'why did you doubt?'" Because of all this, I feel the advice of killing him with kindness is better than killing yourself with bitterness. At least your stress level will be decreased.

When I asked the internet to give me a definition for betrayal, this is what I found: "The term betrayed is used as a transitive verb and is derived from the term betray which means to be disloyal to someone or a cause. It can also be used to mean to give information to an enemy or to deliver something to an enemy in infringement of a trust." This definition describes exactly what this person did to me and too many others. Only he can atone for his sins and find the peace he needs within. Only he can come to grips with the harm and hurt he not only caused but induced on others as he lived a few short months in a dream of his own making. The center will be changed forever, but all those who survived this ordeal will, in time, become stronger and wiser.

CHAPTER 7

Discovering New Horizons

Growing up as a lost penny on the back of a hidden shelf, losing my mom to cancer, losing my first husband to another woman, losing my second husband to abuse and unwillingness to accept my children, and being betrayed by a close and dear friend—all these played a huge role and effect on my future actions, feelings, goals, and dreams. I found myself questioning my every thought as well as my every action. What had I done to deserve all this, and what could I do to change the course that my life seemed to be traveling in?

While visiting my son and his wife in Texas and recuperating from recent knee surgery, I noticed my daughter-in-law using social media, especially Facebook. Because she came from another country (Indonesia), it was her way of staying in touch with her family and friends. It seemed to come so easily to her. I inquired about what all that was about. She quickly taught me how to get a user ID and password and sign up for Yahoo and meet people with your same interest area and pursuits, including available senior males for dating in my local area. This was such a new experience for me that I found myself very intrigued, and I wanted to learn more. I've always tried to keep up with technology, but I was discovering there was a whole new world out there that I had yet to discover. At the same time, I questioned whether I was even partially ready and willing to live in that new world. On the other hand, however, finding a way to screen people who might become possibilities for me to date found its way into my curiosity.

After I returned home, I found that when I was tired in the evening and just wanted to unwind, I would surf the net to see what dating sites and matchmaking sites were actually available to the public. I really liked the eharmony site because you had to spend hours completing their surveys so that they could find only the right or exact match for you. They wanted to make sure only those who complemented you would respond. It took a while, but eventually I received about three match responses. But even though they were matched to me, I assumed I was not a match to them because I never heard from them again. Then there was match.com. They too had you complete a questionnaire to make the percentage of good matches for you increase, not to mention this sight was endorsed by Dr. Phil, who would damage his reputation if something criminal were to happen to you. From there, I went to perfectmatch.com, and then to seniorpeoplemeet, Christian mingle, and many others. There was an annual fee to pay for all these, so I wanted to get my money's worth. I began to get emails, phone calls, Instant Messaging, and yes, even roses sent to me. Of course, all this attention was making me feel very special. And none of them hesitated to send me several pictures so that I would become even more interested in them. Was I interested in continuing this type of communication? I thought to myself, *What was the harm of all this?* Because it was I that controlled how much or how little or in what way communication with these individuals continued, and that meant that I could stop at any time. I even decided it was best to hook up with someone who lived out of town so I didn't have to worry about seeing them in my everyday life if it happened not to work out.

Due to the many illnesses and surgeries I experienced during the past few years, it was great to visit with my children and grandchild in South Carolina after Christmas one year, but like all good things, the visit had to end because I needed to return to West Virginia to go back to work after the Christmas holidays. For my return trip to West Virginia, the weather was bad enough that all planes were delayed that were traveling north, and I ended up spending the whole day at the airport in South Carolina on New Year's Eve. Little did I know that this would allow me to pick up some bacteria that would set off an ear infection that would affect me for the rest of my life. After being diagnosed with yet another type of vertigo (labyrinthitis), I was unable to perform normal duties at work or at home. Going to visit doctors and getting treatment turned out to be an everyday activity for many weeks to come. The specialists I saw put me on medical leave, and I was not able to return to work until I could walk without falling or the dizziness I was experiencing came to a complete halt. Now I have been treated for Meniere's Disease, peripheral vertigo, BPPV (a type of vertigo meaning Benign Paroxysmal Positional Vertigo, which exhibited crystals becoming loose in the ear canal), labyrinthitis, and finally central vertigo.

Each time I experienced a new type of vertigo, it would be accompanied by a new set of symptoms. The first time, I encountered complete hearing loss in the right ear, coupled with very high-pitched ringing in the ears, not to mention the sensation of myself or the room spinning or moving coupled with severe nausea and vomiting. I had difficulty focusing the eyes, severe dizziness, loss of balance, which caused me to fall without warning, slurred speech, and critical weakness of the limbs, which meant I had difficulty walking or traveling from space to space. There was an increase in blood pressure and heartbeat. Loss of balance and coordination continued to be a problem I faced each morning as I awoke. Doctors encouraged me to keep a journal to track symptoms and times of day the symptoms or attack appeared.

After completing many diagnostic tests, including EEGs, MRIs, MRAs, CAT scans, and other hearing tests as needed, and completing twenty weeks of vestibular therapy, my prognosis was still dim. I was treated with antihistamines (Mucinex, etc.) Antivert (meclizine), benzodiazepines (such as diazepam and clonazepam), and promethazine (to treat nausea and vomiting). I was told to keep still, sit, or lie down when any symptoms occur and only gradually resume activity. I was also to avoid sudden position changes, not try to read when symptoms occur, and avoid bright lights. When you experience symptoms like this for twenty hours out of a twenty-four-hour day, you are only existing, not living.

Living alone and feeling ill at the same time gave me every opportunity to feel vulnerable. Once again, I checked out the online dating sites and social media on the internet. This time, I decided to take it more seriously. And I only felt well enough to even look on the internet possibly one hour a day. I did not have the stamina or the ability to do more than that while recuperating. One site called seniorpeoplemeet.com caught my attention because I didn't have to screen out all the possibilities with regard to age and ethnic background and religion, etc. It would be done for me. Before I knew it, I was being contacted by many different males, and I thought, *Why not respond? What or who could this possibly hurt?*

As these relationships began to develop, I continued to quiz myself on whether I really wanted to get involved in something like this. I had a girlfriend who utilized these sites quite regularly and found tremendous success with them. She is actually married now because of one special relationship she found and only one-hour distance from her home. And besides, Match.com seemed to be number one in a number of successful marriages and dating relationships, and they sponsored this particular site (or so I was told).

The first man I met and dated from the internet was a lawyer living a couple hours away in West Virginia near the Maryland border. He had a brother that lived near me, so I thought it would be nice if we got together after writing several emails back and forth and talking to each other on the phone. This was to be my trial run. Even though several others wanted to meet me, I was pretty particular. Finding the right guy was very important to me if I were going to use this internet dating as a screening process. And besides, all the ones living in the town I lived in seemed to be just a little too anxious to meet and wanted to get serious too soon (based on our emails and conversations). I decided to meet him for lunch one day and maybe stroll around downtown, seeing the sites. We made plans to meet Thanksgiving week when I had time off from work. He would drive to the town I lived in for our first date but told me he would have to take the day off. We had talked a lot on the phone and emailed back and forth, so it seemed innocent enough and the logical next step was for us to meet. We met in the parking lot of a very nice restaurant, which chose to be closed on that particular day for lunch and not open till dinner. It was a seasonal thing, so we had to go somewhere else. This guy was tall, dark, and handsome and very intelligent. My first reaction was, "Way to go. You nailed this one." I think we both enjoyed spending time together and were able to carry on a good conversation. We seemed to have a lot in common. After we finished touring the town, he wanted to go back to my place, and I thought it probably couldn't hurt at this point. Plus, he seemed like someone I could trust. Before we met in person, he gave me enough information to check him out with the State Bar Association so that I would not feel uncomfortable. We spent some time together talking and seemed to get along well. It was raining that day, and the temperature was decreasing rapidly. My house was just a place of recluse since the weather was deteriorating on us.

And then the kiss out of nowhere came as I was showing him my house. I wanted sparks but only got surprise at the time. Did I expect a kiss that quickly? I guess not because the date itself seemed so prim and proper. Then an ice storm started to hit the area, and I was so concerned for his safety that I urged him to go ahead and leave. I guess I wasn't feeling comfortable enough to ask a total stranger to spend the night because of the weather and cold. I got the feeling that might be what he wanted, but I let my gut be my thermometer, and it told me to suggest that he head back to the town that he lived in. Then it would be his decision as to whether he stayed in a motel overnight and whether he stayed in this town or not. I was actually hoping to hear from him that he arrived home safely, but we did not speak on the phone again. We just kept in touch by email.

Needless to say, I was surprised when he kissed me on the lips without any warning. Because we did enjoy each other's company, I realized we could make this relationship work if one of us were willing to give up the hours we could get together. He worked weekends, and I worked during the week. So that caused a problem for us, and it seemed as though neither of us were willing to budge on that issue, not because we didn't want to, but because our hours could not be worked out. So I simply took it as a sign that love was not going to be found in this relationship, at least not for now. And what was the hurry anyway? I knew that this was a man who I could have an occasional meal with now and if I desired some male company. We had no problem communicating, but stubborn we both were. And that added an air of mystery to our relationship. We did stay friends, however, and continued to communicate through emails. I was grateful that the afternoon I spent with him was met with no vertigo spells, so that told me the meeting was not too stressful for me. Whether I would consider online dating again in the future would be a question left up in the air. But at least my first experience was a positive one. So I decided to put the next step in God's hands, and he could guide me. In his way, he had allowed me to dip my finger into the chocolate and taste it but gave me a definitive answer that I needed to stop at one taste and not get sick eating too much at one time.

CHAPTER 8

Love in Disguise

Because of the first relationship not working out or one that I felt was going to continue, I opened myself up to screening more applicants for dating. Of course, I was used to interviewing job applicants plus reviewing and screening student job and scholarship applications, but this was a little different. I knew from the beginning that I had been a participant in two marriages that ended in divorce. So there were certain criteria that I looked for if I wanted to develop a personal relationship with someone. I was hoping that this list would allow the computer to do what it was supposed to do—automatically screen applicants for me.

It wasn't long before I met Jerome. He not only responded by emails but also to my Instant Messenger. He would call each day and say exactly what I wanted and even needed to hear. He had a kind of accent that made him difficult to understand at times, and his messages seemed to contain a lot of broken English. That is to say that his emails were nothing short of very romantic. I shared some of them with my friends and my sisters, who thought this guy was just too good to be true. I thought I had met a person who was sensitive and creative as well as very romantic. Yes, of course, I was flying on cloud nine. And then we started chatting with one another each day on Yahoo as well as all the other methods we communicated with. We couldn't seem to get enough of each other.

We finally decided to plan a meeting to meet one another as soon as possible, even though he lived five hours away in Chesapeake,

Virginia. I used to visit my daughter when she lived in Virginia once a month, so I figured five hours would not be too hard on me, especially if we took turns every other weekend. For our first meeting though, we would each drive a couple hours one way and meet for dinner. That was the plan.

Jerome was an engineer and had his own business. He was working on a contract to build an office building in Lagos, Nigeria. When he was called away for business out of the country, he assured me that he would be back in no more than three weeks and hoped that I could wait that long for us to have our first meeting. After I gave it some thought, I realized that three weeks were really not that long. Surely, I could be patient that long for our first meeting together. We were in touch so often that feelings for him began to develop quickly. Of course, he had taken his son out of private school to go with him, and conveniently, his son could keep up with required studies by internet. He was twelve years old. He sent me pictures of himself and with his son to keep reminding me of our fondness for one another.

Eventually, my heart started pounding more often, and thoughts and feelings of love meandered my way. Could this even be possible with someone I haven't met in person? We stayed in touch every day. He made me feel so special. When I would excuse myself from the lunch table with my coworkers to answer his call, my friends knew from my face that I was happy and falling in love.

Being sick was not a big deal when you knew the one you loved would be home at any given moment. It was fun to think before the year was out, I would be married to a man whom had everything I ever looked for in someone. His engineering degree led me to believe he had qualities similar to what my son possessed, and that was a good thing. I knew that this person would never hurt me the way my two ex-husbands had done. His son, whom he adored, appeared to love me just as much. He showed excitement when thinking about meeting my children and family. He would even surprise me and phone when I was in the middle of teaching class at the career center and/or in the middle of a visit with my sisters on the weekend just so he could talk to them and to let them know he loved me. He said he wanted to put a smile on my face. Yes, it was easy for him to grab my heart because I was in love now, and I needed no more convincing. I was simply living in the moment. He was the answer to all my prayers and dreams. He wrote beautiful love poems and literally made me swoon. When I saw my ex-husband out and about, I felt I owed it to him to tell him I had found the man of my dreams and I would probably be married before the end of the year. My ex was so suspicious and actually wondered what I had gotten myself into. He actually laughed when I gave him the news, as if I were dreaming. Of course, at the time, my ex had no idea that I had only met this person online and had never laid eyes upon him except through the pictures he had sent to me.

Everything seemed to be on schedule, and he would return to the States as scheduled. And then I received that phone call of desperation. Jerome and his son had just been mugged, and the muggers had left with all his money, credit cards, passports, and papers. I felt so badly for him.

Jerome was mortified as he expressed his concern for his son's injuries. He made sure he got him to the hospital to assess his injuries. He said the muggers had hit his son's leg with a club when his son tried to get them off of his father. The doctors informed him that they could not treat him and would not operate unless they had the money upfront. Because the muggers left him with nothing, he was asking for my help. He told me he had frozen all his accounts back in the States because his housekeeper had taken his money the last time to the tune of $120,000, so he was not going to let that happen, and his credit cards would not work there in Nigeria. I didn't think twice about it and sent him money through Western Union to help his child. He assured me he would pay back every cent he owed with interest upon his immediate return. I even spoke to the doctor to make sure that all went well and that he had received the money so he could operate. I sent the money to Jerome, and to receive it, he had to have a test question and answer. The year 2009 was going to be the year I found my real true love. I was sure of it. It was unfortunate his trip home would be delayed because of his son's recovery and ability to travel, but I was willing to wait. We continued to send each other pictures and talked every day. While his son was recuperating, progress on the office complex he was building seemed to reach a snag, and he informed me it would be a while longer till he returned. He was having trouble with equipment and labor. Once again, he needed financial help so that he could fix the equipment and finish the contract. Time moved quickly while we continued to keep in touch each day.

Jerome told me that he lived in Chesapeake, Virginia, and he owned a 3,800 square foot home, so it was my plan to move there after I retired. I was able to see the house on Google earth, and it looked like one I could be satisfied with. Yes, we talked about marriage, and of course, he proposed to me, and I accepted. Until then, we would be a weekend couple. He told me he had two vehicles and that I could have the Jaguar to run around in. Since I lived in a 3,400 square foot home, I felt his house would be plenty big for all of us.

After being gone for three months instead of three weeks, Jerome and his son were finally ready to come home. And then as they were leaving the hotel, his son fell down the steps at the hotel and had to be put back in the hospital again, and he needed more money to take care of yet another operation. Of course, I responded. The amount I was sending him started to add up. Sometimes, I had to send close to ten thousand dollars at a time.

Before I knew it, my emotions were being controlled by something that did not seem familiar to me. I was sending thousands and thousands of dollars through Western Union to someone I had not met (in person, that is). I was also lying to them and to my friends that I had previously met him in person face to face. This was totally against my personal ethics. Western Union prided themselves on working with its clients to prevent fraud and eventually started asking questions since so much money was leaving the United States and being received by one particular person. As I heard the questions they would ask me when they called, I started questioning my actions. This was not me, nor did I begin to recognize the person I had become. I continued to tell them upon inquiry that yes, I had indeed met him in person so that he was just not stealing my money and savings from me. I guess I truly felt we had met since we had webcammed, spoke on the phone, and Instant Messaged so much. It was so unlike me to lie, but it was love (or what I thought was love) that did the responding to their many questions. I definitely did not have the kind of money that I could give away at a moment's notice. But after this hospitalization and another month of recuperation, they were ready to come home again. Jerome told me he would come home to be with me and then return to Nigeria to finish the job. He didn't want us to be apart anymore. He wanted to come straight to my house and move in with me. Again, he also said he would immediately pay back all funds I had sent him plus interest. He reminded me that he had frozen his own accounts in the States while he was out of the country and had no access to his own bank accounts. I inquired at a local bank to see if this was possible, and they assured me that no one could touch his holdings except him, and that would not be allowed unless he appeared in person. He could not call them and arrange for them to send him the amount he needed. So I realized that I was his only hope, or so I thought.

And then the call came while I was in the emergency room getting a broken nose stitched and taken care of. I asked him if he was in Virginia and on American soil. He said no, that he had been arrested because he had words with the authorities at the airport. He seemed to have difficulty leaving the country. He was in Lagos, Nigeria, and because his identification (including his and his son's passports) and credit cards and cash were stolen during the mugging, he had to pay immigration to have new IDs made. And that, of course, would take some time to happen. Then he had to pay fees to leave the country. There was also the hotel bill because his stay was much longer than he first anticipated. The authorities there told him all bills had to be paid in full before he could get on the plane. This time, I was able to talk with the hotel manager to inquire about the status of the amount that he owed to them. I found myself sending him money that he would even use to buy a meal. He told me that a plate of lasagna would cost him about three hundred dollars. Because I had had no experience dealing with any of this before, I assumed everything he was telling me was correct. I was in love, so why in the world would I ever challenge what my future husband would tell me? As I think back about all this, he was not even concerned about the fact that

I was in the emergency room or why. This was a big red flag that I seemed to miss altogether.

Because the amount of dollars that I was sending through Western Union was happening over and over, eventually, Western Union said I could not send anymore. I had lied and said that Jerome was my fiancé (which I totally believed at the time) and that I had indeed met him in person and he was someone I knew and had been with. I told them the mugging had prevented him from coming home. I believed each weekend that he would arrive. So much so that I made reservations at Sleep Inn in Winchester, Virginia, so that we could meet the day after he was supposed to arrive. After five weekends straight of making these reservations, the staff at Sleep Inn felt like they knew me well enough to sympathize with me about my fiancé having so much trouble catching up with me. Everyone I talked with showed empathy and had no reason to doubt me or the story I was telling them. Western Union insisted on proof of why he needed any more money from me. When I made the request from Jerome, he sent the invoice/bill from the hotel manager and emailed it to me. I sent it to Western Union, but they decided it was not in my best interest to continue sending money. At the time, I thought how could they get away with telling me what to do with my money. But the truth was, they were looking out for me and my welfare and trying hard to prevent fraud from happening and them being a party to it.

I switched over to MoneyGram to send him the money he needed. There was no need or no evidence to tell me that he might never be able to arrive here in the States. Jerome never failed to convince me that he was indeed coming home each, and every weekend and then, something would happen to him to keep him there, and he was unable to get on the plane. Eventually, MoneyGram said I couldn't send anymore, and I went back to Western Union. I was drilled by their fraud department, and they requested a copy of the hotel bill again or anything to prove where he was spending the money I had sent to him so they would know what he was using the money for. After calling the hotel manager and talking to Jerome, they sent me the needed documentation so that I would be able to send the money he requested. He told me he was up all night preparing it. That didn't make sense to me, but as usual, I did not question it. Jerome assured me over and over that he would pay every cent back that I loaned him upon his return to the States. Before long, I started adding up all the money I had sent him. Months had gone by instead of weeks. It appeared that he had received about $200,000 from me, which included the monthly payments as well as increased interest rates on the remaining balance each month. I was starting to panic because I was realizing I had borrowed enough money on my credit cards and used up all my savings to the point that I would have to mortgage my home to pay off the debts I encountered because of him, a home that was completely paid for and one that I had fought hard to keep during the last divorce. At the time I borrowed the money on my credit cards, I believed he would be home and pay back the loan with interest before I even received my monthly credit card bill. I knew my credit score would be in jeopardy, and I needed to figure out what was really happening and if Jerome was really who he said he was.

The pull he had on me, I could not explain. Finally, on the way to South Carolina to meet my family during the holidays, I got up the nerve to drive to his house, only to find out it wasn't exactly what I expected. And it certainly was not 3,800 square feet. No one came to the door, even though there were three vehicles parked in the driveway, so I thought maybe he does have someone checking on the house each day. And for someone who had his own business as an engineer, the yard and surroundings were not as manicured as I would have expected. This was when the red flags started to make more sense. And I could see my ex-husband laughing at me for being quite the fool for doing what I had done.

Jerome kept asking for more money. He even asked me to pay the membership to seniorpeoplemeet.com for his hotel manager so that his new friend could find someone to help him the way I was helping Jerome. At the time, I started feeling a little used and wondered why the man who I loved would even make a request of this magnitude when I was sitting home waiting for him to appear, going more and more into debt as each day went by because of him. I knew

I had to start paying attention to all the red flags that were going up because I was in trouble with the credit card companies. Every waking moment, I was thinking of him and the results that all of his actions were having on me. I remember even asking my son to loan me some money to send to him or have one of his coworkers in the area to check the man out to see if he could help him to come back to the States. My son said the story sounded like a scam to him and urged me to suspend all communication with this man immediately. Did I listen to him? Of course not. This was just a bad dream, and I didn't want to lose the man I had fallen in love with.

It was time for me to take action to protect myself. So I researched and contacted a private investigator in Virginia and had him investigate to see if Jerome actually existed. I figured the ten thousand I had to pay him would be worth it if I could have peace of mind. After hours of surveillance and finally several interviews and checking IP addresses on the computer from past emails, the investigator found out that Jerome had stolen someone's identity from the Navy, and many women had been scammed by this person. An innocent couple lived in the house at the address he had given me, and I was able to talk with the woman who resided there. I couldn't believe I had given up my savings and my house to this man I had never met, not to mention the thousands of dollars it cost to pay the investigator.

After my divorce, I was so desperate to find someone I could trust and someone who would always protect me and love my children that I became blind to the obvious. After reporting this scam to the authorities (local, county, and state plus the FBI), they had me continue to contact him and set up a sting. When everything was about to go down and I was about to wire him five thousand dollars, they informed me that because he was in Africa, that unless he was willing to come back voluntarily, they could not force him to return to the US without causing a national incident. So I was unable to get the justice I deserved. I even contacted another one of his victims (information given to me from the private investigator), and she was not willing to admit that this had happened to her also, and she certainly didn't want her family to know anything. I guess I thought that if I had someone else who would speak up about the injustice that had been done to them, I could get dateline or some news show to help us locate him and tell our story to the public in an honest and respectful way. It was clear to me, however, after talking to her on the phone, this was not going to happen.

I was alone. I had to face the consequences by myself. I had to accept responsibility for my actions. Thank God I was employed.

A year later, I heard from Jerome through a random email bragging about what he had done and showing pride in the success of his plight. Once again, my trust was shattered. My world was full of people who liked to use others and make them believe that God was the true source of connection. I found myself with distaste in my mouth for all that had happened, and I watched my health continue to decline once more from the additional stress.

I find it is probably hard for anyone (especially myself) to imagine that a bright, intelligent, and educated woman could be taken in by someone to this extent or for this insane amount of money. After taking a glimpse of some of the communications and emails I received, it was hard to understand why I did not become more skeptical of Jerome's actions a lot sooner than I did. I felt like I was watching the ten o'clock news and listening to those who believe and/or say "This could never happen to me." The truth is, and it has been my unfortunate experience that it can and possibly will happen to anyone who finds themselves jilted, cheated on, divorced, unloved, vulnerable for love, or feeling alone in any given situation.

As my story continues, it is hard to feel the full effects of how one is affected by something happening to them like this unless you are able to step into their shoes as they begin to feel the height of emotion felt between two human beings. One year after meeting Jerome online, I applied for a loan to mortgage my house, which had been previously paid off and provided security for my future. After mortgaging my home, the monthly payments put quite a strain on my budget. I had never made a payment that large each month and found myself under a lot of stress. I was able to pay off all my credit cards that had provided me a quick loan to send to him. It felt so good to know I had a zero balance on the credit cards once again, as well as a restored excellent credit rating, but it did not feel good that I had to make twelve hundred-dollar monthly payments on my house each month.

When I finally broke down and shared what had happened with my children, I knew I had shaken up their trust and respect for me. This was during a time when my health declined also. In conjunction with all that, my son asked me over and over about what stress I was under to cause my health to decline so rapidly. When I told him the truth, he came home for a visit and loaned me fifty thousand dollars to assist me in paying off the credit card bills. I worked hard for two years to get myself to a place where I could feel comfortable once again. I also wanted to be able to pay my son back as soon as possible also. He loaned me the money to help pay off the credit cards and take the pressure off the other bills that were arriving each month, but he had no idea about the total amount I had given away. I was in a bind and began to accept the feeling of being squeezed. The stress this ordeal caused me to have was certainly not worth the way it affected my general health. My problems with vertigo started to worsen as well increase in severity and length. I came to realize my declining health would continue unless I could figure a way out of the situation.

As I continued to struggle to meet the monthly payments, I watched my state of wellness continue to fail or make any improvement. I was finding I was unable to work five days straight in a week, so I had to consider the option of retiring as a possible solution. But following up on that option was going to mean I would have to sell the house and move somewhere smaller and a place where I could afford or manage easier. This option was going to be one that I needed to research and investigate. Keeping that in mind, however, made me realize that my friends and family would soon begin to suspect something was not right with my life and the direction it was going.

My son had already demonstrated an act of kindness and rescue by loaning me the fifty thousand dollars. He was looking out for my best interests. I loved him and his wife for that. But I continued to struggle with the decision as to what to do next when I began falling into that big black hole again.

CHAPTER 9

Unconditional Love

About this time something happened I didn't expect. I was checking some of my emails one night and found an old classmate who I was very close to in both high school and college trying to contact me through Facebook. I only checked Facebook maybe once a month if I was lucky, and sometimes I went as long as three to six months. I responded to his email, and after exchanging personal emails, addresses, and phone numbers, we decided to keep in touch on a more regular basis. We both shared dismay that we had allowed so much time and distance to come between us. We talked on the phone every week or as often as we could to make up for lost time. Over fifty years ago, this was a man I dated in high school and college, not to mention he was a dear friend. We learned to love one another, but in a way that communicated through our hearts and souls, not through physical touch or intimacy. It was so good to reach out to a Christian and a friend who had become a pastor in Chicago and married the girl of his dreams. He told me they would visit someday, and he was very sincere when he said it. And as my vertigo seemed to get worse (probably from all the stress), I knew in my heart he would keep that promise. The relationship we developed seemed to evolve as time stood still.

It wasn't long before I received a call from him and his wife that they were traveling to West Virginia. Of course, I was absolutely elated. Not only did he and his endearing wife come for a visit, but this was the first time I had ever spent time with his wife, and she made me feel like I had known her all my life. She was as sweet and kind as they come. We quickly bonded as if we had known each other all our lives, and I treated her as if she were my sister. She knew what I needed and quickly responded as if we had been lifelong friends. Of course, my friend loved seeing us girls become as close as we did. And she realized why it was so important to him to come to West Virginia. He had already known in his heart that the two of us would gel and had assured me of that ahead of time. His wife had such a unique talent. She sat at my piano and began to play. It was music ringing in my ears. Never had I heard such inspirational messages and music coming from any one person or musical instrument in my life. I felt God's presence in that room and the security that he indeed was looking out for all of us. I will never forget that. It was as if we were standing at the pearly gates of heaven and waiting for someone to open the door. Once more in my life, I was experiencing divine intervention.

And my forever rekindled friend showed me the most unconditional love that I could ever experience. All my life, not only had I searched for that kind of love from family, friends, lovers, etc., but to this day, I had never received it or even had a slight inclination of what it was about. That was about to change. He called me his treasure because it took so long for him to find me again. This is the first time in my life that I felt someone being so nonjudgmental, so noncritical, and so full of the spirit of God that he exuberated kindness, generosity, and love. He never put himself first. God was first and foremost in his life, and his actions spoke volumes to validate just that. And now here I was on the receiving end of the most unconditional love any human being could give, no questions asked. In truth, that unconditional love was coming from God himself. Why had I not realized that before? Why did I need a messenger to show me that? Did my children and family think something was wrong with our relationship? Of course, they did. They thought I was having an emotional affair, and they weren't shy about telling me that. I found out later that they even thought I was sending him money to finance his ministry. There was entirely no shame or guilt in our relationship, and I felt honored to have him as my friend.

My dear friend became my confidant, my personal guide to God's Word, world, and heaven. Not only was he the most valued person in my life, but he kept me honest and sincere and never failed to make me laugh or smile. I loved his uncanny ability to always make sure I was feeling high and in a positive spirit before he hung up the phone. We had such a special connection. Every time I was having a crisis or a bad day, it seemed that God responded by letting him know, and he would call me. If I were sad, happy, desperate, or simply in need of a hug or a little understanding, I would receive a personal call or message from him. It was as if he knew I needed him, and he was there. And every time I thanked him, he would tell me, "It's not me that is doing it. I am just God's messenger." And truly he was. His wife loved to shop at any Goodwill Store, and he was happy to drop her off and pick her up at the door. But while she was shopping, he would call me from the parking lot, and it became a joke between us that he called me only when he was waiting in a parking lot for her to finish shopping.

He tried to make each holiday and sometimes just any unspecified day into a day with special memories for me or a day of celebration. Without knowing it or expecting it, a small gift would arrive in the mail, and it would be a message in some way letting me know I was constantly receiving God's love. I remember one time receiving chocolate-covered strawberries. And of course, I enjoyed every bite. He told me he just wanted me to feel special that day.

Since I was going home to attend my niece's wedding in October, I scheduled a stop on the way in Chicago just so I could visit him and his wife. They both made me feel so welcome and comfortable in their presence and in their home. Their family also welcomed me and treated me well. There was nothing but love exuberating from this family of God. He always made a person feel like you were the most important person on this earth. I was so blessed to have a friend like him. They both ended up extending an invitation to me that I was welcome to come visit or stay with them any time I could get away. If there were ever a couple I could be soulmates with, it would be them.

Each month, a package would arrive, and I knew before I opened it that it was from him. It might be something simple like a mirror cover for my iPhone or a shamrock from Ireland. When I called to thank him, he would say, "Every day, I want you to look into that mirror and say to yourself that you are loved." He wanted me to feel God's love, no matter where I was or no matter what I was doing. I loved the attention I was getting and the way I felt every time I hung up the phone from conversing with him.

My son and daughter and even the rest of the family who only could hear my side of the conversation couldn't get over how happy I was every time I talked to him. They also noticed how much I would laugh while talking to him. He had such a sense of humor. Sometimes, the gifts he sent would make me laugh. He knew I loved daisies, so one time, I opened the package, and inside was a tiny little yellow pot with one yellow plastic daisy sticking out of it. The pot was solar-powered, so as it sat in front of my window on the end table in the living room, it would bob back and forth as if it was saying, "Everything is okay, sunshine. You will have a good day." I still look at that daisy even today, and it reminds me of the angel sitting on my shoulder watching over me. I also received an afghan that had the message "Live, Laugh, Love." He practiced that message every day of his life and taught me how to do the same.

Each day, I would ask myself, what did I do to deserve this kind of love and admiration? And the answer always came to me. Just love God as your savior and your Lord.

While I was visiting him in Chicago one night, he could tell I was troubled and asked if he could help. I didn't want to admit or let him know the shame and guilt I was feeling for committing such a disastrous behavior once more. My friend was the one person I confided in and told my story to before I wrote this novel. He never made me feel uneasy and provided me with continued support and guidance. He knew how much I was struggling with what I had done and how hard it was for me to live with my daughter at the time. I was there to help her with her newborn twins. She had the uncanny ability to make me feel like I never did anything right and I was constantly under her critical eye and bruising comments. I was so happy when I was with my grandchildren. I loved them so much. But the stress I felt when around her continued to increase, and I found myself in survival mode each day and not enjoying the time I was having with her.

One evening on May 10, 2013, my friend and I were talking on the phone. He had just told me he wished he were here to rescue me from all that was happening so that I could finally feel that inner peace that I so deserved. That was the last time I heard from him. At that moment, while on the phone, he went into cardiac arrest. I lost my lifetime friend and confidant. He will never be forgotten, and to this day, when I look into the mirror on my iPhone, I tell myself "You are loved" because that was what he wanted me to do! And I know that because of his friendship, support, and guidance, I will always have God on my side, and I will never be alone. I know he is watching every action I take and every thought I process. He will always play an important role in my life, whether he is mortal or not. And I thank God that he allowed me the privilege of having him as my friend. I continued to keep in contact with his widow and maintained our closeness while grieving. I've deemed her my honorary sister.

Due to the situation I was living in (including added stress and accepting the news of his untimed departure), I knew I could not make the trip to Chicago for his funeral without someone helping me or providing assistance. I look back now and wish I had accepted that challenge and asked my friend or sister to accompany me there. It was so hard to say goodbye.

Memories can be a curse, or they can be an inspiration. During this part of my journey, my friend had always been and will always be an inspiration. The lives he touched will never be the same, including mine. Even though I know he is gone, he will never be forgotten. He still brings a smile to my face with every memory I have of him. As his wife mourned his loss, I shared that loss with her. For some reason, God chose to take him from us at this point in his life, but God also chose for us to live on and carry his word to others. I feel so privileged to have been loved by this man and know that the love he received from me was one of unselfishness. He taught me more than he will ever know. And he taught me how to live with God by my side.

I thank God for allowing me to have such a wonderful person in my life. As I listen to his favorite music at Christmastime on the CD he gave me or the sermon he put on CD about West Virginia, I continue to feel the peace and serenity that he instilled in others as he touched their lives. Praise the Lord for the existence of this wonderful man and human being and the woman who loved him unconditionally.

It was over a year since I was able to visit with his wife. She was destined to make a trip to Houston, and we were able to reunite. He lives through her, and I love her just as much as I loved him. Even now as I write, a smile appears on my face. As she played the piano in my house once more, I felt his presence and the spirit of love touch our very souls. I know now that we will forever be friends, and my friend did that for us. He brought us together. God is good.

We planned to keep in touch and renew our friendship every year. When something good happens to us, we can't help but feel his presence. When something bad happens, we can't help but feel his support and encouragement. He gave us the courage to continue. Once again, each day when I say the serenity prayer, he has become part of that unconditional love.

Little did I know that a short time later, this beautiful, talented, and spirited person would join her husband in heaven after suffering a couple strokes. The world is definitely blessed to have both these angels looking after us.

CHAPTER 10

Changing the Path

One day, I received a call from my son telling me he had accepted a position in his company that would allow him to transfer from Jakarta, Indonesia, to Houston, Texas. He told me that he and his wife would find a place that would have enough room for me, and I could sell my house, pay off all my debts, and obtain the medical help that I so desperately needed to alleviate the vertigo that plagued me in my daily life.

It had been a very rough year. When they called and said they were moving to Texas and told me I could retire from my job and move in with them, it took me a while to make the choice of leaving everything behind, including my friends and family. I had to realize that all the things I had accumulated during my life, all the things that I used and/or stored in my ranch style home in the country, were just that—things (material things). Things don't make a home. People do. It seemed to take months for my sisters to convince me that the right thing to do was to move. I finally made my choice. If I were going to have the advantage of good medical doctors available to me, I needed to move to Texas. I hopefully made the right choice.

My son and his wife searched hard to find a place with a mother-in-law suite that would accommodate me, and I was more than happy with my quarters, including a bedroom, living room, private bath, garage, and yard. They found a diverse community a few miles away from Houston that welcomes people of all ages to enjoy a new alternative way of living with access to recreational facilities, water, and other amenities. The biggest advantage would be that I would have family near me in case I would need help or medical assistance (something I didn't have in West Virginia).

Just follow my heart and follow my dreams. This seemed to be a good goal for me at first, but after being betrayed once again, I decided to do what my son suggested. I made preparations to sell my house over the Thanksgiving holidays. I put my house up for sale, and a couple wanted to look at it immediately. I had to go through a lot of boxes in storage and also had a lot of furniture to dispose of before I could make such a bold move. Three living room sets, three dining room sets, and three bedroom sets, plus a lot of odds and ends, including tools and other necessary items stored in the garage. This move was going to be bigger than life for me to execute, and I wasn't sure just how I was going to pull it off. The chronic vertigo was taking a toll on my body, and the stress was irritating the vertigo. So I was feeling like I continued to run in circles over and over.

All this and more meant going to several doctors each week, and many times, I was unable to drive myself. Since I had no one else to drive me, my ex volunteered to be my caretaker and my driver. It was hard to see him in this position since I did not experience a whole lot of this during our past marriage. He asked for nothing in return though and would pick me up at my front door and deliver me back to my home the same way. He watched as it became more and more difficult for me to maneuver around the house and my life. He brought boxes upstairs for me to go through so I would not fall down the stairs with my vertigo. It took weeks for me to go through them and months of traveling to and from the doctors. I began to wonder what I would do without his help since my two children lived out of state and out of country. My sisters did visit at least once a month to assist me, but even that became hard on them through all the bad weather and temperatures. My ex also took it upon himself to mow the grass and run errands for me. Again, he asked for nothing in return. Even though I liked this other side that he was showing me, I knew that I could never love him again in the way I had done for twenty-six years. So I accepted his help, appreciated everything he did for me, and found a kind of love that we could both become familiar and comfortable with and live with.

Finally, in August of the next year, I retired and made my move to Texas to live with my son and his wife. My mission was to find a physician who could help me accept and make valid adjustments in dealing with my vertigo. My wish was to become normal again and improve my quality of life, but the stress I was enduring was playing havoc with my body (to quote a specialist who was taking care of me). My sister was willing to drive the 2,300 miles to get there. So we made the trip together and embraced the new life I was about to experience.

Even though I loved and appreciated my son and his wife for allowing me to live with them, there was still something missing in my life. After seeing doctor after doctor, I was finally able to find a neurotologist that considered my case a challenge and made it his priority to give me back a better quality of life. He was willing to recognize the fact that I wanted to function in life independently, and that would not be possible unless I was able to get my vertigo under control and not be a threat to my own welfare. I worked every day to increase my strength so that my son and his wife would not have to be burdened with taking care of me. I was an individual who absolutely hated depending on someone else for my care or my health. I hated even more asking for help. And I admit it was a big imposition when I moved in with them, and I would be eternally grateful for everything they were doing to help me. I was having so many vertigo spells that it took me weeks to unpack and get settled in my area of the house. I also had to have many meals brought to me and used a cane to steady myself to get around. My sister had driven with me to Texas, and after she returned to West Virginia, I missed the company that she had provided. But even though she was gone, she continued to call each night to check on my progress and be the kind of emotional support I needed to face the months ahead.

My next step was to find a church that I could feel a part of and provide the spiritual support I needed. I was so fortunate to find one within a couple of miles of the house. I also found most of my doctors, car insurance company, and a veterinarian within a three- to five-mile span. That was good for me because I was learning my way around the area, and my comfort zone with driving only included about a six mile range of the house.

After finding a church, I found a group that was church-sponsored who met at the church every Thursday morning. Spending an hour at the church sitting in the upright position was about all I could handle. But I needed to meet people since I knew no one here except my family. After a few weeks, I decided to go to that group on Thursday mornings. The group was called Young at Heart for seniors who were fifty and older. My goal was to attend the group for an hour each week, and after achieving success of driving home, I would begin staying an additional hour each week. I did this until I could stay from nine to one without becoming a danger to myself as I drove home. This proved to be a positive step in my life because I was able to meet other seniors and enjoy leisure time together.

One day, someone told me about a program the local community college offered for seniors. It was called ALL (Academy of Lifelong Learning). The college was also located within a mile of the house, so this seemed like a logical second step for me to take and get involved in. Registration was only twenty dollars for the entire year. The classes looked interesting, challenging, and appealing. So I thought, *Why not? This could be a good way of meeting folks with the same interests as you.* I registered for second semester and found myself making everything, from a birdhouse to taking notes on how to keep your balance. It was so much fun going to cooking and other classes with different topics of interest.

One of the ladies in Young at Heart group told me about the district senior center. They also offered classes free for seniors and provided field trips as well as game and boot camp days to contribute to the wellness program they sponsored. They also sponsored game days, which would allow seniors to interact with one another. Once again, I decided to check it out. It offered different things than the college classes offered, and it also provided me with information that was helpful for seniors living in the area related to legal advice, insurance, and discounts on the metro bus. Besides, I also got to meet even more people I didn't know. What actually happened was there were planned activities available for me to participate in every morning and every afternoon and sometimes on weekends and evenings. It was totally up to me to manage my time and the amount of participation I was exposed to. Each group offered something different with a different set of people attending.

One lady who attended an AARP sponsored driving safety class with me informed me of another group she had become a part of, the Red Hat Society. I had heard of this group but had never known anyone who belonged. So I agreed to be in her newly founded chapter with the motto "It is what it is." This group supplied social activities with opportunities for community service once a month.

There I was, finding all kinds of ways to meet people, and yet there was still a yearning in my heart to be with someone who would make my own life more exciting and more rewarding as well as meaningful, someone who could fill the emptiness that I felt ever since I divorced my second husband. My ex and I shared chemistry between us that I seemed to miss. I wanted to find that again. My son had a life of his own, especially a social life. I envied that. I wanted to have that social life too.

CHAPTER 11

Once Again

It didn't take me long to meet many guys by email once I posted my profile online again. I figured since Houston was so big, having a population of over 2.1 million, I would be able to meet lots of suitable candidates in person and take my time developing a social life that I could be proud of. I came to a big city knowing no one except my son and his wife. So how was I to begin finding that social life? Once again, I was the recipient of such endearing emails, thought-provoking IMs, and yes, even beautiful red roses delivered straight to my door. Of course, I was feeling very special to have this many gentlemen interested in me. It was kind of tiring keeping up with all of them, so I decided to zero in on only one. He sounded so nice.

Meanwhile, a matchmaking company called and wanted to interview me. Upon further investigation, I found out there was a monthly fee, and you had to have a minimum annual income of $50,000. They were located downtown, and I had not attempted to add driving that far to my comfort zone yet, so I told them I was still recuperating from vertigo and would contact them when I felt I was up to driving downtown. Little did I know at the time, this would probably have been the most inexpensive way to find my soul mate. The staff did all the screening, and a criminal check was done to all who belonged to prevent scams or fraudulent activity. Even though this option would probably be the best one, I chose to go the path of dating sites simply because I could explore them in the comfort of my home at times that were convenient for me.

To get an inside glimpse of what I was thinking, I will allow you to walk in my shoes by reading some of the emails and chats that I received in the following months. As I share the many communications I received, a need inside me that had gone untouched for a while was starting to be fulfilled, and I found myself once again falling into a trance that took over my conscience and my everyday life. It was as if I woke up only to check to see if I had heard from that special guy. I couldn't go to sleep without talking to him on the phone or webcamming to say good night. As time went by, we planned to arrange a meeting between us. We were both going to drive halfway to have lunch with one another, which would only be an hour and one-half drive for each of us.

*****

Meet John from Austin, Texas.

I have lived in the U.S. most of my life, but my mom is from Australia and my dad from the USA. I am 57 years old and I got married to a woman whom I lost eight years ago. I have only one son. My mom and dad have both passed away. My elder sister also passed away in the last three years and I have been single till now. I work alone as a business man and deal in timbers. I own a saw mill of my own. I really like my job; but my Lord is always by my side. I am a sweet, romantic man, who loves to play golf. I read and play poker and I am good at it. I am a good cook. I like to fish and I bait my own hook! I also like to veg out in front of the TV and watch movies sometime. I am not a bar hopper or a big drinker. I really can't handle that. I want to meet someone with some of the same qualities. I am a great cuddlier. I am a good hearted man and want to have fun in life. I am a very loving person and want to be with someone that can actually love me in return. I'm not just saying it but time will tell. The color of my eyes is blue. My ethnicity is Caucasian. Also, my appearance is very attractive and I am proud to talk about that. I am a Christian. My dear, for my personal traits, I am serious, kind, confident, smart, responsible, honest, calm, flexible, elegant, communicative, sensitive, gentle, cheerful, optimistic and romantic. I love poetry, books, walks on the beach and cozy candlelight dinners. I enjoy movies, television, music, traveling, and the quietness of the mountains, the ocean, sunrises and sunsets. I am comfortable in jeans or a nice English suit. I am a nonsmoker and don't drink. I'm not into drugs because I don't need them. I live in a natural high. I believe in enjoying the good life and am high on it. I have a healthy attitude about God and the Bible. I am an honest hearted man that is looking for a very stable relationship. I understand it is important to lay down lasting foundations for a lasting relationship. I am an active person who enjoys keeping fit. I believe that keeping fit is important.

I enjoy fine dining and am always looking for someone to share the appreciation of good food and fine wine. I am just as comfortable in my jeans as with my simple shirt. I love to dance, all styles, disco, house or swing. I control my temper easy and cool.

I do not expect a woman to be a servant to me, spending all her time working and cleaning. I believe there is give and take in a relationship, and I realize that at times it's more convenient for me to do laundry, cook, clean, and I have no problem doing that.

I consider myself to be a fairly honest and truthful person and I expect the same in return. I think I am wealthy and can afford all things that will be needed by me or my love or my son.

I believe that time spent apart helps keep things fresh in a relationship and makes the time we do spend together even better. I am not one who cheats in a relationship. One woman is enough trouble. I don't have the time or energy to juggle 2, 3, or 4 at the same time. (Ha-ha) I am generally an optimistic person with a sense of humor, fairly easy-going, and I don't think that I am too critical about things, but I also believe that it takes two people contributing to a relationship to make it work.

My desire is to meet a beautiful, sensitive, sensuous, warm, assertive single woman who wants a friend. My interpretation of a friend is one to whom you can pour out all the contents of your heart, chaff and grain together, knowing that the beautiful of hands will take it all, shift it, keep that which is worth keeping and, with a breath of kindness, blow the rest away. I thank you in advance for allowing me to be that kind of friend to you. I am looking for a special, loving relationship with a unique woman who is affectionate, beautiful, with a shapely figure, sincere, easy going, with interests and characteristics similar to mine and even closer. Someone who wants a meaningful, serious, long-term relationship, not just a few dates is that special woman. I know you are the one I am searching for.

There are many qualities that make relationships, good: support, compromise, and open and honest communication are just a few of these qualities that you may desire in a relationship. Engage only in relationships where both partners can openly discuss their wants and needs; this can take practice. Remember loving relationships grow and only become better; eliminate those who do not meet your needs when they continually fail to support you, will not compromise, and will not be honest... These three qualities alone will help you nurture and develop a deeper relationship with your partner.

Open and honest communication is one of the more desirable qualities you want to have in a relationship. Watch to see that your partner is not secretive, nor are they willing to tell lies to avoid certain subjects. For example, if a partner is married, and fails to tell you that, you can rightfully assume if they can lie about big things, they can lie about small things. While you may not like everything your partner may say; freedom to be honest should be there in your relationship. Likewise, you need to be open and honest with your partner. A relationship based upon false truths is not likely to be successful, because both partners do not have the correct frame of reference in the relationship.

Trust, loyalty and respect are a must for eternal happiness. No matter how much you love someone if you don't have these ingredients you will never succeed. To be in love means being patient but to be patient you must trust in your partner first. You can never find love through the eye or ear, so you must trust the only thing that will never fade until you die—your heart. Love is like trust, when you find your special someone it is as if you're trusting them with your heart. Trust is what you put in someone's hands. Faith is what you hold on to.

Trust is what makes everyone realize that you are always there for them. Faith is what makes everyone realize that you are always there to help them in case they need some help. Love makes not everyone, but the only one in your life who is special, think that you are always there for him, to be with him, to make him realize how much you really love him.

Without honesty, love tends to become cloudy, and without trust, love becomes very unstable. Love is a wonderful gift, trust in it, and believe in it, give into it and it will be returned to you to give again and again.

You can get advice from family, friends and strangers, but the best advice comes from your heart—it never lies—trust it. There may be many people that are trustworthy, but only a few are worth trusting with their heart. Choose wisely. To be trusted is a greater compliment than to be loved…

Nice meeting you and I hope you will want to know more about me as time goes on…

John

So once again, I decided to trust a website. This one was free and was called Date Hookup. After reading the profile and introduction above, of course, I became interested. He was everything, in writing at least, that I was looking for. Once again, I found someone who touched my heart by declaring that God brought us together and it was fate for us to see what could unfold in the future. John also had a son that he adored and I came to adore also. We webcammed and Instant Messaged as well as dabbled in chat and email on the computer. We would even blow each other kisses on the webcam.

One day, during one of our conversations, he told me that his best friend's mother died and he wanted to go to the funeral. He became torn between doing that and meeting me for lunch before he left. Even though I was thinking déjà vu all over again, being the supportive person that I am and always thinking of the other person's needs before my own, I encouraged him to go be with his friend. That friend lived in Cape Coast, Ghana. Of course, he would take his son with him also. It was to be a quick trip over and back, and he would be gone no longer than three weeks. This friend had access to very good species of lumber, and he hoped to do some business while he was there and have the lumber shipped home so he could sell it.

I had to play the role of the understanding and accepting woman. And truthfully, I really wasn't playing the role because I am that accepting and understanding. I am not someone who would keep the person she loves from being with his best friend when that friend's mother suddenly died. Even so, we still arranged to meet the Sunday before he left. Everything was good, and I drove to the halfway point. Then the phone rang, and he told me he couldn't be there because he had come down with the flu. I was disappointed again but understood. Getting ready for his trip was hard on him that week since he was trying to tie up loose ends as well get over the flu.

John and his son traveled to Ghana to support his friend and attend his mother's funeral by the end of the week. They decided to meet afterward and celebrate the wake. Then one thing led to another, and somehow the flat screen TV in the hotel he was staying in became broken. It sounded as though alcohol might have been involved, but I wasn't there, so I don't really know. John begged me to send a new HD TV to him to replace the one that he had accidentally broken. He was told by the hotel manager that he could not leave the country unless the TV was replaced or it was paid for. I told him that would be impossible for me to do. For his sake, I checked anyway, and USPS told me it was too large of a package and they would not be able to send it. When I checked with FedEx, it was going to cost so much (over $1,000) that you could literally buy one over there cheaper than you could buy it here and send it. Needless to say, he was not happy that I was not going to send it, so he asked me to send enough money to replace it so he could give it to the manager. My first thought was why he would be asking me for money to replace something he was responsible for? It just didn't sound right. Many red flags started to go up, but it was as if I was ignoring them once again. This man had too many of the qualities I was looking for to stop my search now. And let's not forget that I had webcammed with him every day before he left.

After that, he said since his stay had to be extended, he would need some clothing and toiletries sent to him because his suitcase was lost at the airport. And again, I obliged him by shopping and shipping the items he requested. Because he said that he did own a saw mill here in Texas, he arranged to buy some wood to sell to furniture companies while he was in Africa and needed some money to pay for shipping it back to the States. He was then given gold by the elders he met while visiting there but needed money for taxes and shipping. He made me believe that I would receive back in gold seven times the value of the US dollars I was loaning him. I truly believed that this would be a good investment, and of course, all money and more would be paid back to me. He would send me pictures of the men cutting the trees, loading them, and even a picture of the gold that he wanted to ship. He wanted me to know that everything he was doing and requesting from me was legitimate. I respected him for that. So I considered it a loan. That was in September of 2011. Two years later I had no gold, no John or John's son, and I was out of another two hundred thousand dollars.

How could this happen to me all over again? John told me he needed funds to pay customs, taxes, registration, and immigration in addition to the shipping costs. It took several months for me to raise the money to send him. Then when I did, the money was stolen by the very people he trusted to hold the gold till he could pay all fees. I even listened to him as he told me to put the money inside the seam of a blanket and send the blanket to him. So when I put over twenty thousand inside a blanket, I actually put the focus of my life on what he needed and wanted and completely forgot about looking ahead at the consequences that my actions would have on me and my family and/or friends. I was dumbfounded and completely speechless when he called and said the twenty thousand dollars had been taken out before he opened the package. Did he not realize that I was giving up everything I had to help him and keeping all of it a secret by not telling my family and friends?

I remember one time he called, and the head of police volunteered to let me transfer money to his nephew who lived in Florida. His nephew would then send the money to Ghana. After I wire-transferred approximately thirteen thousand to his nephew, his nephew kept it and never sent it to Ghana and never sent it back to me. I have his name and address and contacted him daily to send it back to me. He never did, so when I was well enough, I made a trip to Florida to find him and attempt to get the thirteen thousand dollars back to me. The address I drove to was easy to find, but no one answered the door. Neither did anyone pick up on the many phone calls I made. It's hard enough to get scammed by someone overseas, but it is truly heartbreaking to get scammed by someone here in the States.

John then decided to put the gold in my name so that the men involved could not touch it anymore, including customs agents and gold company representatives, etc. At least, this is what he told me. I am educated and have taken care of myself all these years. That's what I told myself. Am I being scammed again or has this man simply run into unfortunate circumstances? And just when I was seeing some red flags, he notified me as well as sending me pictures that his son had been the victim of a hit and run and was taken to the hospital. So somehow, some way, I found a way to help him once again. I thought I fell in love with someone so special. But every phone call, chat, and message ended up being one that requested more money over and over again.

The following emails will allow you to sit in the driver's seat as we share this questionable adventure together.

******

Dear B...

Thank you dear. Oh yes, my son is twelve years old and lives with me. Tell me more about yourself. What is your best color and also what do you like to do on your free time? What is your best food and also what music do you like best? What food do you also like best? Please tell me more about yourself. I guess we can give this a try and be friends first. I am an honest man and I like to laugh and I also like to read. Talk to you soon Hon...

Take care...
John

Good evening... Oh yes, I am John. I have canceled my profile from date hookup and also as you know, I am new to this whole thing, but you can call me John as a simple name. Now tell me how was your day? I have missed you and I am sorry I did not get back to you in time. I have now gotten access to my computer and I think we can talk more. Please, you need to get a yahoo id so we can talk. I will email you and tell you more about myself. Please send me some pictures of yourself and have a nice and great evening. Hon, I have missed you so much...

John

My Dear...

I will stay up tonight but all the same I will need to send you this last email and continue with you tomorrow. Oh Hun I will be happy when you have yahoo so we can communicate on there so you can see me on cam and then in good time we can arrange to meet. I know there are a lot of liars and scammers on here, but just trust in what you are doing. I am an honest man and won't do anything to hurt you. I also have feelings just as you do and it is bad to hurt you, so I will try my hardest to make sure that doesn't happen. I am even happier to meet you since I know we can be a great couple in time. That is simply why I even canceled my profile from the site right away so as not to get involved in this whole thought of being scammed. I thank you and all the same I think that age has nothing to do with love and I am okay with your age. All I need for true love is someone who will love me and love my son as her own…someone who is ready to hold hands with me and walk with me. I am happy to read from you so please try to send me some pictures. I own a house here in Austin, and I will be happy to get to know you better. If you don't have anyone in mind as your love, then I think we are lucky in advance. Just don't worry about who I am and I will always be that special man in your life. Good Night and I will write to you in the morning. Good Night and Sweet Dreams…

John

Hi Hun…

Wow thank you for your sweet mail. I just woke up and just wanted to send this short note to you just to let you know I care and think about you. Morning greetings do not only mean saying

Good Morning. It has a silent message saying: I remember you when I wake up! Have a nice day. I am leaving to work now and hope to hear from you… Hugs…

John

Hello sweetie… Thank you very much for your nice email. The name of my son is Kenny. Kiss… I love your pictures! Wow, you look very cute and beautiful Hun. Wow. That is also nice. Please say hi to your sister and tell her she is welcome.

Honey…

My day was great and cool. Oh yes, I live in an air conditioned office of my own. I told you I work on my own and I work alone, sweetie. I went to my college in Florida. Please try to get back to me Honey and send me an email you're your new yahoo account. Oh thank you Honey for your nice email. Oh yes, I am in Austin sweetie. How was your night Honey?

Hugs,
John

If kisses were water, I'd give you the ocean. If hugs were leaves, I'd give you a forest. If love were space, I'd give you a galaxy. If friendship were life, I'd give you mine for free.

Hello My Love…

Good afternoon to you Honey. I have really missed you. Oh yes, I truly have love to give you. Honey you have let me feel sad and just want to cry. I am sorry for what happened to you and just want you to trust me. Money is a gift from GOD—just as love is also a gift from GOD; so you are a gift from GOD, and I always want you to trust me. I will give you all that I have if you need my help. Just to let you know how I trust you and love you. I know you are not such a woman to hurt me as those scammers did to you. Do I trust you with all my heart? All the same I am happy today because Kenny my son saw your picture and he just told me, Daddy, Mommy is so beautiful and he would like to come and spend some weekends with you. I was very happy and it makes me melt as my only son also loves you as I do. That is so nice. Baby I am at work and surely I will talk to you tonight, okay? Just email me with your number. I have misplaced it. Honey, I love you… Kiss and Hug to you, Honey. With me and you we can make life easy babe. I am so happy you trust me babe.

Your Husband,
John

Wow Babe…

I am happy for that sweetie. Please try and resend me your numbers, babe, so I can call you, okay? I have to get a new phone. I love you so much babe. Just be honest with me and I don't want you to talk to any other man or to hurt me because all I have is you in my heart and mind. Kiss to you my precious baby…kiss… Hope you are enjoying your day, Honey…

John,
your sweetheart

Hey Beautiful… I just wanted to do something simple to say I love you and to put that smile on your face. I love you so much and I want everyone to know how much you mean to me. Ever since you have entered my life, I've been flying on Cloud 9 and I have not come down yet. I tell you this every day, but you are the most beautiful person I know, inside and out. I see that more clearly with each passing day. I love everything about you, about us. You do something to me that no other has… You have made me so happy—the happiest I've ever been. You give me the most amazing feelings inside—the feeling of being in love with you. I still don't know what I did to be so lucky to have you in my life, my dream come true… I am so thankful though. In this short time that we've been together, we have grown so much and I can't wait to see what the future holds for us. I love you, with all my heart and soul, always and forever!

John

Thank you babe… I have also missed you and thinking about you Honey. That is why I am writing down this mail to you. Oh babe, Kennie is so happy and don't worry about him because he also wants you as a mom. I love you babe. Thank you for your address, babe.

This is Mine:

John

Wow babe…

You have a nice voice babe. Today your voice sounded very sweet babe. I will call you with my new cell number, babe…love you…kiss…

John

Sweetheart…

My biggest reward is to see you smile, know you are happy, and feel you are loved. I know life is sometimes cruel, but that's why I'm here, to show you that life can be good when somebody cares.

Good Morning Honey…

I am sorry I missed you online yesterday. I was very tired and also I had a problem with my internet. So lucky me, it's now good, so we can talk. Miss you Honey…kiss and Hug to you… Have a great weekend my love…

Hello My Love...

These are some questions and you can see my answers below:

1. Do you have any fun? I love to cook, garden, travel, go to movies, read, computer, dine out, walk around town, go hiking, camping, or just sit and relax at home having fun with my son.

2. What are you looking for in a relationship and what do you dislike in a man? I'm looking for a good and kind woman who is loyal, caring, thoughtful, creative, compassionate, imaginative, serious, sensual and passionate... But I dislike women who lie, cheat, are dishonest, disrespectful, and who just play tricks and games on their men.

3. Where were you born and raised? I was born and raised in Australia and I have lived in Germany about ten months, but have been here in Austin for almost all my life.

4. Do you enjoy being alone? I don't enjoy being alone

5. Are you a passionate person? I am very passionate about some things, just not a zealot...

6. Are you into a serious relationship with someone special or someone willing to spend the rest of his life with you? Well if you have not been taken by some-

one special, can we be serious with each other by fixing time to meet every day on here to chat and get to know each other very well? From there we will see what God will lead us to...

7. What are your prayers in a relationship to our Lord God? For him to let me find my Soul Mate. I would love to pamper her! For me, a relationship should start with honesty. Then, we will go with the flow. For now we take our time to get to know each other (not too long, but long enough to see if we are made for each other).

8. Do you consider yourself physically affectionate when involved in a relationship? Sure, I love to hold hands, hug and give casual kisses...

9. What is your favorite color? Mine is blue. I love the blue sea... My favorite foods & drinks are Italian food, Fruit drinks and red wine...

10. What are you mostly afraid of in a relationship? To get married to the wrong person, though I'm not in a rush to get married. I'm ultimately looking for a wife and I'm confident God will put us together at some point... Life is short, so we might as well have fun together rather than fighting...

11. How trusting are you? Oh Yes, I know it's hard to trust but I don't give up in trusting

the right woman who I love to spend the rest of my lifetime with…

12. How romantic are you? I love romance and I like being romantic…

13. How do you feel about relocating for a relationship? If I met the right person, I would do whatever I needed to do to move and be with her so we can spend the rest of our lifetime together…

14. What types of music or movies or TV Shows you like? I like all kinds of music, but my Favorites are rock, rock 'n roll, and country. I am a movie nut also…mostly with action packed and drama…

15. Have you narrowed down your specific desires as to what type of person you want to meet? I'm a Christian and I will like to meet someone who trusts God with their life, and someone who demonstrates Honesty, Caring, Respectful, and someone who loves kids very much as well, even if they are not her real kids…

16. Do you have any tattoos or body piercing? No I don't.

17. What do you always want to know in a new partner? I would like to know if everything is going on well in her life where she is living.

18. What's your star sign? Virgo…

19. How often do you lose your temper? Practically never...

20. How often do you find yourself laughing? I'm generally a pretty serious person...

21. If your life partner had a bad day, what is the first thing you would do for him? I would talk with her about her day, or I would take her out on the town.

22. How many female and male friends you had before? I don't like to make friends but I chose a few as my best friend because some friends are very dangerous. They can give you bad advice... Also some can tell you something which you don't like and that's going to tear up your relationship, so I just don't tell my Friend about my relationship but I love to surprise them.

23. If you decided to stay at home for the evening what would you tend to do? I tend to watch TV, but sometimes if I have some paper work to do, I make sure I finish it before the next day.

24. What do you mostly do on weekends? I clean the house, use my washing machine to wash my clothes, and then have some fun with my male friends. Sometimes I go on shopping trips also.

25. Are you left- or right-handed? I'm right-handed and I can also use my left hand to

do many things, example—playing Golf, Writing, etc.

Baby, these are some questions for you. I hope it will help us to know more about each other. Love You Sweetie... Kiss

Thank you my sweetheart... I am online now and just wanted to talk to you baby. I have missed chatting with you. Kiss and hug to you. Have a great weekend babe. I wish I was there to hold hands with you to go walking late this evening...kiss... Love You. I will send you some pictures of your Baby boy Kennie when I get home tonight okay, love? He asked about you this morning.

John

A day may start or end without a message from me, but believe me it won't start or end without me thinking of you... See! I just did. Take care.

Good Morning my Angel...

Can I say I love you today? If not, can I ask you again tomorrow? And the day after tomorrow? And the day after that? Because I'll be loving you every single day of my life. I love you so much Honey, I really enjoyed our chat. Kiss. I love you.

John

Every part of me wants you, maybe because I was made just for you! I thank God I'm rich not with money but with people like you. I may not have the most expensive things but I've got the most precious gem…a friend like you. Good morning my love.

John

Don't let little things get you down. You've got many big reasons to look up to God and say thanks tonight. Tomorrow, it's going to be a great day. Good Night…

John

What is love? Those who don't like it call it responsibility. Those who play with it call it a game. Those who don't have it call it a dream. Those who understand it call it destiny. And me, I call it You. Love You Darlin, John

A lady is a woman who makes a man behave like a gentleman. You're such a lady to me. Good Morning Darlin, Kiss and Hug…

John

Great minds contain ideas, solutions and reasons; scientific minds contain formulas, theories and figures; my mind contains only you! Love You Darling, Have a wonderful day.

Kisses…
John

Begin the day with a light heart. Let all your worries be swept aside at night. Smile a moment and thank God, for every moment He cares for you all the way. Good Night Darlin… My day was very busy and I got home late…

> Your Husband,
> John

There is night so we can appreciate day, sorrow so we can appreciate joy, evil so we can appreciate good, you so I can appreciate love. Miss You My Love…

> Kiss and Hug,
> John

I wish that God would hold you tight. I hope that angels would keep you in sight. Now just to make sure you feel alright, I'm gonna blow you a sweet goodnight. Sorry I had a busy day and was not able to contact you the whole day. Good Night and sweet dreams Kiss…

> John

Each of us is an angel with one wing. The only way we could fly is to hold each other and share wings. So if you have trouble flying, I will always share mine with you.

> Good Morning My Angel,
> John

1000 words 1 could say, 1000 wishes 1 could pray, 1000 miles legs could walk, 1000 sounds a month could talk, 1000 times I'll be true, 1000 ways to say I love you!

When an angel came to me, he asked: "What is your wish for tonight?" I said "Please take care of the person who's reading this message." Goodnight! Sorry I was feeling sleepy so I did not get back online, but I just miss you and saw your offline; I was on the bed then. Sweet dreams and I will talk to you tomorrow.

Kiss and Hug,
John

I asked God for a rose and He gave me a garden. I asked God for a drop of water and He gave me an ocean. I asked God for an angel and He gave me you! Kiss and Hug to you my love…

Good Night…
John

Love is something special, a treasure I want to find… To others, love is blind but for me, it's not true, because when I fell in love… I saw you. I have missed you Darlin; I am not feeling well so I am going to see the Doctor… Love you babe. I am very tired and very weak. Love you…

John

Talk to you later Honey; I am not feeling well, Honey, but don't worry if I can't make it tomorrow. Surely I will meet you next week, babe. You can't believe how I'm feeling now. Kiss to you. I am off to work tomorrow and I will meet a man at my office tomorrow. Love you Hun… Take care. I miss you.

Your husband,
John

What good is beauty without brains, looks without charm, money without happiness, a smile without feelings, a life without you? I Love You Darlin, and thinking of you always… Just pray for me Hun. I am not feeling good. Enjoy your weekend…

John

Hello Darlin…

Good Day, how are you? I have missed you Honey and even more just want to know the kind of question you want to ask and I will give you the answer Honey. Well Honey, you know it is not my intention to go down there, but since he has been good to me, I need to show some love and I think you should understand. Besides, I don't know why you said that you don't want to talk to me till I am back in the United States. Soil does not show true love, Honey. I have no problem and you should even know by now that I am not like the other one you knew. It hurts me and it makes me feel that you are thinking I am like the others. But I am so sad that you have this kind of idea in mind for me when you know I am not that kind of man. Why would I give you my house address if I am like those other men who juggle and cheat on women? I only love you and to be honest with you, I just want you to feel and know how someone who loves just your money is not love. Money helps sometimes, but you just keep it in mind and I am not like those other men or scammers. You should know all this and have more trust in me. This is why I wanted you to go with me. But since you don't have time, I need to go myself. Your words have made me sad Honey. I bet you are just as sad and don't know what to say. If you are truly in love with me, you will know as I do and I have no bad ideas about you Honey. What is money Honey? What can't I do for you? Oh My God, I feel sad and just want to let you know that babe. Miss You…

John

If you're feeling lonely and you think there is nobody there to love, support, listen or show they care, just save this message and every time you realize it, it will remind you that a part of me is always there with you. Good Day… Love You… Kiss and

Hug…
John

Oh yes babe.

You told me to check on your email and I do like what you wrote to me babe. I think I will get better because of this email and then let you come over here to me and kiss you before I leave babe. I love you so much and you have made my day happy and the happiest day of my life, even when I met you today is the happiest day in my life just because of this email. Kiss to you my lovely wife...

John

Good Morning and I am going to see my Doctor. Mr. Daniel says I should send his greeting to you. Love You Darlin.

Your husband,
John

LOL babe. I am always someone who forgives and forever will I forgive you when you go wrong because I believe you are there for me and you are all I want and have, babe. I will never hurt you and I love you forever babe... Kiss... You are like an Angel to me...

Your husband,
John

Happiness is not having what you want, but wanting what you have.—Anonymous

Every day is a happy day as long as you text me once a day. I tell you, this is no lie. A text from you always makes me smile. Good Morning...

Miss You.
John

Oh babe I was just reading your mail about your friend's mom dying and I am so sorry and just feel a lot of pain for my agent, Daniel, but I wish her all the best... Love you... John

Good Evening Darlin, Sorry you missed hearing from me this morning, I was very tired and also busy on my trip... Love you Darlin... Hope your day was great. I am online now waiting for you...

Kiss...
John

Good morning, my love!

My darling... It feels great to start the day by looking at your sweet face and listening to your soft voice. I know that by the time I usually hear your "good morning," most of the people are out in the streets, facing the traffic or being surrounded by a multitude of problems. Yet, your morning greeting gives me the strength to face any Goliath. Your wishing me a good day gives me the motivation to decipher any enigma and to face any giants because it fills me with love and courage. And that's why it feels so great to find you by my side every morning.

You are the reason of my worries and at the same time the source of my courage. Without you around I would be more indifferent to adversities. But you give me the motivation to look ahead with confidence and determination in the pursuit of the options that will give us more tranquility to enjoy the affection we share.

Even when my days don't run as smoothly as I would like, I don't get mad, because I know I will be coming home to your caresses and to be greeted by your warm smile. Even when I face some problems during the day, I always keep in mind your morning wish, your "good morning" and I try to overcome every obstacle just so that I can see you again soon and enjoy true peace in the peaceful island of your arms. I love your "Good morning!," just as I love every night and every hour we spend together. I miss you Darlin and can't wait to be with you... Kiss...

Love,
John

Darlin I am leaving tomorrow morning... I will email you with my information as you say okay... I will be going out now to get some stuff I need... KISS.

John

You are the sweetest woman in the world and I love you forever. Babe your words make me smile and make me feel so happy. Oh yes babe. I love you with all my heart, so just keep it coming and be careful Darlin. Kiss to You...

Your Husband,
John

A smile to end your day, A prayer to bless your sleep, A song to lighten your dreams, A cheer to praise his presence, and a peaceful night to a wonderful Lover like you. Good Night... Love you... Kiss...

Love,
John

See outside the Window, Sun rising for you, Flowers smiling for you, Birds Singing for you, because last night I told them to wish you Good Morning. Kiss and Hug to you my Darlin… Have a nice day…

John,
Your Husband

Hello Darlin… I am leaving now. I will miss you Darlin. Please be by my side in spirit… You know that you are all I have and I never want you to let me down. Babe I love you deeply from my heart and with all my soul… I guess I need to go now. Have a good day… KISS… MISS YOU… I will contact you when I get there Hun. My hotel is Golden Tulip Hotel, East Legion, Cape Coast, Ghana. Flight Info: 18:00 Houston (George Bush Intercontinental)—20:55 Minneapolis (Saint Paul Intl.). Aircraft type: Bombardier 900… Transfer time: 0h50…21:45 Minneapolis (Saint aul Intl.)—13:05 Amsterdam (Schiphol)… This flight arrives one day later. Aircraft type: Boeing 767, Transfer time: 2h10

Good Evening Darlin…

Thank you for your mail. Oh yes I had a safe journey and I am now in the Hotel. My internet is not yet fixed, but I guess they will do that for me tomorrow. So I am using Mr. Daniel's computer just to let you know I have missed you and am thinking about you. Oh yes I Love You Darlin and I have missed you so much. So badly that I left my bag which contains all my belong-ings I had on the Flight, but I will go with Mr.

Daniel tomorrow and check at the Port. Love you Darlin… I have not gotten a phone yet, so I will let you know when I get my bag and I will get a new sim card so you can call me. Love You My Lovely wife… Thank you for your kindness. I Love You… It's 8:59 pm here and I am going to bed. As you know I don't know anyone here and I just want to take good care of myself as you told me to do… Kiss and Bye… I will talk to you tomorrow. Okay? After we get back from the Port…

Your husband,
John

Good Morning My Love…

Thank you for your nice mail Honey, but it hurt me when you say I should not let this feeling you have for me end? Darlin I always tell you just trust me I will love you and forever will I love you Honey. I will never do anything to hurt you either to do something to break up this babe. You are mine forever and forever will I be your love. For once just put this word in your mind and know I am yours babe—truly yours and no one else's. We are just coming from the Port. We woke up early this morning and went to check on my brief case, which contained my stuff, but was unable to get it so I think I need to get some items tomorrow from the store with the help of Daniel who will take me out since I don't know any-where here. I seriously need the phone because you know I will be busy. Not because of the funeral, but when I am in the forest when the log truck is loading the timbers and the logs to the port to get them shipped. I can only make calls because I can have no access to the internet there only use of the phone. That is why I need it but I am going to try and see if I will get one nice cell phone here tomorrow. Daniel is saying that he knows of big shopping mall here so we will go and check it out. So please don't let this make you feel bad about me Darlin. You know I love you and I can't do anything bad to hurt you Darlin. You have my heart and mind and soul babe, so you should not think badly of me and always keep me safe there. Kennie says hi to you, mom. The funeral is this coming Friday, so afterwards, he will just see to it that I get my items from the forest and ship them and then come home. Love You... Miss You...

John

Good Evening Darlin...

It's 10:20 p.m. here Darlin and I am online waiting for you. I'm so lucky I have Daniel's laptop with me so we can chat. Honey we went there but I don't like the items there babe and also it cost a lot while it is not as good as those in the states. I just want you to get me some babe. I know you are going to get me the goods once and that is even going to put a smile on my face once I get it babe and please try and get me the boxer shorts but please wear one pair before you send it so I will feel you in anything I wear. Lol... I love you so much babe and you are all my life and everything. I am still waiting for you Babe. Just buzz me babe. Kiss and hug to you babe. Daniel says Good Night. He is going to his house now. Now I am here with your son Kennie. Kiss Darlin... I am waiting for you. This is the address to send the items. DB, Post Box, Cape Coast, Ghana. Love You...

Take a deep breath, stand near the window, look at the sky, there will be two stars twinkling brightly, you know what they are? They are my eyes always taking care of you... Good night. Miss You... Love You... Kiss...

John

Good Morning Darlin...

I just came back from breakfast with Daniel and Kennie... Oh yes, I got your mail picture babe, and we are just looking at it now. Daniel is very happy and he says you look very pretty—better looking than I am. LOL

Darlin these are the items and some Brands I need: Any brand of shampoo, Deodorant—Spray—POLO BLACK, Lotions—DOVE or NIVEA, shaving crème—Any Brand, soap—DOVE, 3 Large T Shirts, 3 Med 10 T Shirts, 1 pr sandals size 9, 2 pr sandals size 7, Lg Boxer shorts underwear—Med, Briefs for Kennie—small size, 2 Belts—white and black—size 34, and 2 flash Drives. Please Darlin try and add some two or three jeans so Kennie will wear since he doesn't have any now. Daniel has given me some, so I am okay with the ones I have. I guess you are still on the bed. I dream about you and I have missed you so much. I am going out to print your picture large and place it in my Hotel Room. I will talk to you when I am back. Kiss... Just send me a mail when you can, okay or after you send the items with the tracking numbers. Love You...

Your Husband...
John

Hello... Good Evening Darlin,

Well I am sorry I did not get back to you in time as I told you I would. I had to visit the forest where we have the timbers so I am just coming from there. It is far from the hotel. This is Daniel's number: DB, Post Box, Street Pink, Cape Coast, Ghana. Please send it through Express mail okay babe at the post office USPS Express Mail. That will be faster... okay babe and write this address okay? Kiss and hug to you...love you Darlin...

JBW

Use this babe this is the address he just gave me so there is no need to use the first one, okay? This is what you should go with and send it at Express Mail USPS. Kiss and hug to you. Love you Darlin...

John

Please Darlin, I am grateful for what you have just done and I feel more in love with you and feel like you truly love me from your heart and I will always be there for you. I promise to die in your hands my lovely Babe. Please this is the right address okay? Good Night Darlin,

Kiss and Hug,
John

Hi Darlin… I love your "Good morning!" just as I love every night and I guess you are sleeping by now. I just woke up. Oh thank you for your mail and Darlin I always want you to know and feel how I love you. I really know how you feel, but I always want to let you know how I am. I am born to love you, not to hurt you. Please please put your trust in me. How on earth can I hurt you Darlin? I can never do this to you. I love you more than I do myself. Please just understand me and know you are all I have in my life. You know water kills, but we still drink it, so keep in mind I am not that kind of water to kill you. I am the water to give you life of love and love you forever. Please Darlin, as I told you, Please send the items to only this: Express Hun, EMS EXPRESS or EXPRESS MAIL. Daniel says that is closer to him and he can get it fast to me. Please, You have the right to do what you want to do. Just don't talk a lot, but prove to them that you know what you are doing when you get there, and make sure you have the right address, okay? And email me with the tracking number. Love you Darlin. I am going to take my bath and go get some coffee.

I admire all that you have done Darlin, and thank you for being so kind to me. It shows how you trust me and love me. I will never disappoint you or hurt you babe. You are all I want and all that I need in life.

Kiss and Hug…
John

Thank you Darlin…

I feel happy when you ask me anything you don't understand. Oh yes babe you know because of my trip I have a friend called Stephen Walter. He is dead. He helped me to get my landline, but I was on a trip and I wanted to talk with Kennie so he did that in his name. That is why I was very surprised when I met this man called Steven Walter. So I even told him about my friend. So it was very surprising and he even felt sad. He was my only best friend I have, Darlin. You have my house address and everything. To be honest why on earth would I play games with your heart Darlin. I love you and some words make me sad—very, very, sad. I feel shame that you don't believe me and trust me. Please, this is my promise. Just take your time. You will see me for sure and know I am who I am. I need to stay online to talk to you but I feel sad. All the same thank you for your kindness. I really appreciate what you have done. I will never get upset with you because I Love You. But please just make me feel happy and believe all that I say and count on me. I will be with you soon. Miss You…

John

Don't love for fun; love me for reason AND let the reason be for love. I love you and I'll be forever loving you. Have a sweet dream. Thank you my Darlin… Kiss…

John

Hello Darlin…

I left offline yesterday because I was very sad and I was not expecting you to say no to me. It makes me feel like you are treating me like those other online scammers. To be honest with you, I love you deeply from my heart and there is no way on this earth I can hurt you. I love you Darlin. It was my fault and I am just sorry I did not intend to spoil the Plasma TV, but I was very sad yesterday. Please please I know how you feel babe, but you can count on me babe. Just trust in me and know I am a gift from God to you as you are the same to me. I promise I will never let you down. Darlin thank you for the e card you sent me. Please hun, the plasma is just 42 inches. Please Darlin, you know I have paid a lot of money here and I am almost running out of money, but I just wanted to get everything done and come home. You have my house address and how on earth can I hurt you babe i love you and i cant do that to you babe you can just keep a receipt and I will pay you back babe… Trust me Darlin… The Hotel Manager called me this morning and ask me to try and get the plasma there but I just confirm to him I will.

Darling… You are all I have but it hurts me if you think I don't love you, or when you compare me to others. I swear and vow I love you and I promise to make everything possible to be with you as you also promise to me, so don't give up babe for true love there is a lot of problems. Trust

me that it will not happen again... Kiss and Hug.
Hope you are on bed and sleep soundly.

Your Love,
John

My love...

I thought I would give it one more shot to
see if you would even take time out of your busy
schedule to understand. Like I said, all of this is
in God's hands. When I said I can't help you, that
was what I meant. You seemed so wrapped up
in the problem itself that you failed to see I was
sending you a message that I was unable to perform many daily functions at this point. Stress
exasperates the problem and becomes a terrible
symptom of continued immobility. I came to
Houston to see if I could get more answers concerning this condition. When I am happy and
free of stress, the symptoms become dormant but
can arise at any time. Maybe I will never be normal. I don't know.

I have to tell you I was disappointed that
all your focus was on the plasma and none of
the focus was on us. I was interested in how the
funeral went, how your day went, what is going
on in your life, and all you could talk about was
the plasma TV. I know you will work something out, my love, because if we had not met, I
wouldn't be here to help you, and you still would
have to solve the problem. I liked being your
angel and hope that somehow this angel would
give you strength to solve your problems.

If you do decide to have nothing more to
do with me, just keep the things in the package I

sent as a gift, and we will call it even. There is no need for you to have to deal with me again. But you do need to know that you mean the world to me. But I am tough and have accepted this condition as one I won't give up on, and right now, all my efforts will go into getting myself better and back where I was last week before all this began. So do what you have to do. I have given you my heart and soul. I have to admit I haven't liked you getting so upset with me because I said no. I also didn't like that you could cause damage when you were drunk since I lived with someone that was abusive when he was drunk. I thought I knew you better and hate to think that every time you get sad that you feel the need to get drunk or hurt something or someone. You are so much better than that. I thought we were a lot alike. This whole thing really gets me to the core. But if I have to suck it up, I will. I have always been a survivor, and I will continue to be one. Yes, I have been stepped on, spat on, and taken for granted. But all of it has made me stronger. It's also made me very vulnerable and cautious to trust and love someone. I thought I found that special someone to love and trust in you.

You can stay mad at me if you want. You can be sad if you want. But what I really want you to do right now is figure out a way to solve your problems, be a good role model for your son, and face up to any consequences you have caused yourself. I want you to be proud of your actions, your thoughts, and most of all yourself. I love you, John, and I want you to remember that even if you don't have room for me in your life anymore, you have a good friend in Daniel. Let him see how you handle situations that are challenging for you. I was not sent to you to solve your problems. I was sent to you to be your partner and be part of the inspiration for you to solve your problems. I was sent to you to give you love and support so that each day you grow stronger as a person. Do take care, my darling. I'm really sorry all this has had to happen. Now, chin up, face your demons, and move ahead. You can, and you will do it. I have faith in you. If I don't hear from you, I will understand. But at least now you have the rest of the story. Take care and God bless.

Your love,
BB

Never cry for those who don't deserve your tears, But those who deserve them won't let you cry. Love is Crazy. Love is Stupid, Love is Mad, Love is Hurt, Yet love is Caring. Love is understanding, Love brings joy, It takes two to Love, Love is Pain and Pain is Love. I love you and I am sorry for the pain I made you go through. I love you Darling and please forgive me.

I wish you a speedy recovery. I Hope by Monday you will be fine so you can try and get me the Plasma. I am off to bed now. Good Night.

Your Love,
John

I love you endlessly, with you I can breathe, with you I can do anything, without you I can do nothing, and I only have three words to tell you: I love you! My eyes miss you, my feelings are of love, my hand needs you, my soul calls upon you, my heart is just for you. I'd die without you, because I love you... I love you so much that I can't write in words how much I love you... I love you,

Hello my love. I just read your mail and I feel very happy that you are always there for me. Oh God Bless you. I love you and I will never let you down Hun. Trust me and take my words. I will be with you in Spirit to help you to drive. So you can get what I told you done. Love you.

I am off and will be online tonight okay. Kiss to you...

John,
your Husband

Hello...

How do I start Darling? Thank you and I am so happy for your coming into my life. Oh yes I should be the one to thank you day in and out. I love you so much and always want to be sure you are doing great. You are all that I have and all that I want. I love you every second. Not money nor anything but just love because my love is for you. I have been on the computer just to say Hi and send my greetings to you but sorry I missed you. Hope you have a great Day. Kiss and Hug. I will talk to you when I close for the day. My day is busy but I think I am okay with that just to get home very soon and be with you as my wish...

John,
Your Love

Good Night My Love. I have also missed you and yes my Day was great. I have not received the package yet but hopeful I will by Monday. Oh yes, I just woke up and am trying to go and talk with the Truck Drivers who are going to load the timbers babe. There are five drivers with five trucks but they say the price I gave them is less because they charge $45,000 for the whole week. They will load the timbers but now they say they will take $50,000 because the road to the forest is very far. So I am going to talk to them because I want them to start so I can come home soon my love. I love you and I am counting on you Hun. I will tell you how it goes, okay? After I go to the tax office and find some things out Darling, they called me because I have some balance to pay them babe. As you know almost $18,000 Daniel took to one of his friends and he agrees but the boss himself wants to see us so we will pass over there Darling…and talk to him. I guess I need some money, but I don't know. I will let you know Darling. Let's pray that it's not more money because I am damn broke Babe. I will let you know how my day will go. I love you and I keep on missing you and the more I love you. Kiss…

John

Hello Darling…

Good Evening to you. I just came home Darling. Oh yes I had a great and busy day. I have talked to the truck drivers and they still want the $5000 so they can work but they have started working since I talked to them. Also we went over to the tax office and I talked to him. I will be there on Monday and talk to him again. I love you Darling. I have missed you so much my love. This is a picture of one of the trucks loading timbers babe. They start work today. I need to talk to you Hun. I have missed you. I don't have any coins on me Darling. But all the same your love makes me happy and always strong. Love you… Kiss and hug…

John,
Your Husband

Good Morning Darling…

Thank you for your nice mail. It makes me feel more and more in love with you and it shows me how much you care and love me. Thank you Hun. Well it's Monday and still busy babe. I need to talk to you Darling. It's very serious, please. I am happy you are doing fine babe and always part of me my love that makes me more and more happy. And know I will do my possible best to marry you as I always have promised you. Besides, I thank you for the trust you have in me. Oh yes I am doing my best even when I don't have anything left. Please don't forget I need to talk to you Darling. I am almost done with everything. The trucks are still loading babe. But there are a number of timbers we still need to cut. Please let me know when you will be online so we can chat. I need to talk with you and besides, I have missed you so much, babe. Guess and tell me how much I have missed you my love. I love you Hun and take care babe. Kiss and Hug to you my lovely wife.

John

Hello Darling…

I have missed you and think of you all night babe. Oh yes babe I received the Package today and so sad that there was no money in it. They must have changed the teddy bear, but all the same I feel happy I have you in my life babe. The drivers have asked for their money today babe and also the Tax babe I have to pay about 13,700 dollars. That is all I have to pay and come home babe. I was very sad today but all the same I think the money should be covered with carbon paper and also cotton and black rubber, but please try and ask more about the VIGO babe. It will work and you can try there babe. I am serious babe and I am almost done babe. Just trust me babe. The love and the trust you have for me—just keep it up babe. I will never let you down babe. Please try and send some units on Daniel's number, okay babe? So we can call the customs. Please babe, Please try and do that for me babe. Love you and check on the Vigo for me. Love you my lovely wife,

John…kiss

Hun… Thank you for the Airtime and it makes me feel like I am truly in love and that you care about me. Oh yes babe I love you so much with your words after all the pains you have been through, I just thank you for the trust and belief you have for me and I will never let you down as I always promise to you. Well Darling I am still trying to find a way out so I can come home safe, babe. But I am trying to find out from the Vigo and you can also try and see if there is any other express way, okay babe? Thank you and may God Bless you so much for the kind way and the love you have for me babe. I will always be your love and forever will I be faithful because I love you more than anything in this world. I will talk to you. I am going to see customs and afterwards I need to talk to the drivers to have patience, I hope. I will talk to you after so please just be there for me and try to be by my side to get me out babe. I promise we will make a whole lot of money. You can't believe the number of timbers I am coming home with. I am more excited and I always say to Daniel that you are the luckiest woman I have ever met. I love you and Daniel says Thank you for the gift. Kennie says that He has missed you too Babe. Please take care of your self for me my lovely wife. Kiss…

John

Hello babe… How are you? I have been waiting for you and no mail no call why Hun… It seems you are playing with my heart and also you don't trust me. I have taken the Gold to the FedEx office so it can be sent very soon but I have not heard from you since you told me you will send the money. I am waiting to hear from you. I learned they called you from the States just to verify your address, so when they call you, please answer the call. That is what they told me. This is the number they will call you with, but I told them you did not pick up because you thnk it was the Fraud Department. So please pick up the call when they call you and make sure you send the money Hun love you…

Your Husband…
John

*****

Emails continued to be exchanged back and forth, and the phone calls continued to be even more often than before. It was always the same plea. "Please, babe, send the money. We must get the gold home to pay off all your debts. Why won't you pick up your phone?" Even now, if I were to contact John and give him my new phone number and email address, the message would be the same: "Send me more money." I never seemed to get past the thought that the gold and the money always meant more to him than my health or emotional wellness. This is so sad but true. In summary, John left me holding all the debts that he borrowed to pay for the gold, which never arrived. Now he is only part of a nightmare that I have trouble waking up from.

CHAPTER 12

Love Like No Other

Wondering what could happen next and what would my children say (especially my son) if they knew I had used up my life savings and sent them to someone I hadn't met in person once again. Would he kick me out of the house? I was at an all-time low, feeling both sorry for myself and angry at myself for allowing this to happen again. Thank goodness I had a pension and social security to live on. And now it was getting hard to make the one-thousand-dollar payments to my son each month to pay back the fifty thousand I owed him. I had paid off more than twelve thousand by now and knew how important it was to not only set a good example for my son that I pay off all my debts, but also to know that he could believe in me and trust me that I now make only good decisions. I need to be clear about something. Not once during this journey did I think that my son or daughter would need to bail me out of anything. I also did not think that they were acting as a safety net for me if I should ever fail at my attempt to congeal a long-term relationship. As I have mentioned before, I put everything I have and feel into a romantic relationship and am always optimistic about the outcome. Sometimes, that might mean I am not being realistic, and I may be living in a fantasy. If I didn't feel both parties were into this relationship equally as serious in their approach, I would never get involved in it in the first place. I always thought I would be making my children proud of the choices I made, and I never once thought I would disappoint them or cause them embarrassment. My last relationship allowed me to make what I thought was a great investment. And I would be paid back seven times over by selling the gold that I received as payment for the money loaned to him during his business venture. I believed with all my heart that this was and would be a good investment. But as you know, I was swindled, because I never saw John or the gold ever again.

Eventually, another gentleman from Date Hookup sought me out. There was something about him that made me reach out and want to get to know him better. I wasn't sure whether to respond or not, but this one really intrigued me, and he only lived a few miles away from me. I felt instant attraction and chemistry with him. Because his job location was so close to me, I would be crazy not to check him out. I just had a gut feeling that this one was the one. I took the big leap and responded. If there ever was a fairy tale romance, I had a feeling this was going to be the one. He knew the exact things to say. He knew exactly what to do and how to do it. He drove an arrow right through my heart and captured it in a way no one else had done. This man was special, and I wanted to know as much about him as possible, because after only knowing him one week, I fell madly in love with him. And he was so very handsome.

*****

Meet George from Houston, Texas

Hello B…

Thanks for taking your time to write back. I love your smile and I won't lie. It got my attention. How are you and your family and friends? My name is George. I'm a widower with one daughter. Her name is Jenny and she is 17 years of age. My grandparents are from Scotland and Germany. I have one sister. Well I've been a widower for five years plus now. I would like to know more things about you—like what is your birth name? Where are you from? This is my personal email. You can give me an Addy or send a message to me as I am sure things are more personal there than here on the dating service site. So I can even send some of my recent pictures to you, since I find it very hard trying to upload some on the site. Meanwhile I might not get on the dating site for a while, but usually check my email address daily. So most definitely my email is the best place for us to keep the communication going...

Hugs...
George

*****

After responding to George's personal email address, I failed to notice that red flag number one had just popped up (writing to my personal email and not directly to dating site so it could not be traced). The journey began with both of us emailing one another more than once a day. Immediately after I sent him an email, he decided to respond quickly. Here was his response:

*****

Thanks for your time. I have been waiting to read from you—don't know why though. I really can't explain why...smiles... I'm so pleased to hear from you. It has warmed my heart and I'm hoping to always hear from you. You have shared very lovely pictures of yourself with me. You have really lived a very interesting life and I must say—you seem very nice and welcoming. I plan to seek happiness that will last for a life time with you; (smiles) but I guess time will tell. I hope this will take us to the next level and we can build a relationship that will last forever.

Distance between us does not bother me as I know we could meet someday if we wish to. I liked your profile and all I read about it was awesome and you seem very close with your children. I share a very strong bond with my daughter too and she is a great kid. I'm sure you will love her when you meet her. I would like to tell you that the sick dog is doing better but still won't eat on her own so I have to force feed her. I was up at 5 am to give her the 4 medications plus get some food down her. She is much perkier and even jumped up on the window seat which is a far cry from how lethargic she's been the last 5 days. I'm encouraged. It will be my pleasure to get to know more about you. I want to get to know you and meet you and see how interesting things can go between us.

With much Love,
George

*****

Red flag number two popped up, but of course, I ignored it too. When he shared with me about the condition of his dog, it must have been someone else that he had talked to about it because this was the first I had heard about it. Yet lovesick me appeared and wrote back to him once more. It was like everything I was doing was involuntary and did not require a lot of thought, just a quick response to keep him interested. I didn't want to lose this one because he was so very special, even though I felt compelled to tell him about my concerns about him being real or just another scammer. He looked exactly like the captain on the TV show *Below Deck*. Once again, the next day, when I woke up, I checked to see if I had a response from him, and once more, the following appeared on my phone.

*****

Morning...

It was so nice hearing from you. I hope you are doing great this morning. I would really love getting to meet you in person. In your answer you sound like someone I would like to spend the rest of my life with and you have a way with words that I like. I can picture what I'm up for even with the small distance between us; but I just want to clear your mind about me being real or fake. It's really giving me a turn-off on my side. I know what you have been through and I want you to have a thought that this is the year for the real thing. I think positive and I see positive answers. It's my own little secret and it's been working for me. (Smiles) I have never even kissed or hugged anyone but my late wife; as she was my first girlfriend and only one in my life. I'm still working and thinking of retiring soon too. I think when I find love, (smiles) we can both go on vacation with our phones switched off and mind at rest. I hope you know what I'm trying to drive at.

I am financially secure and have no credit balances except for my new little red Chevy Cobalt I bought about 7 months ago. I took advantage of the $4,500 government program and traded in my 11 yr. old car. I had to go for it as my car was falling apart though now I have two cars. I do not like bills and I have credit cards, but I pay the entire balance when the bill comes due. You really made my day and I can't stop thinking about you. Every time I read from you, I hope everything is cool. Sure I can be your Man while you can be my woman. I will be so loyal to you. Well you do know a relationship is not something you can just run into—in the case of not getting hurt. As I told you my heart had shed a lot of tears. All I want is joy and happiness. I need a woman who could just be the angel of my life with all my heart. I am telling you this—I would love to meet you in person. I will always tell the truth and be willing to discuss just about anything. I am not a fighter and like to get along but it should be a partnership of equal sharing of everything. Agree?

By the way, I don't drink at all but have no problem with someone who drinks moderately. Just so you know, I also am quite liberal in my views both politically and socially. I hope that's not a problem with you. I have attended mostly Lutheran and Episcopalian churches over the years which are actually quite close to Catholic, except for the allegiance to the Pope. Let's just chat on yahoo. Nothing to it. I'm not saying we should not meet. Mind you, no man would not want someone as sweet as you in his life. Let's chat and share more things with each other. You are so easy to write to and I can tell that you will be very interesting to know more about. So if you are up for chat, just tell me when you are.

*****

Oops! Red flag number three pops up when he says he is turned off by my thinking that he could possibly be a fake and might only be using me for something he wants. Once again, I ignored the sign.

I look back now and wonder where my head was. Did it go on vacation this time? I had just experienced two different relationships in the past three years who chose to scam me. Why was I thinking this person could be the one that only had my well-being and my good in mind? After giving him my response, I received yet another email from him.

*****

My dear I'm doing fine and alright... I would have loved to get back to you sooner than this time but I've been very busy with the contract I am working towards getting. I don't want you to feel that it's going to be in our way. It's just getting some of my time for now. Oh less I forget—I reread all your emails. Not that I did not get it the first time—I just enjoy reading from you. Sounds to me like I'm reading a love novel and we are still on chapter one—how Romeo met Juliet...smiling here... I just hope and pray they give me an approval on the contract. I just joined the site five days before I saw your profile and then I went through your profile the third time I was getting on the site...

Really enjoying all that we have shared and thinking my search for a woman has ended. My favorite color is purple, I enjoy all kinds of English food but my favorite is rice, spaghetti, beef and little of red meat... Of course yes, I believe in love at the first sight and that is why we are still keeping this conversation going. I still feel the same way I felt about you after going through your profile. Like now I am just completely sure it is just meant to be... Ok, I could not keep the secret from Jenny long enough. She found out about you and got me to talk about the wonderful woman that has been making daddy smile on his laptop. She is a good kid and I'm sure you will like her, because she loves whatever makes daddy happy…smiles. Like she wants me to be happy and having a woman in my life is what can complete me again. So she's quite alright with me and also I've been telling her about you but didn't tell her much beyond where we are. I hope that is alright by you? Well I don't really think your cure for our loneliness is selfish. If I get hold of someone I can give all my heart to and I get hers in return, I will spoil her and bring down the moon for her. Okay, that was a joke. But if she really wants the moon, I will draw one for her… smiles. I'm really enjoying the bold step I took by writing you on the site. I was having doubtful thoughts—like what if she does not like me and all, but I can tell that my boldness is really paying off now.

I'm talking to one of the most wonderful women on earth. I hope to hear from you and to know how you are doing today. And I pray that my notes bring a bright and fresh smile to you this morning. I really hope we get to talk on IM today; I really can't wait to talk to you soon.

Hugs,
George

Our relationship tended to move quickly as George became the center of my life. Receiving responses from him several times a day did nothing but put a continual smile on my face all day long. The following email came from him wanting to know even more about me.

*****

It will be my pleasure to get to know more about you and I am putting these questions to you. What do you seek for in a relationship? What are the basic qualities you seek for in a Man? What sort of relationship do you seek for? What interests you? Got kids?

What do you do for fun? Do you like public intimacy? How long have you been single? What's being single like? How do you treat your man? Why do you need a man? Can you love this man? What is love to you? Would you hit your man for any reasons? I'll hopefully want to know what your consent is about these questions. I want to get to know you and meet you and see how interesting things can go between us.

With much Love,
George

*****

And after answering all his questions, I received his response of appreciation.

Thanks for taking your time to write me and I enjoy reading from you. You have a very nice way with words that I sometimes feel you are here telling me to my face...smiles... You share a lot with me and I think that's really important in a relationship. I understand what the online dating scene has turned into, but have not had any of those sad stories yet and I pray I never do, because I want my search to stop with you and that's a secret...smiles. I think meeting each other would be a nice thing to do too, because I know how it feels giving out your mind and time to a man and finding out it's all a sham… You shared a lot with me and I think I should just call it over with the search… Again a secret… smiles… I'm glad you like Jenny and will love the three girls in my life to be happy…smiles… You, Jenny and Debbi (my sister)… Jenny is in the Senior high school and she has some friends, but she still remains my best friend…smiles

My lawn guy who does all the outside stuff on the one acre of landscaped yard is coming tomorrow to plant lots and lots of flowers. We've had such a mild winter that things are starting to bud out already. He thatched and fertilized the lawn yesterday and it rained for about thirty minutes right afterwards which was great. I told him I'd do my rain dance for him and it worked! I'll send you pictures of the yard, house etc. as soon as it all gets done, if you'd like… What a good response to the questions. I adore you and I am opening my heart to you now as what I had read from you so far has made me feel much confidence in you. I just need you to be at ease with it. I feel so safe and secure in you. Can you be the woman you have illustrated in your writings??? I hope you can. Since the questionnaire reciprocated, my answers are below here.

What do you do for a living? I work as a Construction Engineer.

What do you seek in a relationship? I seek trust, honesty, understanding, sincerity, love and sharing, sharing the good and bad times together with no fear of what the world might put upon us—compatibility is the most of all.

What sort of relationship you seek for? Well, the relationship I want is one to be built on the solid foundation which is love and trust. I do believe in these two ingredients of a relationship. So many relationships have come to success unlike ones built on false truths and pretenses.

What are the basic qualities I seek for in a woman? The basic qualities are Honesty, Love, and Trust.

What interests you? Wow! God interests me. All the things he has created interests me. Nature really does.

Got kids? Yeah, I had told you before I have a daughter and her name is Jenny.

What do you do for fun? I like playing basketball, playing billiards, dancing, writing, reading, watching movies or TV.

Do you like public intimacy? Public intimacy is my thing. I miss that though. I still like to walk while holding hands. It's fun I guess.

How long have you been single? I have been single for about five years plus back.

What's being single like? Being single is the dullest and loneliest thing that has ever happened to me.

How do you treat your woman? I treat her with respect, loyalty, adoration, and treat her like a Queen.

Why do I need a woman? I need a woman because I feel two people can make things worthwhile. It's always good to have a shoulder to lean on.

Can you love this woman? Yeah, most definitely I will love her.

What is love to you? Love to me is everything. Everything that has made up this world is love.

Would you hit your woman for any reasons? I won't do that. I would rather discuss it rather than fight.

Do you like camping? Do you like to lie on a blanket on a warm summer's evening and look at the stars while holding each other? Do you like to sing and dance in a warm rain or just put on some music and dance under the stars? Or even sit near a lake or ocean and listen to the gentle waves roll in (maybe with some cheese and a bottle of wine to share?). Yes, I am a hopeless romantic! LOL. To leave little love notes for one another each day, just to let them know how special they are to you. I long for that kind of love to share!

I hope I have answered the questions to your satisfaction and if not, bring on more. Well I believe what matters most in a relationship is that the person must be very honest and loyal so that you could have a long term relationship with one another. I believe talking through email and/ or chat cannot be like meeting in person. I can't wait to hear from you soon. With all my heart I'm telling you this—I will never do anything to hurt a woman in my life because that is what my dad told me before he died. So tell me what do you think about chatting on yahoo messenger? I think that way we can get to know more about each other and I can bet that you will love it… smiles… Send me some of your pics, okay?

With much Love,
George

*****

Our emails and text just seemed to flow and be so natural. It took little effort on my part to stay in touch. I liked being myself when I responded to him. He made it so easy. I truly felt we were meant to be. I felt as if I was part of a love novel every time we communicated. I loved hearing from him. Everything I longed for in my marriage was suddenly being handed to me. I got another response from him.

> You are so easy to write to and I can tell that you will be very interesting to know more about. So if you are up for chat, just tell me when you are free. I can always talk from work too, when I'm less busy. Just give me your yahoo handle and let me add you. You sure seem to me like you enjoy life and use the lemons that life has to offer well. (smiles)
>
> I would love to go to Disney World someday with Jenny. Oh less I forget; she knows I'm talking to someone on the internet. But I can tell she will ask today, because she noticed me smiling when writing to you (which I don't do normally before). I don't want to talk much about you for now, because I want us to grow bigger and see what time has got for us. Ok, I just wanted to say Top of the Morning to you before I started sharing my mind. (Smiles) I enjoy reading from you and hope to read more. Enjoy the rest of you day… Hugs.
>
> CAN I TRUST YOU? CAN U TRUST ME?
>
> MUCH LOVE FROM George

I had shared with him about a family trip I was taking to Disney World. Since this last email kind of tested me on being able to trust him, I jumped into the fire pretty fast here. So once again, I heard from him.

I'm so pleased to hear from you. It has warmed my heart and I'm hoping to always hear from you and I'm very happy you enjoyed getting a mail from me in the morning. I was actually up to get some paper work done for a meeting I had this morning. I'm bidding for a contract and we had meetings today with the other party, so, I'm hoping I get the contract on our last meeting. Ok, that's all about my work today. How has your day been? Just got into my office and I got the lovely mail from you. You have such a nice way with words and I think you can be a poet writer too…smiles… From the initial contact there has been you and I. No eye contact, no hand holding, no dancing or physical attraction. Just a union of the minds, without prior knowledge or infractions. The words however were sincere, and sent across the air waves onto the monitor. I read what was not stated, what was overly reported… I knew I had a winner knocking at my door way undistorted. Now, some time has passed and we write our own poetry, and type dreams of a positive future. A friendship that has surpassed any and all we were used to. We laugh, we explain and confide… For we are oceans, mountains and valleys apart… Smiles… But one thing we shall not forget is how this technology has won our hearts and has helped us share a lot. So far I think the race for making things happen in our lives is getting better and enjoying every moment with you. Your insecurity will not really turn me off, because there is a word that goes like this. If you really want love to happen, you have to look like you have found it…smiles… I don't know if you know what I mean by that and I like the kind of spirit and that your children are giving you—Telling you not to judge every man the same way, because you came across some bad ones. Being protective is very good too and I like that. It shows when I'm part of your family, that I'm part of a caring family that looks out for each other's mistakes. You did not send the yahoo handle. Thought we agreed on chatting—just so you know I will be very free from 3pm today on and you can add me as this same mail on yahoo or you send yours so we chat… Ok? Glad to talk with you. I must admit I do get lonely some times.

Hugs… George

*****

As I read each email, this man George fell deeper and deeper into my heart. He was on my mind morning, noon, and night. Could I have possibly found the man of my dreams? I was beginning to think so just as another email arrives.

*****

Heh Sugar…smiles… Thanks for the mail and the sweet compliment… I can sometimes just go on sharing so much with you in a day…because I just feel like I'm in safe hands… smiles… Really glad you like the fact that I told Jenny. I thought you might not like it… From the look of things, your family really wants you to have a wonderful man in your life… I feel very good about that so when they meet me, I can tell I'm part of a wonderful family. My busy schedule can never get in between both of us. I like the fact that you know I can get busy at times too, and you give me the time for work. Thanks for that. I love to work, but can't allow it to get in between my happiness. I really love to see you and Jenny get along very fine, because I can tell she needs a mother figure who she can share some more things with. You know how teenagers do, right? They don't share all with the dad…smiles.

Hey…now I need to get back to work. I was just on my laptop to check something and took that time to see if I have gotten a mail from my wonderful woman… So I will do all I can to see that we chat later today around three, ok… I do not need to set an alarm, because you run in my mind all day long…so have a great day ahead…

More hugs from George

*****

After sending my Yahoo address, we were able to chat online. It didn't take long after our little chat for me to hear from him again.

*****

Really enjoyed all that we talked about today. You are making this man happy and never pray to stop that… We just seem like what we have both been looking for and not looking at the right places…ok, I guess my words are getting too heavy for you… Please Tell me if they are… I will just drive on yellow, instead of Green. I guess I just can't hold what I feel for you and have to

171

burst out...smiles... I have enjoyed everything we have shared and hope we share more...

> Hugs and kisses...
> George

The next morning, I awoke to the following:

Hey Hon...

Good Morning, thanks for your mail. But I guess the food won my time with you and I'm very jealous... Smiles... I waited for you to come back, but I guess you were having a great time with your family. Sounds good though, so tell me how did you know I was watching a movie with Jenny...come on, don't lie; were you here with me?...smiles...pretty woman. I think I've seen the movie before, the one with Julia Roberts and Richard Gere, right...it was in the 1990's though, but a lovely film... Don't know if it's the same one you are talking about anyways... So your son has noticed the change about you, sounds nice to me, so let's still go as planned and don't tell them about me yet, until I come over and hope they like me... Do you know that I can be shy at times, but not with that lovely family of yours...smiles...ok... I will be free today too for some chat and thinking of taking Jenny to the place I told you about, because she has been on my neck like forever... Smiles, I will have to let you wake up now; just want to say Good Morning and hope you had a nice rest...

> Hugs,
> George

Sugar…

Thanks for your sweet note. I woke up around 4 a.m. to do some more findings and I stumbled across your note, Wow!!!! Can't remember the last time I have been cared for this much… You watch over me before I go to bed and are there first when I wake up… Ok now tell me what more can a man ask for in a woman… Really enjoyed last night chat… The more we talk the more we enjoy. Like we see things the same time and we want just the same thing in our life… I'm not scared to give out my love, because from the look of things I might be getting more from you and your wonderful family… Jenny will really love this and at last she has found a good Woman to share her inner thoughts with… you know with her age, she will have some things she will only be comfortable telling a woman… I hope you understand what I mean… Ok

Our relationship seemed to grow closer by the minute, and these notes were one of many I received as we began to bond even more.

*****

Today is a big day and I'm hoping I go with your prayers. Well, it seems like I have it already because for the past few weeks now things have been in my favor. I prayed for you and you walked in and now I prayed for the contract and it will be mine…smiles… I just want to wake you up into your wonderful life…

Hugs and kisses to you from George

My Sugar… The first thing I will have to say right now is please I'm on my knees and I hope you accept my apology. Because in everything in life, I think my family comes first which you are part of it and we have not talked for almost three days now. Very bad I will say… Just so you know, my laptop started acting weird again and I had to get it fixed this time around. OK, now to the news of the day. We won the contract and I have been very happy since Monday night. I was hoping I could share the news with you and then my laptop broke my heart. I knew you would be up waiting for my return… Honey, I'm very happy. But there is a little problem there. I know it's not one for me, but you. I don't know and I don't want anything to come between us right now, because my days have been filled with joy and my nights with love.

I will be traveling to U.A.E, Dubai for the work… I told you I applied for two contracts, right? One in Ohio and the other in Dubai, so got the one in Dubai. Though this pay is better than the one in Ohio, but this one might cause some kind of a distance for us you know… But you won't get to miss a thing, because I will be there with my laptop and we can talk from time to time honey…please I need to talk to you when you wake up, because right now I'm packing already. We need to report there on Friday and I will be going with nine of my crew members… Ok… I just want you to know how well I'm doing and really missed talking to you my

Sugar...smiles... Oh less I forget, Jenny says Hi...hope to read from you when you wake...

Hugs,
George

Hey Love... I am overwhelmed and short of words out of happiness and being over-joyed!!!!... But I'll just search inside of me and let the words just flow... I believe there is nothing as important in a relationship as loyalty, commitment, devotion and communication in a relationship... Love and affections grows with each passing second... My love for you grows with each heart beat... I want to be the one to love and protect you till the end of time... I feel special having you. I'm so blessed. You are everything I have hoped for in a woman and more... I have prayed in my heart to find one woman who will need, want and deserve all the love I have inside of me.

I have been lucky in life to have what I have today... I have enough saved up for a life time. I started out as a lucky young man with a background better than average, earning more than many of my pairs...and have been lucky from being an employee to being an employer... I own my business, no partners...just me!!... I have been managing my business for about 20 years... I am a contractor that has worked on different construction projects...roads, bridges, towers... structures mostly... I have worked with individuals, corporate bodies and different governments... I have been lucky all through but like you... I miss one thing that is more important than all of these. One thing that would actually complete me... My life misses the presence of a diva, a queen, a lover, a friend and a companion all in one...but you came along!!!!!... What did I do right?? What have I been doing wrong? Where have you been??

... I wish I had met you a long time ago... My heart skips at the thought of you... I am a much happier person now... I walk around with a smile... Life is just perfect for me now... I guess God decided to answer my prayers and he sent me an angel... One I will cherish forever!!...

Sweetheart, Really happy that Jenny feels very right about you too... She is such a sweetheart. You will love her! She's understanding and has a good heart... When she was younger and even now she would give her stuff, her toys and clothes out to her friend who she felt was not as fortunate as her... I'm thankful I have her!!... She always asked me if she'll be getting a new "Mom" and I would tell her that Yes, when I find someone that will love us and care about us genuinely she would... I am happy and thankful that I eventually found her and Jenny has found a Mom that will love her like her very own... I spoil her with everything she wants but she is very self-controlled and learns when she's corrected... She not a typical spoiled brat!!... You'll love her... I know in her heart she cares about you already because like me, she wanted this to happen! She'll love and cherish whoever makes me happy!... I own my home in Texas and also a Sea side Condo in Berlin, Germany... It's our getaway place... I also have a yacht down there... I have plans of selling my condo in Berlin home and buying a new place that will be where ever we decide to live... I am also talking with some Realtor in Europe. I have plans of buying a place that will be rebuilt into Studio flats for rent, but maybe these plans will change a bit now that I have you. You have 50% right on every decision I make now... Everything I do now will be decided by the both of us... It's us now, not just me or just you... Tell me, what do you think about marriage...do you think you'll like to walk the aisle again?? Or who would rather just live with the man you love??... I'm just curious because I have always had dreams of a wedding. Whatever you want honey, as long as I have you in my life, I'll love you and be dedicated all the same... I am blessed to have the things I have but they don't mean the world to me, these are just material things...

Your Love is most important to me right now... You're my better half! and I have gained more trust in you... I have never shared any of this with any woman before, apart from my wife. So when you said we must see, I was like you are seeing the relationship from another angle. But I can understand what some men have put you through. I do not tell women about my fortune too, because some out there are just out for my success and all, so I seek a true love and I found that in you... Smiles...

Working with you on my mind will just work out fine for me believe me. I try to create a good relationship with my workers, also good pay and so they are always happy to work... Smith, my assistant and project manager is wonderful. He has the brain and attitude I need to work with... His Wife and kids are very friendly and happy to take care of Jenny while i'm at work... Jenny likes it there too but prefer to be with Debby when I'm out of the states... She has a good heart and never looks down on people who are less fortunate… I can't wait!

My home is locked when ever I'm out of the states. In the past I had an housekeeper who took care of the house while I was away but then, my identity was stolen…someone broke into my files and money was stolen from one of my accounts, about $120,000 so I became more careful…now when I travel, I lock my accounts so no one can take money from it until I am back in the states, not even me… I usually use my credit cards when I'm outside the states… I have a card for personal expenses and another for business… I have also had gold diggers in the past who just wanted the juice… I am happy to have found you because I know you don't care about the money and you have your own but still, I will spoil you!!!!…

I am happy that you are so beautiful and have a good heart… People will just envy us… I'm so happy and excited! Baby, I want you to do me a favor. Let your friends and family have their first impression from me. Let our love be our little secret while I'm still here as we have been doing it… I really don't want to be a picture you painted in their minds! I want them to see me as the man I really am…lol… I need you in my life like the air I breath, I will cherish you like life itself!!!… I will be here thinking about you!!… Love You…

Your George

*****

This man is absolutely too good to be true. However, I became blinded by love. This experience was everything I had dreamed about.

I wanted to do everything to preserve this relationship and do nothing to damage it. I was enjoying this ride so much. He was saying all the right things. And with every word, my feelings for him became more cemented in our journey to be with one another forever.

*****

Hi Hon…

I guess now you realize you are stuck with me. Once you get in my veins, it's hard to get you out. I hope I am in yours too. I guess the sugar will hopefully make us both sweeter to each other. I'm so glad I heard from you today. I was even more happy that you made me smile and helped me realize it is worth it to stay with you and explore what we have together. I know now I can't give up on us, because we are just beginning. And we will never know what we could have had if we don't stay with it and nourish it a little. It's like you said, don't let my past experiences slow us down or come between us. I know now you are so right. Falling in love is always a risk but as they say it is better to have loved and lost than never to have loved at all. Will chat with you later.

Your Sweet Sugar,
George

My dear… Glad to read from you again. It's always a pleasure to read from you and the flight was really interesting. I got talking a lot with my crew… Like you and I had my share of fun and adventure growing up and I still seek after more… I have to work here in Dubai for five weeks but we'll be able to keep in touch as much as we care to since there's internet in the hotel.

Now to tell you little about me... I grew up with practical parents. A mother, God love her, who washed aluminum foil after she cooked in it, then reused it. She was the original recycle queen, before they had a name for it... A father who was happier getting old shoes fixed than buying new ones. Their marriage was good, their dreams focused. Their best friends lived barely a wave away... As I close my eyes I can see them now— dad in trousers, tee shirt and a hat, and mom in a house dress, lawn mower in one hand, and dish-towel in the other. It was the time for fixing things... A curtain rod, the kitchen radio, screen door, the oven door, the hem in a dress. Things we keep. It was a way of life, and sometimes it made me crazy... All that re-fixing, eating, renewing, I wanted just once to be wasteful. Waste meant affluence. Throwing things away meant you knew there will always be more. I wanted more and I strived hard and worked for it... I got every-thing I ever wanted in life... Life got better or so I thought...after all, Life is life... But then my mother died, and on that clear summer's night, in the warmth of the hospital room, I was struck with the pain of learning that sometimes there isn't any more... I have learned to get happy with what I have and would never cause you pain or hurt... Sometimes, what we care about most gets all used up and goes away... Like losing my wife, never to return... So...while we have it...it's best we love it...and care for it... and fix it when it's broken...and heal it when it's sick. This is true for friendship, lovers, marriages...and old cars... and children with bad report cards...and dogs with bad hips...and aging parents...and grand-parents. We keep them because they are worth it, because we are worth it... There are just some things that make life important, like people that make us happy and those we care to see smiles on their faces... That being said... When I saw your emails about what the under world men have put you through, I could not help but cry. That I have not done in years now; one of my employees walk in (Mr. Lawson) and asked Sir what seems to be the problem? I could not help but say nothing is wrong with me... My share was not that much... I just met a woman, that all they want is me and even want to take Jenny as their daughter. Just talking at some fancy restaurant of their choice and when they hear me talk about Jenny, they all don't make comments on her. So when you said you were happy that Jenny is being taken care of, you can't know how happy that made me... Honey, what we have is very important to me and I can't let go for anything in the world... My stay here would be a splendid one, as I will be going to the site this morning to have a view and hopeful we get some labour around here... My love, I will write more soon... ok, You run in my veins. Hugs,

Your Sugar
George

My Love, I'm so glad I could wake to your email... Awww!! What more would I ask for my love, your words are just so captivating and makes me think where have you been all of my life? I saw the preview of the film too; that was shot in the tallest building in the world. I have not been there yet, because it's not in the same city as me... So you pictured me here...that's very lovely honey...smiles. Since day one we've shared something incredible, something that most people only dream of. I had been searching for you all of my life. You have made me the happiest I have ever been. You are a sincere, caring, loving woman, and I wouldn't trade you for the world. I am so thankful and blessed that you love me as much as I love you, and that you made me your Man. We have been talking for days and now it feels like years. If you ask me I would say, Our souls have been connecting even before meeting each other. Do you agree with me? And I have cherished every moment since the day we met. I love you more and more every day. Thinking about our future fills me with anticipation and excitement. We make the perfect husband and wife team, and I cannot wait to bring Jenny and your own children into our world. We are going to have an amazing life together raising a family. All of our dreams are coming true, baby!

Don't worry about the times that we will be tight on money. I know that we can make it through and get to that place where we'll have all we ever wanted. Look how much we have already! We have so much to be thankful for! We will just continue to lean on each other, loving and supporting one another with all of the love we have, and we will be just fine. Our life together is already amazing, and together it will only get better and better. I will forever be grateful that you came into my life and made all my dreams come true. Together we're perfect, and I will enjoy spending the rest of my life with you. I love you more than words can say. I love you and nothing can change that... I hope we get to talk on Im later today... Hugs...

Love always,
George

Hey Love, You are just making me float on cloud 9. I really do not have much to do today as I have told you before. I will be signing some documents today as well... For payment and I will let you know as things go here honey. I ate some nice spaghetti last night and took diet coke, and had a nice time with my friends and crew. I call them both because before things get out of hand here they are the first to know, so right now, we are more like friends... Smiles... They all want to meet the boss's woman. They said the charm is really making prince charming smiling all day and you should not change him for us... Don't mind them they are just bunch of crazy dudes, that sure know how to lighten up, when things get boring... So baby, I woke up this morning and said my prayers. I included you in it and Jenny...the lovely women I have in my life right now... I will send the pic to you... ok, Talk to you soon...oh less I forget, Good Morning My love, I am writing you this letter to tell you how much you mean to me, and to thank you for coming into my life. You are something I never thought could exist for me. You are one of the best things that has happened in my life, and I don't regret being with you. At first I was confused, and didn't really know what I wanted, because I was very new to online dating. I didn't know if I would want to take a chance again and actually take you seriously. So, I decided to come close to you as a friend and find out who you truly were and what you were like. You seemed cool, nice and funny—some things I really liked in a woman. So I took a chance and got with you and we talked for long, and that moment, I knew something good is knocking on my door. In the beginning, things didn't seem that good; you actually had your doubts about me. I wasn't sure you were actually taking me seriously. But, it was too late to look back; I had already fallen for you since the day we shared things online and I wasn't really looking forward to giving up too soon. I tried so hard to have you; I wasn't going to let you go so easily! Well, time has passed and I have discovered new things and a new me. You have truly changed me. Still, in a way, I'm not scared because I am actually growing a true feeling inside my heart which I just can't explain. But I know it's there waiting for you to come and uncover it. Now that I am with you, I sleep thinking about you and the next morning I wake up smiling. Mainly I wanted you to know I will wait for you. I don't need fancy gifts or 100% of your time, all I need is to know you care, and you do that already. I love your ways and comforting words and I want to say thank you for everything. I have loved you as my friend for some time and I would cherish the chance to love you even more as my lover.

Love always…
Your Sugar

Do you know that I picture you in everything around me too. I saw a couple yesterday and I was thinking Hummm…that can just be me and my love here for vacation. I think that would be a great idea, after my work we can just come here next year or so for our vacation, just the two of us and Jenny's big brother can watch over her for us by then, what do you say Honey? Last night after our chat, when I got to the dining room, my crew were all smiling and saying, anyone can ask George anything now and he will grant him, because he just spoke to his woman. You know they sometimes act crazy just to get at me. Well I think it's good anyways, the place won't get bored. I said she has told me to fire you guys and get new members... They all started laughing... But then waited for me anyways and it was to my surprise... I really loved that they respect my time with you. That's very nice. I watch that show sometimes back too. The one with Donald Trump, right? I think some times you have to create a good relationship with your workers, because there is a saying that goes like this... You have to give respect to earn some... I hope you understand what I mean... I sit right here, thinking of you, and how you make my heart beat and how I am in love. I could never have thought that I would feel this way. You know all too well how surprising this is. I just love you so much. I don't know how it happened, and frankly I don't even care. I just want to love you and you to love me. I'll love you forever and never leave you. You'll be in my arms soon, I promise you.

This may start sounding like a poem, I don't know; must be the rhythm of my heart that's calling for you. I just wanted to tell you, and the world, 1) that you are my heart and my every thought, 2) that I love you with everything I have and hold dear, 3) that you mean more to me than this bright blue sphere. I miss you so much. You're probably sleeping now, but when you wake up, this will greet you. In this little letter I'm pouring my heart, can you feel how I feel for you?... My Love, You mean the world to me... I'll never forget you. I'll be faithful and never leave you. Ok I need to go back to work now and I wish you a safe trip on your road trip to Austin and hope you have a great time with you in my veins. I sure will...smiles...and we can chat maybe later on your phone if you are not home yet...ok...

Love always,
George

... I was on my way to the site and wanted to write you a little note. Thank you so much for having so much faith in me and in us as a couple. Thank you for making me a better person, and for giving your heart to me and opening up so much. I'm very happy that you had a good time on your bus trip. Just to let you know, even we do not chat, I know you have me in you and I do the same...what if there is no computer and all that, so I always have you in my veins and not even chatting can meet up with that. Though I ate early and did some men talk with the boys, but I still had my happy face on. You are not dreaming and you need not to be pinched. You have what it takes to be a happy woman. Please don't go out of that... Your happiness connects with me, so when you are happy, George is sure happy...smiles

Over the last 2 weeks, it's been wonderful; I never expected to feel this way nor actually be with you in this way, experiencing life with you.

You are wonderful...to me, to my friends, to my family. You make me really happy and even though we are apart for now, it's made up each time I will use with you in future. The feeling that I get is overwhelming every time that I do get to see you for the first time in such a long time and as time goes by my feelings for you grow dramatically. I am so happy that you respect my beliefs as I respect yours. You say that you are going to make me a happy man... Well, you have already done that, just by being you and showing me love and being so open with your feelings. You are what I dreamed of when I was a little boy, someone with integrity, honesty, love, affection, beautiful and with such a charming personality. I never thought I would find you, but here you are. I guess you went single just to meet this man in a fairytale...smiles. I love you so much, and can't wait to be with you. I want to give you my heart and soul. I don't care about anything else in the world because I am in love with you. I love you. Thank you for you have made all of my dreams come true. I could not ask for more. I am the luckiest man in the world to be called your Sugar, I'm truly honored. Thank you. I hope we can chat today honey. Missed that too...smiles and keep smiling. Love always, George

I can almost feel you beside me as I write this letter, and I can smell the scent of wildflowers...smiles... Last night, in my dreams, I saw you on the pier. The wind was blowing through your hair, and your eyes held the fading sunlight. I was speechless as I watched you leaning against the rail. You are beautiful, I thought as I saw you, a vision that I could never find in anyone else. I slowly began to walk toward you, and when you finally turned to me, I noticed that others had been watching you as well. "Do you know her?" they asked me in jealous whispers, and as you smiled at me I simply answered with the truth, "Better than I know myself." I stop when I reach you and I take you in my arms. I long for this moment more than any other. It is what I live for, and when you return my embrace, I give myself over to this moment, at peace once again. I raise my hand and gently touch your cheek and you tilt your head and close your eyes. My hands are hard and your skin is soft, and I wonder for a moment if you'll pull back, but of course, you don't. I know that this is the moment I have been waiting for, and I pray that the moment never ends.

Love always,
your Sugar

Good Morning Here honey…

It was really nice to chat with you last nite… Oh it was four hours and felt like one…smiling here… I just want to you know I love you and I will everyday be proving that to you. I fell in love with you when I realized how blissful love is. It is rare; but when your heart finds it, there is nothing that detours you away. You have baptized me with your love. What a blessing. What a priceless gift. How did I get to be so lucky? Lucky to have found you. My love, always, forever… I love you.

As we travel on our journey, hand-in-hand, there is no obstacle we cannot get past. With you, I am strong. With you, I am happy. With you, life is good. I love you and want you beside me, always. I want you to know that God does not look at our past to judge us. So far we have prayed for forgiveness. All is done; so those things that happened in the past, please let them remain there and we have so much in the future to look forward to. So who wants to dig up the past again... I hope you understand what I mean honey... I really love your son too. He saw it like your mistake and it's good that you want to hold on to your mind by paying him back, that is what a good mother will do to a son. Awwwww... I just fall for you everyday and night and your ways are just too good for me... I love you and you are my world. You are the sweetest, most precious woman in my life. All my life I prayed for someone like you and I thank God that I finally found you. Love, I feel so comfortable, secure and easy in your company. Your words give me all the pleasures of the world. Your smile has a certain thing that makes me listen to everything that you say. You intoxicate me in every way. I forget about the whole world when I am with you. I guess I have become addicted to you. I need to go work now...and you on the other side as my team mate handle the other works... and that is the construction of my heart, smiles. I hope we get to chat later today honey... Love you loads...

Smiles,
George

Wow, I don't even know where to start. You make my heart pound so fast and I can't even catch my breath. You give me goose bumps all over my body and you're all I think about. I've never had a love like this before and I've never felt this way. I want to keep you forever. I can't explain how all this distance and time apart has made my love for you grow.

My feelings are growing stronger and stronger every day. You confide in me. That melts me inside. No one has ever in my life talked to me about their hurts and sorrows and I love that. We both have gone through so much, and I feel like I relate to you on a much higher level than I have ever felt before. We have the same interests and the same likes. I know I am a person that needs gratification, and you seem to fulfill my needs in every way. I think that if we take our time and do everything right, this love could blossom into a fairytale romance. All I ask—and I know I have said it before—is that you be true to me and be true to yourself. I have put all my trust in you, and I have opened every fiber of my being to you and only you. I also said I don't care about looks or money, granted they are nice things, but I am after a love that will give me a reason to breathe. I want a future wife in my life, someone to hold, confide in, laugh with, cry with; someone I can watch football with, fish with, walk along the beach at night with. I want it. I deserve it, as do you. And I sincerely know that you feel the same as I do about you. You are beautiful, you leave me speechless, you turn tears into happy bliss, you make bad things seem not so bad. You astonish me and you brighten every aspect of my life. Like you said, it's amazing that we've grown so close in such a short amount of time. The feelings blossomed rapidly and I don't want to lose that. I have fallen madly in love with you. You are everything and more than what I have dreamed of my entire life. You would make me happier than the richest person in the world by sharing your love with me. With love from your Sugar… smiles.

My love… I know I am not perfect, but I do have goals in my life. I take good care of myself and my Jenny and you have done the same to your children too, and that makes our primary mission in life complete. I'm sure your dad will be smiling like a fulfilled man, because he gave you a good hand in life and you transferred that to your own children—some reason why you could run to your son when you needed a loan. Honey if he was smoking pot or on drugs on the street you won't have summoned that courage to meet him for loan… I hope you understand what I'm saying honey… So I feel very proud of you, because it takes only a strong woman to accomplish what you have done in life and that's superb. I'm really sorry to hear about Dad's health. I hope he's feeling better now. When do you plan on going to meet him at home and stay with him for a while? Your staying with him might just be a healer you know baby. So sometimes we go through tears and pains and it does not actually change a thing about it… It's just the echoes of Hard times in Life… We complete one another; you thought that no good man existed and then you met me. How I long for you to know that the feeling is mutual; that I have never met a woman that can read though me and explore my inner core. Please keep in mind that I will not take your heart that I hold for granted. I will replace it with mine, so you know I wouldn't be able to breathe without it. You are a splendid jewel that He released and

I grasped. Never would I let a soul take you away or bring harm near you. The day I looked into the blue recesses of your soul—correction: my soul, I knew no force could ruin the joining of two souls... Ok I think I need to join the boys again, this mail took me two hours...smiling... working and typing with you.

... One stone for two birds...so they say... so you have a great time learning golf and I we can chat around 12 your time ok...

Love you loads...
Sugar

I want to take a pause from George's emails for a bit and explain a little of what happened next. You will see some samples of email communications from a foreign bank and a law firm from which I believed that George had initiated contact. Of course, I had never had a large amount of money in an online bank account prior to this put in my name, and I thought I was simply providing a simple way for this man to show his love by opening a bank account to start our future. I totally trusted him. But as you read the emails and communications (and I will remove specific bank account numbers and information for legal reasons, obviously), you will notice how I became involved in something that I had no information or intention of doing so. Ignorance of knowledge was not an excuse. But trusting a total stranger should not have been an excuse either.

13-JUN-2012
Dear BB,
European Finance Services eLectronic Notification Service (EFSeNs)
We wish to inform you that a credit transaction occurred on your account with us. The details of this transaction are shown below:

Transaction Notification—Account Number: -0709

Transaction Location: Ruwais, Abu Dhabi, United Arab Emirates

Description/Origin

Depositor::WT_Abu Dhabi Commercial Bank

GlobalSantaFe Corporation

Amount: 430,000.00

Value Date: 11-JUN-2010

Remarks: N/A

Time of Transaction: 05:27:13 PM

Document Number: 0

The balances on this account as at 12-JUN-2012, 12:37:35 PM are as follows;

Balance Before: USD $619,017.50

Current Balance:USD $1,049,017.50

Available Balance: USD $1,049,017.50

Please logon to your internet banking portal to ascertain this credit transaction.

Thank you for choosing European Finance Services.

Ref: 04/27/2012/enquiry on deposited funds

ATTN. BB

Your email has been received and acknowledged. Please be advised that the said payment was deposited in a fixed account for further remittance to you upon your request. Kindly note that before the proceeds of the account can be credited to your designated account, you will be required to set up a non-resident account with us due to the amount involved. This measure is for safety and security of your funds and also to ensure that you do not encounter tax issue's in your country as an affidavit will be obtained in effect of this wire transfer as well and will be sent via fax or email attachment to you for your review.

Please visit our online website to download the account opening application form, fill and return the completed form so as to enable us proceed with the necessary arrangements to get your funds to you.

You can as well complete the account application form on our secure website if you don't have a scanner/fax to send in your application. We will also require you to send a copy of your scanned passport or driver license for verification purpose. Click here to go directly to the online banking application page. Anticipating your earliest response in this regard.

Respectfully,
eBusiness Department. Corporate
Office, European Financial Services

4th Floor Berkeley Square House, Berkeley Square, London. W1J 6BX—United Kingdom.
Tel. +44 (702) 409 9216... Facsimile/Fax: +44 (203) 300 7602... Web Address: www.euf-services.eu.com... Email: ebusiness@eufservices.eu.com

This message contains confidential information(s) and is intended only for the use of the individual to whom it is addressed. If you are not the intended recipient of this email, you should not disseminate, distribute or copy this e-mail. Please notify the sender immediately if you have received this e-mail in error and delete this e-mail from your system.

Ref: 04/27/2012/account application received
ATTN. BB

*****

This is not your account information
email. You will receive your account information including username and access-code within
24–48 hours of the receipt of this email.

*****

Seems pretty official and authentic, doesn't it? The sad part is
that my health has not been good enough to travel and find out if
this bank actually exists and if the account is real and in my name. I
also do not have the funding to finance a trip of such origin.

Keep in mind that blind love and trust played the biggest role
in this relationship, which allowed me to be manipulated and drawn
into the biggest money scheme and, who knows, possible money
laundering that continued to dominate this whole relationship. So
now I will share some personal emails filtered in with those from the
bank and lawyer at the same time.

Good Morning Honey…

I'm really sorry about last night. I slept off
while waiting for you to troubleshoot your P.C.
You won't believe that I slept on the couch while
waiting for you. I tried locating a church this
morning but a bit far from me, so I just said my
prayers in the room and ate breakfast. I need to
tell you that I was not a complete man last night
for not talking to you. I missed you like we did
not talk for days. When I got the mail that the
P.C. is now working you don't know how happy

I was. All I can say is thank you for bringing life back to me and I know someday soon, I will be able to say that to your face with a big smile on mine...smiles. So Jenny told me you wrote her and that you sound very pleasant. I told her you know I have good taste. I just went for the best one out there...smiles and I hope she does not go asking you too many questions. Oh less I forget, you guys are the same on that page; you ask questions a lot. But don't get me wrong; I'm not saying it's bad to do that. It's good to ask when you don't know. We live and learn and that's Life baby. I hope you get to talk to Dad today and help me to find out about his health. I hope he's getting better because I need to see that Big smile on His face when we get to visit Him soon. Honey, Earth moves with such apathy that only Our Heaven can keep the pace of our devotion for one another. As slow as the heart beat of a Goliath at rest. Why would the world seem so passive? I believe it is a chance for us to make our own time to spend together. It is love. It is what binds the thoughts of all beings trying to understand it. It appears that you and I have fallen into love, without having looked for it. This is Heaven and we are the Angels of Our Name... Affection Always, Your Heaven's Angel

After hearing from the European Financial Intelligence Unit telling me that I am suspected of money laundering and that I must pay fees to get access to the money and provide a job completion certificate to the authorities, I was mortified. The mission of the European Financial Intelligence Unit is to safeguard the financial system, so this is when I relied on George to obtain the name of a lawyer to help us. After doing this and paying the lawyers' fees as well as court costs, etc., which amounted once more to almost a $100,000, I was told that the money would once again become accessible to me.

So now I am petrified. What do I do? And how did I ever allow him to put this account in my name? As it turns out, I never asked him for anything, let alone putting my name on an international bank account. So now the fun begins, and I become even more manipulated to avoid international criminal charges.

And George speaks again.

> Honey… Please understand that we have so much to give to each other and I look forward to that day. I believe it is closer now than ever before. It is just that there may be a few more obstacles that we need to clear up, and I think you know what I am talking about. Besides that, we can and I know we will survive. There have been hard times, bad times and good times, but with that comes lonely times. We have reached new and higher grounds with what we have shared in the past few weeks, and I would do it all over again with you if I had to. I have no regrets and how we will solve this will show us how we can handle things in the future honey. I hope you know what I mean honey. I cannot wear a lie on my face and I know the most questions I will get today will be what is wrong with you George and most of their questions are: Hope your woman did not hurt you, because from my face people around me can know what I'm going through. But I won't be able to share this with anybody honey. Because I know we are both in this and we will surely get out of it together…we can and I know we will survive… I know somewhere down the road things will change but for right now we have to be patient. No matter what we did wrong

to one another, we've always made it through and that just goes to show my love for you. I just want you to know I love you and always will. Tomorrow's hopes and dreams will never die as long as you believe in yourself and follow your heart. The kindnesses in your heart will guide you to accomplish many things in life and overcome all challenges and all obstacles. Never give up, always have faith in yourself, and you will gain the greatest gift of all, the gift of hope and love you rightly deserve. I will be online and in case you have time to talk before you leave the house that will be fine or we can just chat around 12 your time. I need to go see the expert working on the equipment, but again, I hate this face and do not love to be walking around with it. As we travel on our journey, hand-in-hand, there is no obstacle we cannot get past. With you, I am strong. With you, I am happy. With you, life is good. I love you and want you beside me, always… Talk to you soon. Hugs…

Love always,
Your sugar.

My Love… Hope you had a nice night. You sure have the right words to wake me up with. When I woke up to your mail, I was just smiling again…and it sure put me in the right mood for today's work… There are so many reasons for me to love you. I love the way you find humor in the darkest of clouds. I Love the way you make me smile… Last Night was fun, even though we have issues, I'm very happy about you. Please have faith in us that we can make it through anything. After our fight and make up, Smiles, I still slept like a baby. Your words sure make me strong and happy. I admire your inner strength. I could list reasons from here to eternity, but I will not. Let's work together…together forever and always.

Honey, I really hope the bank will help deduct the funds needed. I have just been very prayerful and hoping we get past this dark cloud we have in front of us or should we call it our past, because everything in our present will still be our past honey… I have been trying all I can here to get this through with, but still to no avail. I know God will come through for us. He cannot watch his own suffer. He made us fall in love and gives us a test. You know the teacher is always silent when they give a test, but they are always watching… I hope you understand what that means…smiles… I hope we get to chat today. I checked my calendar of you…smiles and I saw what you will be doing today… Love you loads, Honey…

Kisses and Hugs,
your sweet sugar

*****

And once again, I receive that dreaded email from the bank.

*****

Ref: 04/05/2012/SAR_Error Code 991
ATTN.: BB

Your email has been received and acknowl-edged, Please note that the funds cannot be deducted from your account because the

European Financial Intelligence Unit (EuFIU) has placed a hold on the funds due to the amount involved, pending payment of the requested fee(s) which will be used to obtain the requested documents.

Please visit the terms of service page on our website, under RULES OF THE ROAD Def. 11, sub section (i) which reads as stated;

11. For the benefit and security of our Customer(s) and to comply with applicable laws, we have a few mandatory guidelines that we call rules of the road. And conduct that violates the rules of the road is grounds for termination of this services and the bank may for whatsoever reason vary these terms and conditions. For this reason, the customer undertakes to:

(i) ACKNOWLEDGE AND AGREE THAT WHEN WE ARE EFFECTING A BANK TO BANK TRANSFER OR AN INTERNATIONAL WIRE TRANSFER FROM OR TO ANY OF YOUR OR A RECIPIENT'S ACCOUNTS, WE ARE ACTING AS YOUR AGENT, AND NOT AS THE AGENT OR ON BEHALF OF ANY THIRD PARTY. You agree that the Bank, its affiliates, service providers and partners will be entitled to rely on the foregoing authorization and agency.

YOU AGREE THAT WE WILL NOT BE LIABLE FOR ANY COSTS, FEES, LOSSES OR DAMAGES OF ANY KIND INCURRED AS A RESULT OF (A) OUR ACCESS TO THE ACCOUNTS; (B) ANY DEBIT AND/ OR CREDIT OR INABILITY TO DEBIT AND/OR CREDIT THE ACCOUNTS IN ACCORDANCE WITH YOUR BANK TO BANK TRANSFER INSTRUCTIONS; (C)

ANY INACCURACY, INCOMPLETENESS OR MISINFORMATION CONTAINED IN THE INFORMATION RETRIEVED FROM THE ACCOUNTS; (D) ANY CHARGES IMPOSED BY ANY PROVIDER OF ACCOUNTS; AND (E) ANY FUND TRANSFER LIMITATIONS SET BY THE FINANCIAL INSTITUTIONS OR OTHER PROVIDERS OF THE ACCOUNTS.

For detailed information please visit any of our under-listed affiliates,

http://ec.europa.eu/internal_market/company/financial-crime/index_en.htm

http://www.imf.org/external/pubs/ft/FIU/index.htm

After much deliberation by our institution in this context, we have made arrangements to help you with a 20% waiver, please note that this is solely on the institution, we are hereby pleased to inform you that your fees has been reduced to $52,736. In order to facilitate the fund transfer to your designated account, you are requested to make available the aforementioned payment for the procurement of the basic instruments i.e; Stamp duties, Tax Clearance, C.O.T and all other official notarization with the appropriate authorities, to ensure that your account does not stay dormant and your funds confiscated.

Do ensure you get in touch with us as soon as possible to clarify these issues and we strongly apologize for all inconveniences caused during this period and continually thank you for banking with us as we are honored to have you as a customer and will strive for your total satisfaction.

Respectfully,
eBusiness Department.

And my response was sent back to them:

Dear Sir:

I am sorry when I wrote to you earlier I forgot to include my ID as you had requested on all correspondence. Below, please see my previous email sent to you. I just wanted to make sure you received it because your response is usually pretty prompt. I have asked my fiancé, who named me next of kin, to send me the document in which he contracted payment from the company he is doing work for in UAE. I am hoping that will be enough (along with a copy of my driver's license) to release the funds and provide a certificate that all is okay. Regarding the fees you request for procurement, I would have no way of getting the requested fee to you since I am in the US, so I am requesting that you would be able to deduct the amount requested from my funds there. I would be glad to give authorization to the bank to do just that so that we will have access to the remainder of the funds. I appreciate your attention to this matter, and thank you once again for explaining everything to me. I do admit ignorance of the global laws and therefore apologize for not doing everything correctly the first time. Hoping to hear from you soon.

BB

Dear Sir:

Thank you for explaining the situation to me. I am in the process of obtaining documents that will satisfy your requirements. To obtain any of the funds though, is it possible after sending you the required documents that the amount required for procurement of funds could be deducted from the amount in my account pending my authorization? Because I am out of the country, I am concerned how you would get the required amount otherwise. Can you please tell me if sending a scanned copy of the documents would be acceptable so that we can complete the requirements you requested? Also, would you explain what you need to complete court undertaking requirement? Your immediate response is appreciated. Thank you for your assistance.

BB

*My Triple S…

These days cheating on nature for another nature has been easy… Smiles. My sleep must have been so jealous of us, that this lady has been taking this man's time and won't let him come to me…smiling here. I sleep late this days and wake up on time and very strong and healthy… My Computer was acting up all of a sudden again last night. I think that too is a bit jealous of us… Hhahahahahahahah

So sometimes your medications make you feel sleepy too?? wow!!! Guess I'm not the only one that will be sleeping when I get home tired… Sorry, some times all I will just need when I close from work, might just be a good shower and my B's food…then off to bed… Hope you won't mind sometimes, Smiles. I'm sure you won't because you are always worried and caring about how I'm feeling… Hummmmm, guess I got a mother plus a wife, smiles… Not mom, not stealing anyone's spot…smiles, I'm sure I will still get your guy's secrets out very soon. I have my way around Jenny and I will try the same thing with you… I know it will work. That way I will know what you guys must have been talking about… Guess what Jenny said she wants from here, you won't believe… A perfume… I was like wow!!! Did you guys talk about that too or she just wants that? But she just said, I know now… Hummmmmm… But I was really amazed that my girls want the same thing…smiles

You are like God's dove, so beautiful, so pretty, so loving, caring, and that's what I love, the fact that you love me for who I am, not what you want me to become. Thank you, God, for this special woman, you gave me—I can't thank him enough for the love and beauty that I found. I've said it before and I'll say it again, words cannot express how you make me feel. I make this promise to you, my B, to love you the way that you love me. I now look to the future and forget the past. Your life is mine and we will make it last. I love you more today than I did yesterday, and I'll love you more tomorrow than I do today. With all my heart I am forever yours.

So baby when are the handy men coming home today and when will you be back from the bank, because I will not be doing so much today on the site, because the things needed for work are still with the expertise and not much work to be done today… So in-case you want to talk, I will be online. Just buzz me and wait a bit for me to talk to you, because I might be far from the computer then, but like I do with you when you are on mobile, Just be patient, Ok baby… Just want to give you something to read from your Sweet sugar… Hope to talk to you soon… Love you loads… Smiles and kisses.

Baby… I just read your mail and am very happy that the bank is being considerate too. I think the universe will surely see us through honey. I felt really happy when I read all you sent. Your words I believe in and your faith I hold on to baby.

The most important thing I've learned is that love is a whole lot more than flowers and candlelight. It's sticking together during those times when you're short on money, patience and confidence. It's sacrificing something you want for something the family needs, and always being willing to listen. We've been through so much together yet we've always emerged closer and stronger than before. Baby, I will still be online, Ok… Just Buzz me and I wish you luck baby…

Love you loads baby

*****

And then the emails from daughter Jenny begin.

*****

Good Morning Mom,

Thanks for adding me to your fairytale. So
you all want to go to Disneyland. That will be
great, but we can do mine when Dad comes. You
know you are just who I know among your family
for now and I can be shy if I'm not free with people. Ma, You are just my one and might not be
very comfortable with others. You should know
what I mean. I want to shop for my prom gown,
but can't do that with Aunty Debby. She is so
old school you know. I will be needing someone
like... Hummmmm, maybe your daughter-in-
law? Dad told me about her too that she loves to
wear good things and loves designers. Will she be
open to do that for me? Don't worry you and dad
might be scared that we might spend too much,
as the two of you are just old fashioned... The
lovebirds... LOL. Now about me, I met a guy
and he seems cool. We have been talking for a
while now, say a week, and he's very cool. But he
always wants us to go out togther but I have been
turning him down. He has what I really do not
like on him a tattoo. So i just want to take things
a bit careful. He comes around to my aunt's place
and we talk and spend time together. Though
I have not told him I do not like body arts, I
just want to know your take on this and what
you think I should do and please do not tell dad
yet... Though he won't get mad, I just want to be
sure of him before showing him to dad or telling
him about him. His name is Brian and he seems
cool. Guess I'm jealous of you and dad. So I just
need your words and tell me what you feel about
body arts too, because I really do not like it...
Ok... Thanks Dad told me you stay with your

son and there is nothing there. So far you like it there ma, but did you and dad talk about moving in with us? I will be glad if you can, because that way we can talk and I can have my own counselor at home. Lol… Dad seems busy, because he did not reply to my mail since last night. I hope you guys are communicating well, because I know the love birds will always meet up in the sky… LOL… Ok I have to go now and will be waiting to read more about Brian, ok… Please mom, just tell me…your baby…hahahahah,

Jenny

*****

Now here it all gets interesting. G had me send 5000-plus dollars to the "wife" of one of his crew who was working for him. He conveniently supplied the account number and routing number of the bank to which I transferred the money. When the fraud department of one of my banks checked this out (long after I realized a scam of his doing had been successful), they found out that this was one of G's girlfriends who sent the money received from me to him (her boyfriend) or at least that is what she told the fraud department.

Baby…where did you go again… I'm still online and you are not talking again… Here is the information he gave me, honey…
Full Name: RMB, Full Address: Elkins, Arkansas.72727, Routing no: _____8, Account no: _____3, Bank name: C Bank, Bank Address: Fayetteville, AR 72703

*****

And then I hear from his daughter again.

Good Morning Mom,

Thanks for your sweet words and your care. Mom, I knew you had it in you. You know I was thinking the same thing about not judging a book by its cover. We only can judge people when we are close to them and share thing with them. So far Mom, Brian does not use bad words or is abusive to people and I do not know if he drinks. Did I tell you that he's two years older than me? He came around last night and it was magical. We got to talking about his family and he seems to have a good one too mom. But I still do not need to rush into his arms right now. I'm glad I have my private Counselor and she will be living with me very soon… LOL. All that comes with just getting a mom… I can't help but smile. I know you think I got my funny ways from dad, because sometimes he can make me laugh and forget my plenty of questions… He does that to me a lot.

So sorry to hear about you health situation. I hope you are getting better now, because I can make you feel better, by taking you up and down of the whole area, so they know I just got myself the best Mom in the world. Now I see that patience is very big virtue, because dad said, Jenny is getting a good woman to love. It's not like going to the mall to get clothes that will still tear. He wanted something forever… I'm so happy for both of you. So his computer is bad… I hope he gets to fix it soon, because I have missed him. But you have filled the space. Writing to you every now and then has really helped me not to miss him much… Thanks again for your advice and I will step carefully now with Brian. One step at a time... About the prom, thanks for wanting to help me order, but it's not very important that we do that fast. I will check on the ones you sent though and see the one I like. That's like shopping from home, Mom. Do you think they will have my actual size? We can always go down there, when your Husband is back... Lol. Oh did I just let the cat out of the bag??... LOL When Dad comes back, we can always go.

Have a good day mom,
Your Jenny.

So as Jenny and I continued to correspond, I became more glued into the web of deceit as the bank and lawyers continued to make contact with me, and I felt even more pressure to raise the money needed to pay the fines bestowed upon me.

Dear Sir:

Please note I have attached my state ID as per your request. I still am unclear what the signed court undertaking document is though. Can you please explain that to me? We are working on getting you the other required documents and fees for taxes. Thank you for your help in this matter.

B

ATTN.: B

Following on your recent email letter to us, we acknowledge receipt of your state ID., Please be informed that the signed court undertakings, i.e; AFFIDAVIT FOR CHANGE OF

OWNERSHIP/NEXT OF KIN, DEED OF LODGE as well as the AFFIDAVIT OF CLAIM, would be obtained by the European Financial Intelligence Unit (EUFIU) once the fee(s) for the Stamp duties, Tax Clearance, C.O.T as you are already aware of. Awaiting your response ascertaining payment via your fiancé (G). Thank you for your understanding and co-operation through this period as we are doing our best to ensure that this issue is resolved in the quickest possible time, We are honored to have you as a customer, and we will strive for your total satisfaction, first class and effective financial services.

Respectfully,
eBusiness Department. ID: ____6

*****

Good Morning Sweet Smart Sugar,

You write me letters that brings me joy and I wake up in the morning just to give God thanks for what he has done in our lives through the rough times and happy moments. Just be very glad we have more happy moments than we have the rough ones and I'm so happy about that. Our fight has really been funny. We fight not to make up, but we fight to get stronger and happier... I will really love to go to the play with you sometimes, and I'm glad that you were not feeling very lonely last night when you knew what is at stake for you...smiles.

Ok, I wrote to your daughter last night and am still expecting to hear from her...smiles. I told her how much I have been enjoying you guys and all... I'm very sure that if we were together when you were sick, you would recover very fast honey, because they say sweet minds are always easy to please and that will surely help you get stronger... Smiles. I really enjoyed our chat and still did not forget what you said... It's not the quantity but it's the quality...smiles. That really got me honey. Tell me, will you teach me all these words when we are together? I hope so honey and I'm sure I will learn fast. Those words travel very fast to my head and my soul... I want to say a big thank you for that... Texas is really making both of us happy and I can't even let you leave unless we both decide to buy a house else where... But that will be later honey, My night was good. You were all over me here baby and helping me to sleep good, I'm so glad you had a swell time with your friend and her husband... You have gotten it all, even my heart. You make me feel like I am in heaven in the arms of an Angel... I see that I can only love you more and more every day. You're my inspiration each and every day. You are what keeps me going when I just want to give up. You are my meaning for life and love. I love the way that you love me. I wish you luck in all you do today and I'm trusting you to make a today a good one for both of us...smiles.

Kisses and hugs...
Your Sugar

You and I have connected on such a higher level. Our souls have exchanged caresses and hearts beats and I can understand why you would not value someone who will not give you forever because, sometimes in happiness Forever is the smallest... Smiles

When I am in pain she is my remedy. She replenishes the holes made by others in my heart and the death of my Wife, mending them with her thoughtfulness, kindness, and I've experienced both love and what I thought was love, and found pain and hurt. The real definition of love is you, who's given me everything and more. The time we share with one another is breathtaking. I feel safe in her arms; she embraces me with her words; touching every bone in my body as it tingles to the touch of her warm flesh. Her presence lingers in my mind when she isn't physically with me, she's always on my mind and in my heart. She cares for me the way no one can and ever will. Our time spent with each other is blissful. SHE is perfect in every way, shape, and form. Happiness describes every moment we share. We've gone beyond our limits, surpassing each others barriers. What we have may become stale at times but will re-make and once again be fresh. She quenches my thirst, whatever it may be. She serenades me as if I were a King in a royal family. Oh, how I cherish her. We were once strangers, but have become the love of each others lives.

There is nothing that I wouldn't do for you. Everything that I feel runs so deep that I don't care about your past and all the things you've done that you feel you should be ashamed of, because it's unconditional love that conquers our souls today.

Thank you, B, for stepping into my life; you mean so much to me. I love you!

*****

212

And once again I hear from my daughter supposedly.

Good Morning Mom…

It was really good reading from you Ma, and you have really made me smile, so I'm a part of your happiness. So you would love for me to wear them with you. That sounds very nice to know that you will be in the stores and tell me which one looks better on me… I'm really glad that you have shared your secret with me and it's safe with me. So they will still be surprised… LOL… So your husband wrote me last night and he told me how much he has missed me and all. Then I told him you already told me about his computer and I have missed him too. Then I told him how nice and sweet both of us have been talking on here… I'm sure he will be happy. I really missed him though and can't wait for him to come home soon… Thanks for sharing so much with me and I feel not left alone. You have really made my days. Thanks ma. Me and Brian have really been having a nice time. But nothing intimate for now… Aunt Debby knows his family and she said they are really nice. They even attend the same church. But Brian won't come to church. I think I can convince him to come with me someday. He says it's too boring and all… LOL. The first time we talked, I called him a rock star… LOL…beccause he has a cool face and I don't know why he has got that Tatoo anyways… LOL.

So the big day is coming and I really wish we could spend it together very soon. I mean Mothers Day, Mom. I have missed it… It's been years now that I have had to celebrate that with someone. But I'm sure those days are over now that we have you... Lol. I'm sure I won't miss the next one with you, Lol... So will you still be able to write me from Florida? Because it will be a big punch on my face, if I get to miss the two of you at the same time ma... Ok I have to go now and I want you to have a good day ahead...

your Jenny.

Good Morning Sugar...

The Good news about your mail, was when you said now let's talk about the most important thing of the day. I want you to know that no matter what we are going through, the love we share is the most important thing and you can see that too. That is a very lovely thing to know and I want to say I'm very sorry for trying to keep something from you last night and I still failed at doing that. You know me too well I guess and I'm always myself when I have nothing to hide. I know we are both in this and I want you to know that we will surely get through with this, Ok... I was really happy when I woke up today. I guess you wake happy when you sleep happy. Your words were very comforting and I give it to you. You surely know how to talk to me and make my sad face smile again... Thank you B.

Now to the least important matter of the day, smiles... Baby, I know how this will be for you and I know how smart and hard you are working on this. I trust us on this, even when we thought nothing will come out. We still have to raise 30,000 and I believe in you baby and I will not want this to disturb your trip honey...

So did they say we have to wait for seven days? I mean the credit card company baby…you mean Chase stopped all transfers? Does that include the online of today too baby? I know you will be trying really hard today. I just want you to know that I do appreciate what you have done in my life. I read a mail from Jenny again last night and she said so many things about you. I never knew she could love you that much. She talked about some advice, though she won't give me details. Honey, I almost shed tears, but don't be scared. They are tears of joy. Right now as I write to you, I'm filled with joy and happiness from above. You baby are doing very good here honey. What words can describe the sweetest, most beautiful part of my life? You are my certainty, my comfort and hope, without you I would be lost. I know we have our ups and downs but if you'll let me know that this is just the test of love and the examples of forever, we are just getting prepared for anything that comes to us in the future. I want to make you feel how you deserve to feel, like a queen… The one I was put on this earth for. You are my soul mate. When you told me that you loved me I was beside myself with joy. You are going to make a wonderful wife and mother, and there is nothing I would love more than to be your husband.

I was forced to respond.

    After forwarding George a copy of the most recent email, he approached his supervisor on the job, and he asked that we contact you immediately to assist us in gaining access to our funds in a most expeditious manner. I am requesting that you do anything possible to help us gain access to our account so G will be able to complete the contract on schedule. Your cooperation and response to this matter is both appreciated and needed. We will look forward to hearing from you.

Sincerely,
B (fiancé of George)

I then received the following message from the lawyers George retained:

HOLBORN CHAMBERS, ATTORNEYS AT LAW, SOLICITORS & ADVOCATES

Hello B... Following on your previous email, we have attached some documents for perusal. Please note that the Affidavit of Claim, Affidavit for Change of Ownership and the Letter of Administration will be obtained from the Ministry of Justice, upon payment of the mobilization fee as stipulated in the Terms of Service document emailed to you. We also communicated with the European Finance Services in this regard and they await the neccesary documents so that copies can also be forwarded to the European Financial Intellignce Unit for approval and release of your funds. M Thank you for your understanding and hope to read from you again.

Sincerely,
Barrister Steven Stuart (Esq),
Holborn Chambers

As the emails continued from George, there was no indication that any of this was fraudulent, only part of a nightmare that we seemed to share together.

*****

Good Morning Love,

Hope you had a nice night. I sure did after you tucked me in. I just slept like a baby. You know I woke up late today. I guess you spent much time on my bed today again… Smiles… So I got two outstanding mails from you and took my time to read them here on the Site. I could just read the short one in my room then I knew I would find time to read this long one, WOW!!!!! Baby you have a very good way with words that whoever is reading it, will understand every word you use. Tell me. What does that magic for you? Told you mine last night… If it's me I guess I will have to win the first page of your book too… smiles. I must tell you that every word you used in your mails made me feel very special, even when you use just "my" it does bring me very close your heart every time… I want to say thank you, because we both find time for each other every time. You see what makes a relationship work is when we have two fighters in a ring. Not when one is fighting and the other is looking. I hope you understand what I mean… We both give into each other and give our whole mind and heart into it and see where it has landed us… Ok the Island of happiness… Smiles… More than anything in this world I want to spend the rest of my life with you. We have both been through a lot of distrust and discomfort from our past,

217

and we have seemed to finally find that trust and comfort in each other. We are always knowing what each other is thinking whether something is wrong or right. We are both birds of free spirit, but we fly together forever. It is you who I am so sure of spending the rest of my life with, to marry, to raise our children with, to love and to cherish forever and eternally. Your love has made me love my life. Everyday seems like a blessing since I've met you. I feel so lucky and honored to be in love with such a talented, beautiful, intelligent and respected woman. I love you with all of my heart. Thank you for sharing your love with me. It is a truly wonderful gift. Thank God for the sweet Gift... Hugs and kisses...

Hope we talk later today, your Sugar...

*****

I continued to correspond with the lawyers.

Mr. Chambers,

We have not heard from Global SantaFe Corporation or yourself since your last email. Could you please update us on the status of the completion certificate being processed so that we can obtain access to the funding that the company placed in the bank. We need access to the funds to complete the contract in Dubai. The supervisor (Abdul) has assured us that you are the one to make sure that all goes well for us. We both appreciate your speedy expedition of this matter.

Sincerely,

B

*****

From: Holborn Chambers [mailto:holbornattorneys@lawyer.com]
To: B
Subject: Re: Urgent Matter
Hello B and George,

Your email has been received and acknowledged to the letter, Please be informed that we will look up your case file and email you immediately this issue has been resolved with the requested documents. We have sent a printed copy of your email via fax to GlobalSantaFe Corporation for authorization and hope to hear from them in earnest. Thank you for contacting Holborn Chambers, we appreciate your business and hope for a lasting relationship with you.

Sincerely, Barrister Steven Stuart (Esq).

My Sweet Sugar,

Good Morning Sweet one. It was really sweet talking to you last night and also knowing that my prayers on DAD is working smiles... I really long for his blessing and happiness and very sweet that he can feel that in you. Thanks for your sweet note this morning and for your always reminder... Hhahahahahah. My heart does know someone cares and even if you do not say it in a day, it knows I meet one girl everyday and that girl, I fall in love with her in different ways too… Smiles… We are already making our dreams work. Now we will be 65 together this year, what a sweet News flash…smiles… So was it your favorite person that won in the Apprentice?? Because we never even talked about who you like most… I really did not take my time to sit and watch the show, so I do not have anyone on mind for the medal and with the love you have for it, I can tell that we will sit together next season to watch it…smiles… I know baby that things are hard right now and we are doing our best and God has been crowing that for us too, I feel very glad for all the effort we both put into places to see this work for us… What a Team mate I have in you… But the echoes of hard time is finally over when we are done with this bank stuff… We are just matched from heaven. I was really surprised when you told me that Susan was your favorite in Desperate Housewives, you know each day we find out new things about each other and it's very sweet things to know… Earth moves with such apathy that only Our Heaven can keep the pace of myself or to put it together in one, the only easy thing to think of it is loving you. For just one look into your eyes makes everything in the world and in my life seem to disappear. You make me want to see the sunrise every day, to know it's another day where I can maybe have you by my side. I just keep up my hope, 'til then I'll think of you just like now; your touch will forever caress me with tenderness, and your kisses will keep the flame in my heart alive in and I know soon you and I will be together… I can't even begin to explain how you have enriched my life. I'm so very proud of you. You are a very strong person. It is really cool that we are strong for each other in different ways. We totally understand each other and feel for each other. When you hurt, I hurt. When you are happy, I'm happy. I just love you so much sweetheart and I never want to lose you. I give you my heart, my love and my life for now and forever. I love you... You are always there for me no matter what. I do not know what I would've done with this contract without your love and support. You are the most loving, caring, compassionate and absolutely most awesome person that I have ever met. Jenny holds a special place in my heart, but you have gone way above and beyond her, because it's about my happiness and she comes after that and you come with that... Smiles... Ok just wanted to bring your early Morning Coffee to you on your bed. I hope you just wake up to my arms and say thank you baby... Love you honey... Talk to you soon... Hugs and Kisses, Your Sugar

Baby, Thanks for the Information and I will try to pay in all the funds today and get back to you on what ever happens ok my love... Once again, your Sugar...hahahahhahahahahahah, Have a great time... For you my love:

She moves through my dreams as a star in the night; Her hair soft and long, Her eyes glowing bright; Her countenance sweet, She is patient and kind; And yet has a strength, That you don't often find. This smile of hers, I have never seen; a mischievous child, with the grace of a queen.

Her laughter rings, like a sweet love song; A voice that is soft, a heart that is strong; Compassion and love. For all living things; Like moths to a flame, Her loving heart brings. And I'm drawn to her too, As though under her spell; sweet lips soft and full, In the air her sweet smell; Her Kisses like morning dew, Lightly touching my face. Her warm gentle body, Make my sleeping heart race; I hold her so close in this dream. In the night, I don't want to let go; As she holds me so tight. But as morning dawn, Slowly peeks through my dreams; Time to start a new day, And the same old regimes. This soft tender beauty, I don't want to leave; Just a dream, but it seems;

Is so hard to conceive. But wait... What is this, something stirring, Soft hair tickles my face; I don't think I'm still sleeping, Yet I feel her embrace; No longer dreaming, My dreams now subside. In my arms is my dream girl, My lover, my bride. So here in my heart, In my arms in my life; I have all I need, My dream girl, My sweet wife.

My Dearest One,

I know we are so far apart, and it has been two days since the last time we were together but you know the flow of you in my vein has really been my savior... Smiles. You would think that I have gotten better at not missing you as much. I can't explain how all this distance and time apart has made my love for you grow.

I'm very glad that you had a great time with A and others... You know how much I enjoy you having a great time Honey... Smiles... So, here is what happened with me yesterday. I was with the Supervisor, when I was trying to get some things from my front pocket and I brought out your photo along with it. Then he saw it and said,

Who is that Mr G? My reply was, what would you put so close to your heart even while you are at work and everywhere? The man is just a very funny clown. He said My Money or my wife... I could not help but laugh. Mr Abdul just knew when to show up, when all the guys heard at dinner, they were like... So he loves money that much that it has to come before his wife?? But I explained to them that he was just kidding around with me. Then he looked at your photo and said, She looks really good. But you need to hear him say that. I bet you would laugh too... smiles. The boys were like, Now we know someone is not happy with the Hotel and their internet. I was just like No not really. B is busy too. But really we miss talking but we had a great time together... So Honey, My day was boring without you in it... You can say that again...smiles.

So I got the mail and asked Mr Abdul for the completion certificate. He said I'd have to ask you to talk to their lawyer. That he's the only one that can make that process happen. I hope you understand what I mean honey... So I will just give you his information and you can write him and explain to him..., I guess the company uses him every time for something like that... I will send you that later...ok baby... I know that we are going through a lot now and I do not want you to be very worried about me honey. I know it's hard baby. Just know that I will try to make ends meet here baby. The Generator Guy said he trusts me and really feels for me. I'm happy he said that. He said I will just have to pay him when I'm ready and the Boys do not know anything about this. So when I woke up today, I do not feel I have big problem. I just felt my God

is bigger than what ever we are going through…
Smiles

Baby, just know I will never get tired of anything from you baby. All your mails, made me feel like I did not miss much. I got them and I was busy reading them before bed… Honey you sure have a very sweet way with words. It was like you are saying everything to my ears… Smiles… how did you do that? My very Good partner, Give me the secrets… Smiles… Today, you are so far away and I'm not being able to hold you, kiss you, or even able to tell you I love you every day, as we go through the hardest thing we have ever had to go through in life. Well there is a saying that whatever will be sweet to the End always has some rough patches. Yes, I miss you and can't wait till I come home to be able to wrap my arms around you and hold you close to my heart. Days go by and nights get longer. It makes me stronger and stronger. I just want you to know that I will be here as long as it will take; one thing I want you to know is I love you and you will forever be in my heart… Even if we do not get to talk today again, Who cares when we can talk forever…

Smiles… Your Sugar

Baby… I will want you to give me updates about the bank stuff, but I know we will be successful on that too, because God has been smiling on us…smiles… Talk to you later my love and Still feeling high here too, with lots of smiles the boys can't find reasons for… They never knew the private enjoyment I had last Night… Chuckles…smiles… Love you more.

Good Morning Honey,

The formula working for us began with God. I love that a lot, because everything you do in life, we have to had a bit more of God. That sure makes it work all the time, because he made so much happen in our lives and he will never watch what he has done fail… Smiles… Your words this morning for me were really a good push to work with and I'm loving that a lot. I love you so much, Sweetie. You are the best thing that ever happened to me. You are like the best poetry ever composed, the best song ever played, the best picture ever painted. I never thought that someone like me could get so lucky; you choose the right words at the right time and I know when we meet, we will just get along really fine. We have done so many things that even some couples have never been too and with the miles between us, the hearts connects even better… smiles… A few times we have crossed so many troubled bridges and that shows no matter what troubles we have in life, we will surely smile at the end of them all. Life comes with so many puzzles that we have to fix ourselves. Like on what took us so long to meet each other and we fixed that ourselves with God's help. Then The Euro comes again and we have been fixing that too. All that happens when we have each others back, support from both sides. What more can a fulfilled man like me be worried about again? Smiles… Some of the most superb feelings and tingling emotions come from what love an Angel, such as yourself, and I make. Our world, as we have come to see it, has no bearing and an infinite boundary when we are locked lips to lips. No one person can sever that bond of nothing but pure affection and intimate passion. We are the Angels of Our Heaven and with merely our names to live with. A name, which consists of nothing more than symbols of a language taken for granted. I would soon rather speak nothing. A true test of love of which we have accomplished merely by the elucidation in our eyes. Earth moves with such apathy that only Our Heaven can keep the pace of our devotion for one another. As slow as the heart beat of a Goliath at rest. Why would the world seem so passive? I believe it is a chance for us to make our own time to spend together. It is love. It is what binds the thoughts of all beings trying to understand it. It appears that you and I have fallen into love, without having looked for it. This is Heaven and we are the Angels of Our Name... Baby, I will get you the Information later today, so we can do the transfer today... Ok My love... What matters most is that we have the Money already... Ok my love, I hope we get to talk soon... I love the fact that I love you... Smiles.

Kisses and Hugs,
Your Sugar.

And again, I end up falling for his story and sending the money to one of his crew's wife. Again I receive the following correspondence:

Hello BB and GWD,

Your email updates have been received and acknowledged, I have been away from the internet for a while to make arrangments for the propoer notarization of the obtained documents from the Ministry of Justice. Upon reciept of the mobilization fee, i'll email you all the copies received and also proceed to ensure that the lien release certificate is obtained from the European Financial Intelligence Unit and also contact the bank to know the status of the fund transfer to you. I will communicate a feedback to you in the quickest possible time.

Thank you very much for your business and i hope to read from you soon with payment confirmation.

Sincerely, Barrister Steven Stuart (Esq).

HOLBORN CHAMBERS, ATTORNEYS AT LAW, SOLICITORS & ADVOCATES
6 GATE ST. LINCOLN'S INN FIELDS LONDON WC2A 3HP

His sweet emails continue.

My Sugar...

I want to start by saying thanks to you; you sure made my night a good one, after my wait last night. I know we did not have much time to talk and baby you are not being selfish; you just want to enjoy the great life God has given us everytime, which I love too...smiles. So you think I feel selfish when I get to wake you to talk to me or when you have to stop class to talk to me? I see like I need to enjoy the great life we both share everytime, because when we get together, I might have to just show up at your class section sometimes. Just like you coming to my office too on surprise visits… Smiles. Hummmm… Did I just let some cat out of the basket. Awwwwww… Smiles. I can still catch you unaware…smiles. I know B that much.

I know you don't need another reminder because I tell you a thousand times a day how much I love you, but I do and that is my only way to show you. I love the million ways you show me how much you love me, and I know my simple words can never compare. From day one, I knew there was something in you that no other guy had. You are the most AMAZING girl I have ever known. Thinking back to the strange way we met, because I never believed in meeting someone on the dating site. Imagine, some days on there and you sure proved me wrong, Hummmmm, Made my No to yes, Smiles, how we grow so close in just a few short days, and how you were the first one to show me the meaning of true love, it makes me smile and fall all over for you again, Just like I meet you everyday and telling you Hey My name is George, 'cause you are always new to me everyday. Sometimes i feel like we have finished talking, But the next day we still talk for hours, Never done that before either and you made all this happen, Showing me when you are in love, you always have things to talk about. Ever since you walked into my life I have been smiling. There hasn't been a night when I have gone to sleep with a frown on my face, and it's all because of you. Honey, I am glad that you came into my life. I have always wanted the love of my life to be understanding, loving, caring, and faithful. I wanted someone who would accept me for who I am. I know that I've found that person in you. My heart told me that my princess was there when I first said hello to you over the site it all started with my Bold "Hello" Move, you know what they say, when you love something go for it and think positive. It will surely bring back positive things. I didn't have to think twice when I asked you to be my wife. I knew that you were the perfect match for me. I don't think that there is, or that there ever could be, anyone better than you out there for me. You mean so much to me, and my only desire is to make you as happy as you make me. With each passing day I fall more in love with you. You can do the slightest thing and it warms me; most of the time you don't even realize it. You are always in my thoughts and in my heart. I never knew that love could be so wonderful until I met you. You have given me a new perspective on so many things. I will always treasure our love and keep it safe. I love you, Baby. Our life together is already amazing, and together it will only get better and better. I will forever be grateful that you came into my life and made all my dreams come true. Together we're perfect, and I will enjoy spending the rest of my life with you. I love you more than words can say. I hope we get to talk later today. We will surely do it...anyways... Will have to turn the Computer on even when we are on the Site... Love you loads...

Kisses and Hugs,
Your Sugar

Good Morning Honey,

You know when you sent the last mail, I was actually already up. I just wanted you to go and rest and enjoy your time... Wow!!! what a concert that was. I was sure in the concert with you baby, Thanks for the Lovely smiles you sent to me, Honey. I could feel your happiness from the Pics, Glad that you are happy about going. I sure do not miss anything, Hope it was not too crowded for you baby, So did you get to hear your old songs you have missed... Hummmm... I guess you were singing along with them... Smiles. So you had a nice time and that is the Most interesting part of it all. Smart move you made by going twenty minutes before the end of the show. I'm sure that sure helps with the crowd... Hummmmmm... My smart and loving woman... Smiles

We tend to share so much with each other and more great than even a partner; Honey I'm so happy about what God has given me, which is you. I guess you were right. I was just very sure about you from the first day, But needed you to join my league, Smiles, cause I need you on this Team and not the opponent, Smiles... With you by my side, I know there is nothing we can both not conquer, Right baby... We have done so much with each other... Hummm less I forget, guess what... Weekend is here again, Yuppppiiiiii... Have really missed you honey, I mean I've missed you in me, you know what that means don't you, Unless you wanna act, Like you don't smiles, Silly Girl... When I am with you, the world and its troubles are nothing to me but a blur. When I have a bad day I know you are there for me. Just the same for you if you are having a bad day; I'll do anything to make you smile, to kiss your soft, sweet lips—to look into those beautiful eyes that sparkle with happiness.

In those eyes I see a fire of passion and safeness. I was about to give up all hope on love until I laid eyes on you. Love and friendship is what I feel with you, it is not just that we are lovers, we are also friends, and that is what makes our relationship much better. The greatest of lovers don't make the best of friends, remember that, and when there comes a time when you feel that things can't get any worse, think of me, for I can try my best to bring you all the happiness in the world, B. I grow to love you more and more every-day, and I do not know right now what I would do without you. Sometimes I would like to think my love for you is like a great dream, I don't want to wake up because I don't want to lose that love. I will be by your side whenever you need me and I hope I am and always will be in your heart and in your dreams forever. But when I wake up to reality I still have you again, so no time passes by without you in me, Even on the site I have always been wearing a shirt with front pocket, so I can have you in there 24 hours, Things could not be any better than having you in my life. You are my inspiration and my shoulder to cry on, you're the one who stands by me through every-thing and most of all, you make me know that I am loved. There is no one that completes me the way that you do. You mean everything to me. There is nothing that I would not do for you and there is no one else I would want to share my life with. You are the reason I get up each morning and come to work, and you make me look at life with a new perspective. I have never met any-one as wonderful as you. I really miss you. There are so many things that I am grateful for I can't even count. You have been there for me through thick and thin and I thank you for giving me that opportunity to get to know you and for always being there for me. You mean so much to me, it's so unbelievable that I have someone such as you. Even when I am down you are there for me. Things have been so hectic that I could not have wanted anyone to be there for me but you. You have been the stability in my life and this is just a note to let you know that I love you... Love always your Sugar

Our love is infinite, A bond everlasting; Two heart's in love, With deep passions. Love is our destiny, A life now together; Love shall conquer, The stormy weather. Our love is so pure, Outlasting all time; I'll take your hand, And you take mine. A journey together, We'll walk through; My star from above, My wish come true. From all of our joys, And all our sorrows; Love shall guide us, My heart will follow. Our love is endless, I'll be by your side; I'm your soul mate, And I'm your guide. You will always be, Forever in my heart; A lifetime with you, Till death do us part. Good Morning My baby... How was your night? Mine was in the moon...smiles...with what we had... I was just flying on Cloud Nine. Though we started yesterday on a rough part, we were able to clear things between each other. Baby no matter the issue we are having, I must tell you that it's bad to walk out from our problems. We better just sit down and work things out. So baby when we stick together nothing can come in. I totally understand what you wanted and happy that we could sort things out. Baby I understand the past, but we have lived past that too in the few months we have been together. I found out that I can hardly remember my past pains and fears, because with your thoughts on my mind, so baby I let the past remain in the best place and that is the past… Smiles.

Honey thanks for the sweet songs you shared with me, I love that I need your love. You know I had it on my laptop and I never knew who sang it… Hummmmmm. We are so much alike I would say and each day we amaze each other with different things, smiles… Now when someone now asks me why I'm so in love with this sweet lady, I'm so very proud of you. You are a very strong person. It is really cool that we are strong for each other in different ways. We totally understand each other and feel for each other. One thing for sure is that I fall in love more and more in a different way honey. You know if someone had told me about our pleasure, I would say it's not possible. How can you satisfy a man with the miles between them? But baby, I just did not hear it. We actually do it… Smiles… Baby, you are my inspiration; you are a gift from God. You made me believe in true love in my lowest moments. Meeting you is like a source of light that penetrates through the end of a dark tunnel. I love you so much…forever, through eternity. Love is huge. I will work hardest to reach it. My love is only for you. I will present it just for you. When I met you, my heart shook. I haven't been able to escape you. I will hold you all my life, it's my promise. I want to show you how very big my love is for you—everyday, every night, every time, all my life. I love you! From time to time you ask me why I chose you? What is so special about you? Well, the reason is simple. I chose you because you are YOU!!! I have never had anyone treat me the way you do. I have never had anyone just look at me and make me feel so good. You do that to me! You make me feel special and wanted. As liberal as I can be, I would never do anything to hurt you. You mean more to me than you realize... Honey I need to work again... Oh less I forget I finished your coffee here on the site...smiles, Hope we talk later today... Lots of love... Your sugar.

I hope you will love this song... I have it on my laptop too and sometimes, when I want to sleep and we are done talking, I just play it... Smiles

"Forever And For Always" By SHANIA TWAIN... In your arms, I can still feel the way you want me; when you hold me, I can still hear the words you whispered. When you told me, I can stay right here; forever in your arms. And there ain't no way, I'm lettin' you go now; And there ain't no way, and there ain't no how, I'll never see that day... [Chorus:]'Cause I'm keeping you forever and for always. We will be together all of our days. Wanna wake up every morning to your sweet face.—always... Mmmm, baby In your heart, I can still hear a beat for every time you kiss me; And when we're apart, I know how much you miss me. I can feel your love for me in your heart, And there ain't no way—I'm lettin' you go now; And there ain't no way— and there ain't no how, I'll never see that day... [Repeat Chorus] (I wanna wake up every morning) In your eyes—(I can still see the look of the one) I can still see the look of the one who really loves me (I can still feel the way that you want). The one who wouldn't put anything else in the world above me (I can still see love for me). I can still see love for me in your eyes (I still see the love). And there ain't no way—I'm lettin' you go now; And there ain't no way—and there ain't no how I'll never see that day… [Repeat Chorus (2x)] I'm keeping you forever and for always, I'm in your arms.

Love Always,
Your Sugar

My sweetness, A poem just for you…

To live a fantasy in our reality, This love is just not a formality; For now we live a fantasy of love, A reality so strong we take hold of. So within our hearts this love is real, The test of time we will totally feel; Our hearts and soul will always know, Love has its truth and time will show. Your refreshment for life, Is sent "I think" from heaven. Your vim is worth the strife. The friendliness is just you "A Special Person"; I can feel the touch of spring coming, It reminds me of you. The life flowing through the pretty flowers, Makes you know when you leave earth, You're not through! Never change your "cheerful ways," They uplift people, just to know you. They're contagious to people every day. That's why I know "You're sent from Heaven"!

An Angel, maybe, Who knows, but one can dream. But as I can see, When I get to heaven, I hope they're All like you!

Good Morning Sweet thing,

Really got me smiling this morning, reading your mail and knowing you were a bit tipsy when writing that… Smiles… I know S was just going to know your response to the wine I guess and I'm sure he must be smiling when he noticed that mom is a bit on the edge… Smiling here too. I really can take that out when I thought of you getting high… Well, I guess what thrilled me the most about all this, that despite the situation that you are in, you still could drop me a note and make me understand how you are feeling. Baby believe me, that really thrilled me. Thanks Honey for that. We all have conditional gears and I love that. No matter the weather or the condition we still have each others back… I love the fact that I love you…smile. Since day one we've shared something incredible, something that most people only dream of. I had been searching for you all of my life. You have made me the happiest I have ever been. You are a sincere, caring, loving woman, and I wouldn't trade you in for the world. I am so thankful and blessed that you love me as much as I love you, and that you made me your Husband.

We have been married for two months, and I have cherished every moment since the day we met. I love you more and more everyday. Thinking about our future fills me with anticipation and excitement. We make the perfect husband and wife team. Our life together is already amazing, and together it will only get better and better. I will forever be grateful that you came into my life and made all my dreams come true. Together we're perfect, and I will enjoy spending the rest of my life with you. From the moment I saw you I knew you were a gift from God. You constantly shower me with unconditional love and you always understand my shortcomings without criticism. Just looking at you is enough to make me happy. My life is now full of promise, every day is worth looking forward to, and it's all because of you. I really look forward to the day when the both of us will be walking down the red carpet hand in hand and in the name of love, we exchange marriage rings looking into each other eyes saying, "I do not regret for choosing you in my life. I took this part out, because it's the most important of them all…smiles. Talk to you soon honey, Your sweet sweet sugar.

When I read that you went out with R, believe me I was happy, because I know at least it will help us with all this big stone on us baby. So I just read your note before I slept and it sure helps me to know that I have the best wife in the world. I'm really trying not to make all of this wear me down and you have been helping with that. All thanks to you. So hope you had a great time with each other, I think she just loved seeing the sweet looks on your face when you talk about the love we have. Smiles. Really when I woke up this morning and read your mail, I have been smiling a lot, said my prayers when I woke up and I'm sure within somedays God will make a way for us. So I'm staying very positive. Hope you slept well. Your notes did make me do that well. Slept like I have nothing to worry about. Ok, I will have to keep it short, since we will still get to talk more later today, you know… I love that I love you. And please keep smiling.

Hugs and kisses, Your sweet sugar

Good Morning Honey…

Hope you had a nice time with S and A yesterday. I waited for you and believe me baby, I could not even play Solitaire while waiting. I was just thinking and don't know why I got so depressed last night. You could even feel my tiredness from here baby. I was just too worried last night honey. Ok, you sure can tell that I did not sleep very well and was just rolling on the bed. Hope I did not push you down the bed. Thanks for the song lyrics you sent. You sure made me happy reading that one too. The most important thing I've learned is that love is a whole lot more than flowers and candlelight. It's sticking together during those times when you're short on money, patience and confidence. It's sacrificing something you want for something the family needs, and always being willing to listen. We've been through so much together yet we've always emerged closer and stronger than before. I don't know if I could have made it through without you there by my side. You're my lover and my friend. No matter what life holds in store, I can handle it as long as I have you. I know times have been rough and things have been said but I hope deep down you know how much you truly mean to me. Please have faith in us that we can make it through anything, together forever and always. Our love has proven to be true even through the worst of times. Every single day that passes, I thank God for you. I love you more than you could ever imagine. Baby, you mean the universe to me and I want to be with you for all time. Together we can do anything. Our love is what keeps a smile on my face, knowing that you care and will always be there. I can't imagine where I would be right now without you. I love you! Just remember... Ok your man needs to go back to work now baby and hope we get to talk later today, Ok baby. Love you so much.

Hugs and kisses, your sweet sugar.

Hello Good Morning,

This is a letter from your husband George. He tells me to share some valuable Information with you. First, He said the first thing you need to know is that he loves you and nothing can change that... He said these words while he was filled with smiles and from the look in his eyes, I bet he has his world already with you, So now to the Message of the day... Now I can tell I got you... Smiles... So I need to know what you were thinking while reading my first Paragraph. Got you I guess. I just wanted to add more spice to your Coffee this Morning... Smiles. Hope you had a nice night. Mine was really good... After our chat, you won't believe I slept there and did not even shower. Guess you really did a great job tucking me in last night, with a sweet bed time story...smiles... Baby, I know it's hard staying here with out so much to live on, but what can I do? I know how hard you go to make things happen and I hate to see you worried about things we have in a million folds. I believe this is just a hard time for the sweetness we are going to have in the near future. So sometimes I just enjoy the hard times too. So far I have you and we have our love. Nothing matters to me again my love. Talking about Jenny, Debby wrote me

that she's fine and not just getting on any laptop for now. That she has this friend she borrows
from and that one too got bad again, So baby, do
not be so worried, honey, I know a good mother
will always be, But Debbie assures me she's fine
honey… I know she will be missing us more and
I have so many reasons to want to get this done
and come home… Oh less I forget, did I tell you
the company saw our job here and was telling me
about another offer… That happened yesterday,
I guess it spiked my mind… But I told them, I
can always do that when I'm done with this one
and go home first… Did turn it down baby, but
they said they can wait… I guess we are doing
great here honey and some people are loving your
husband more for the good things he's doing…
smiles. You know what? I think I will just go with
anything that you choose for Jenny as a gift for
missing mother's day. I trust your decision on
that honey…you do great in doing things like
that…smiles. I truly could not live my life without having you to talk to and to confide in. You
know more about me than anyone; you know my
thoughts, and you know my heart inside and out.
You have a way of making my heart skip a beat,
and I want you and the whole world to know,
that I love you, B, and I will be forever yours.
Thank you for showing me what kind of love all
men deserve. I'm in love with you even though
I am thousands of miles away from you; I am
forever by your side. You've touched my heart
and wouldn't let go. Our relationship has given
me a lot of dreams, and now I feel hope. You
entered my thoughts and magically erased all of
my fears with your sweet and caring ways. Now I
look forward to each day and feel so much at ease

with you. I'm so grateful that we're able to share our problems and aspirations with each other. It truly seems as if you're a part of me, as if our time together was a melting of souls. The thought of you fills me with smiles, and I can't wait to hug you each day... Have a great day honey and hope we talk later today... Guess how time flies, the weekend is here again... Hold on to more enjoyment... Smiles. Only you and I understand that... Ahhahahahahahah... Kisses and hugs, from your sweet sweet sugar

Oh baby... Good Morning and you really do a lot with the cards you sent. I just can't thank you enough baby. You are the best woman on earth baby. Thanks a Million times.

Tell me what can I do without you. I'm feeling both of you girls around me on this special day. All thanks to you my love. You did great in making this home a good one baby and I can't ask for more than more love and happiness. It's really helping me everytime... One of the best fathers day of my life believe me honey, even without my best girls around me. I still feel warm and comfortable here. All thanks to my home maker... Smiles. I know we are facing some hard times now, but I will always be happy that it is not shaking what we have honey. I can proudly say, we can always dance in the storm and not be afraid. I know we have problems, and everybody does—that means I will not give up on us or you. I love you so much! I can't stand being away from you, sleeping without you. Just having you there reassures me that everything will be alright.

You are like God's dove, so beautiful, so pretty, so loving, caring, and that's what I love the fact that you love me for who I am, not what you

B. F. CHRISTMAN

want me to become. Thank you, God, for this special woman, you gave me—I can't thank him enough for the love and beauty that I found. I am sending you this to let you know that I have been sent an angel to be with me, and you are that angel. Please understand that we have so much to give to each other and I look forward to that day. I believe it is closer now than ever before. It is just that there may be a few more obstacles that we need to clear up, and I think you know what I am talking about. Besides that, we can and I know we will survive... Hope we get to talk soon my love and hope and pray that T agrees to help us. I am attaching a poem I wrote for you... Hope you like it... Hugs and kisses, your sweet sweet sugar

    She is a sunset over the horizon, Her waves will lift me higher; Into an ocean of deep pleasures, In waters of passionate desires. She is a star in my constellation, Her beauty, seen over the miles; She is a star, shining so bright, That star that gives me a smile. She is rare as a rose in winter, Nurtured by warmth and love; A rose, with an exquisite beauty, Simply a blessing from above. The beauty within every dream, When I close my eyes to sleep; My love goes beyond eyesight, I see her beauty that is beneath. You can be so charming, even when alarming; you can be so sly, that eye cannot deny. You can be so sweet, on the day we meet; you can be so grand, finest woman in the land. As like a moon lite summer night, admiring the beauty I see within; In my arms I shall hold you tight. Our love only blooms with color, With beauty that's beyond sight. The heart whispers of love softly, To lovers in the silver moonlight. With time, true love only grows,

242

Into the rarest form of emotions; It's felt so deep within our heart, Our love is deeper than an ocean. Let your heart's desires unfold, With me neath the moon tonight; Open all of your heart's secrets, It's with you I will spend my life. I really hope you enjoyed reading this poem written just for you.

Love,
Your sugar

The more you open up to me, the better you will feel. How do I know that? Because the more I open up to you, the better I feel. And I am so glad to have found you and let you enter my world. That world has become our world now. So don't close your thoughts. Take a breath and let God show you the way to solve this problem and this situation.

He will not let us down, love. You will finish this job and come home very very soon, and we will have that wonderful life together. I am just hoping and praying that we don't lose the million dollars that has been deposited for all your hard work. I will continue praying for you, love, and in just a short time, you will see the light, because God will provide it for you, and you will come out of the dark tunnel you are in. Take care, my love, and believe in yourself and believe in us. I will talk with you soon. And enjoy this cup of coffee. I serve it with a smile. Love you so much.

All my love,
B

After sending this email, I have to question how I got myself in this predicament. How could I become so gullible? And how could I possibly get myself in even more debt than I was.

Morning love.

> Words cannot express how much your friendship means to me. You have always found the time to cheer me up via e-mail and/or messages, and chat lines. You always seem to know just what to say and I really appreciate that. I know that you are so sincere with your thoughts that you write to me and I know with time we will see each other and I can't wait. Thank you for your love and for being there when I need you. Whenever I am down, I can think of you and it seems to work. Thank you. No matter what happens in our lives, I know that you made my life so much better and I love you—that it has been three months, three whole months and forever. Forever I know you'll be here in my heart, in my arms, and when years go by I want you to know how much I love you each and every day. You are a miracle, each and every day with you I treasure in my heart. Every beat of my heart fills more and more with your love.

*****

And even more reality comes to the surface. I asked my best friend for a loan of forty thousand dollars. When I explained why I needed it, she immediately told me I was being scammed, and she would help me prove it. I didn't want to believe her. I wanted to continue living in the fantasy I had created for myself. She forced me to make a personal visit to the address of his office to find out that the person who is writing to me is not the person in this office or at this business, and I have no idea who he really is. Thank goodness my friend gave me the courage and confidence to investigate the premises of where he worked in Houston. I was so nervous. I met his son, who worked side by side with him, and waited to speak to George, who was apparently out to lunch. When he entered the room, I almost fainted. He looked exactly like his picture, but he was here not in Dubai. My words stuttered, and my body trembled as I listened to what he had to say. He told me he had had problems with someone stealing his identity and that he was happily married and had no daughter. I was in shock, and as he hugged me and offered to do anything he could to help me straighten things out, I felt like I was going to faint after hearing the news. Feeling very emotional and drained, I decided to send the following email.

Dear George,

I don't even know how to write this. I don't know what to say. I feel as if the problem of not getting the funds for fees pales in comparison to what happened today. I can hardly breathe. I can hardly accept what is right in front of me. I am in so much pain. My heart does not have any feeling at the moment. I believed in you. I trusted you. I loved you with all my heart, soul, and mind. I thought we were going to have a future together. I don't understand all this. It's hard to accept you could even think of doing this to me. I don't even know if I can hit send. This is too much to accept right now.

Good Morning Love,

Really when I read this mail, I was really dumbfounded, because I'm lost. I do not know what I have done wrong this time again… Please can you tell me, because right now, I'm indoors.

I'm not going to the site, because I do not think any one can stand the chance of me not being myself today...because your mail this Morning, was just too harsh for me.

Please I need a reply asap... I need to know if loving you was wrong or trusting you, because right now I can't point to one thing from what you have said...still love you and will always do...

Hugs,
George

Good Morning Love,

I'm really sorry for not dropping you a note yesterday. I left in a hurry, some havoc was caused at the site, two days ago. I guess that was why the boys were knocking on my door, while we were talking and my face was bad. You remember that right, so when I got there, lots had to be taken care of and I left my laptop in the room. I did send you a chat but, you were not on site... So hope you had a great day without me yesterday, because mine was really hectic and after the tummy filling, just slept off... There are so many reasons for me to love you. I love the way you find humor in the darkest of clouds. I Love the way you make me smile. I love the way you accept me for who I am. I admire your inner strength. I could list reasons from here to eternity, but I will not. We are in the darkest days of our lives. I have made mistakes as have you. However, it is during this time, at our weakest, we can also be our strongest. For we have our love and if we remember that love, draw on that love, we can get through this and truly be one. Let's work together, trust each other, honor each other, respect each other, be faithful in our love for each other and we can conquer all that life throws our way. I am so happy, I feel complete. You are the piece of the puzzle that was missing in me. I didn't know what would fill that void, but I know now that it was always you. We've become such good friends, I trust you, and I care about you so much and I know that you feel the same way. It is so wonderful to know that you love me as much as I love you. I feel so over-whelmed with emotion that I'm speechless. I really am speechless. I just want you to know that I love you so much. Thinking of how much you love me brings me such comfort when I'm not feeling so great. Everything seems so right these days; everything makes sense. Thank you, my sweet angel… I hope we get to chat today,

Kisses and Hugs, your sweet sweet sugar.

Good Morning,

Thanks for taking your time to write me, wow!!! I think you got me wrong when I said I had tears dropping from my eyes. I wrote that before we chatted online yesterday. I felt I was making you go through a lot and I never planned for that. But when we talked in the morning, you sure made my mind calm about everything. Tell you what, I felt heavy relief after talking to you yesterday… My love, I'm so sorry that we did not have our pleasure time yesterday "WINKING" Smiles… I know we can't get together right now; we are just too far apart and I perfectly understand that. But somehow, I still have faith (BIG faith) that in due time, this will all come to an end and we will be together...forever (as what I'm always asking from God). Being far from you is not that easy, Honey. It sometimes drives me crazy and makes me want to be with you at this very instant. Though we're apart now, believe me, I can assure you that it doesn't change the way I feel about you. You're such a blessing for me. Thank you for everything...for loving me; I mean it, Honey. I really appreciate you. You are too smart to fall in love with me, but I guess I am much smarter than you are to make myself fall in love with you so deeply. Smiles, Though the miles separate us, the bond we have is far stronger. You are the very one I have spent all these years looking for. You make me smile. You make me laugh. You make me whole. I cannot describe the giddy feeling I have when you are near or even when you cross my mind. I am so amazingly happy and content and forever I want to spend in your life, in your world, in your family, and in your arms. My love we worked so hard yesterday, due to the havoc at hand...you really do not know how much I enjoyed talking to you yesterday. I enjoy every time we spent together, against all odds we still enjoy talking and enjoy each others company.

Hey baby,

Good Morning, thanks for all your effort on me and on this to see it work... Smiles... Honey I'm so sorry to bring this up... But for real I will be need some money here, Say 3 to 5k... You know the havoc caused then?? I'm trying to get things together and that cannot work without money, again I'm very sorry to bring it up, But i really need it... Please Honey, I know you can still go around for that amount Pleaseesssssssssssssssssssssssssssssssss, Like on my knees right now, Not even for the way I have been living for the past few days... Just imagine asking you in your early Morning coffee, which I do not do normally... Honey, I'm really counting on you right now baby... Again I'm so sorry baby, Just can't help it,... You are my best friend and confidant. Together we are one union, that of love, a love that is unlike any that I have ever felt or experienced before. How did such a blessing evolve? I fell in love with you when I realized how blissful love is. It is rare, but, when your heart finds it there is nothing that deters you away. You have baptized me with your love. What a blessing. What a priceless gift. How did I get to be so lucky? Lucky to have found you. My love, always, forever... I love you...your sweet sweet sugar.

Hey baby...

Thanks for your mail, Hope you are having a great time there in WV. Do not worry about me, because right now I think only God is my strength. You think I do not care because you cannot give me some funds...well it's not like that if you are in my shoes B. You might even do more... I'm a frustrated man right about now and all I can do is just be looking... Ok got to go now and hope we talk soon, you mean you cannot chat there?? love you so much... Hugs and kisses, George

Good Morning Love, How was your Night? I waited for you last night and you were not here… Tell me what is going on baby… I'm really worried… I hope you are doing good, because that is what matters most to me honey. Please get back to me and let me know what is going on,

> Ok…
> Love you,
> George

My baby,

Thanks for the lovely note, for days now. Have not had my coffee so sweet and I must tell you that I'm happy to get this. I enjoyed talking to you yesterday and when I lost you I knew something came up, because I know that the B I have will never leave me…smiles…you mean so much to me honey and I want you to know that. I know you have been going through so much with me and we are the end of or our worries. I enjoy every step you take to help take me out of here and I must commend you on that, B. I was thinking that since we have money on credit, why not buy some things; I sell them back. Just think of what you could buy and sell them back to get cash, because Honey, really cash is the only way out for me here, I swear. I hate swearing I just had to do that right now, because I'm in a fix here and I'm trying to explain to you my darling, because it's only you and I that can understand all this. Since we already have 1k in cash and you can sell the things you bought to get cash, then we can always look for a way to get it here, you know how we do right, the team mates…smiles… Right now, all I have in mind by this time, was to be at the Olympics with you and Jenny, Gosh!!!!! Will there always be another one anyways, what matters most is that I have you and you have me… So honey…what do you think and let me know, I will be online later today, Ok My love… Love you loads and thanks so much…

Hugs and kisses. Your sweet sweet sugar

Hi Sweetheart,

I just wanted to tell you how much I enjoyed our conversation today on IM. I love talking to you anytime, and I know when we are finally together, we will talk the night away. Honey, I have checked all my credit cards, and I do have up to 5,000 to use as credit on them, but do you have any ideas how to get that credit turned into cash? I also checked on the internet, and VIGO does not operate in Dubai. It does in Europe and Africa and other countries, but not Dubai. So we have three problems: 1) can't get the credit turned into cash, 2) can't send the amount of 5000 without being flagged, 3) can't send it to you through money transfer if we do get it. So we need to come up with a new plan to get you home. Why don't you tell me the bills that need to be paid to get you home and let's see if they would take a credit card possibly? Or could you talk to them so you could give them an IOU and you will wire them the money upon your return? Just because of your previous good reputation. Then you come home and straighten it all out from here. What do you think? It is getting harder and harder to come up with solutions. I am surprised we haven't heard from the lawyer or the bank since it has been a couple months. Anyway, I don't want to spend my time always talking about the money you need. I really like it when we can be honest with each other and express our feelings. It is obvious each time we talk that the electric connection still exists between us. And, honey, if I were honest with you, I tried so hard to get rid of my feelings for you. To put them aside and start a new life, but I just haven't been able to. Every day, I hear from my kids how I need to be with men face to face and to stop meeting anyone on the net because they will take advantage of me. Little do they know, right? I never want them to find out what I have been through (not with you or with the other guy). Sorry, I am not supposed to talk about my past. I want to look only forward to the future, our future. I hope you are really doing okay, my love. I think about you constantly. I know you don't think I do, but I do. And no one can ever take away the memories the two of us have created in the last five months. Our times of pleasure can never be replaced. You still are able to do to me (or should I say make me respond) like no one else. Sometimes, I wish I weren't so vulnerable around you, but like I have told you a million times, you make me melt. I never want to imagine my life without you. I know I gave you the cold shoulder more than once when things weren't going well for us. But I am proud of you that you hung in there and understood why I was doing so. Thanks for reaffirming our love today. I needed to hear that. Call me crazy, call me lost, but just as you need affirmation from me, I need it from you. As I told you before, I respond to the love being given to me, and then I give it my all, so you are very important to me, and I want this to work out for us. My only regret is that we didn't meet before you left for Dubai. I think we would be twice as close right now if we had. I will let you go for now. I hope when you are back in the café or have internet access, you will take time to write to me and give me my morning coffee once again. I always enjoy that, and I want you to have yours on time, so here it is. Take care, my love. We must have faith in each other and in the future that all this will eventually work out.

All my love,
B

Good Morning Love,

Hope you had a nice night, mine was not very nice though, cos my hopes were up all through yesterday... Honey I know you have to be there for others, cause this time she needs you the most and i really wish i can be there too, But believe me honey, My prayers goes to her...so far our plans did not work and i can't even think of anything right now... Talked to Debby too and she was up to nothing, This is really getting me frustrated here honey, I know you have been my only pillar and I want to say a big thank you to all your effort, but i need you to try more honey, I know when i come home all of this will be sorted out with, I can't even think of what to tell you to do, cos i know my smart lady must have done the thinking herself...so honey, what is the next line of action of getting cash baby???? Your baby is getting sick here... Honey, I await the day we will get together as I miss your tender touch i ought to be having by now, kiss, and most of all—your hands as you would use it to caress my body. I want the whole world to know that I love you honey and nothing will ever change that. There is no other woman for me and there is no other man for you...we were created for each other, to ease each others pain and sorrow and replace our sadness with love and happiness... I love you loads baby... Talk to you soon,

Hugs and kisses your sweet sweet Sugar.

Hey baby...

Honey so you mean you drove there?? Believe me if I'm home I won't have allowed that. I hate long distance driving especially you being alone in the car. Please Honey, That got me really scared and next time tell me before you do that honey, ok baby... My prayers has really been going to her. She is part of my family and I always pray for every member of my family... smiles... I missed talking to you and our leg pulling...smiles... Thank God we got back better, you now understand me more. Everyday we live and learn more about ourself and time has sure been of great help to us. Please honey I want you to know that so far, I Have not gotten anything about coming home. I know it's a sad news but I need to share it with my one and alone love... Ok let me leave you now and hope we talk better later, ok love...can we still chat on later, will try sending you a message on IM, oK... Love and will always do... Smiles...

Hugs and kisses, your sweet sweet sugar.

Hi, G.

How are you? I haven't heard from you for a long while and just got a letter from Holburn Chambers and bank that all money has been paid and I can now transfer funds. Thank you for taking care of that. I changed my password but will begin transferring funds. I guess you are in Houston now.

Hope you are well.
B

B,

Thanks for your mail. Well, since you left me, God has been with me and Nope I'm still in Dubai. Thanks for your care

Dear George,

I don't know why I was thinking of you, but you have really been on my mind lately. I went back and read all our emails, and we seemed to have found a love only found in a fairy tale. I am not sure what happened except the fact that I drained all my accounts to send money to you to help you but never was able to get a return on my investment. It appears as if you wanted nothing to do with me once I could not come up with any more funding. Now I am in the hands of a debt consolidation company and will pay back the funds in four years (I hope). When I heard from the bank a few weeks ago, I thought they told me I could start releasing the funds, but that was not true. It seems they will only release very small amounts at one time, and they put another hold on the account. Anyway, when you said you were still in Dubai, I wondered if there was anything I could do to help you come back home or are you working on that other contract you talked about. I also wondered if you wanted to pick up where we left off or if you wanted to call our relationship quits for good. We had so much good when we were together. I miss that, and it is hard to find. I also wondered how Jenny is getting along. So if you feel like it, let me hear from you, and we will see where this can go. All we have to do is work toward each other, and we may be able to rekindle what we had. Hope to hear from you soon.

B

Hello B…

Thanks for your concern about me here. I must commend you on that, upon all that you have been told about me. You still have second thoughts of my welfare and my family. You are such a good person and you deserve to be happy. I'm sure God will always repay you for all this kindness. Jenny is fine and Debby too… They have really been trying their best but I guess their best is not working so much to get me home and believe me, B, when I think of any other woman, with what you have been through with me, learning things that would make me a very bad person in your sight and in the sight of our creator, I just stopped talking to you. Because I know what you are going through with the banks and all. I know how it feels to be monitored and all, and if we talk I will ask for more money, because I need to come home. So I hate to bother you about it anymore, so the best thing for me to do at the time was to stop talking to you and plan to surprise you when I come home... But I guess it's not been working for me as I thought... Well for so many reasons, your thoughts always make me happy and makes me have more than a million reasons not to give up, because you never gave up on me... I love you B and will always...checked on you around 4pm your time last nite...so are you working now or what... I know I must have missed a lot... Can you fill me in... Sweet Smiles...

Hugs and kisses, George

Hello Darling,

Thanks for always taking your time on me. Yes I'm still in Dubai and you really made me remember old times, when I got angry with you and your questions... I felt really bad when I got your latest mail and did not even know my reply to it... I enjoy your friendship, because you are very rare to come across in real Life...things have just been not good with me here, But this time I leave my problems to myself... You have done more than enough and would not want to involve you again. I know someday you will still sleep next to me and laugh with me; I hope that day comes soon... I owe a lot out here dear and please do not put all this in mind. I need you to be happy with yourself and believe me, that will surely make me happy here too... Love you loads...

Hugs and kisses,
George

Hi George,

It's been about ten days since I heard from you. Are you still in Dubai? And do you plan on staying there for a while? I wondered why I didn't hear from you and thought maybe something happened. Then I remember how upset you got with me every time I asked you for your address, so is that what is happening again? I would think you could trust me by now with all I have given up for you. So let me hear from you and tell me what is going on. I think you will feel better if you have someone to talk with. Take care and God bless.

BB

Summary:

George and I exchanged emails, phone calls, texts, chats, and webcams. So it makes sense that when we planned to meet one another at Barnes and Noble one day, I would be surprised to get a phone call that he just received word and needed to go out of town to fulfill a contract he had been working on. When he called, he was actually dropping off his daughter to his sister's house so she could stay with her while he was out of town. Once again, just like other possible suitors, G said he would be gone a few weeks, but we would stay in contact with one another, and it would be as if he had never left.

One night, he told me that he had met with the contractor and filled out a paper naming me his next of kin. He convinced me that he had an oil business here in Houston and did lots of business internationally. A quick trip to Dubai to complete a project was not out of the realm for reality. He even had his daughter send me an email and ask me to help her pick out a dress for the prom. He told me if anything happened to him, the money from the project would come to me, and he wanted to assure me the importance of my role in his life. So naturally, we talked about our future together a lot. He would even disapprove if I ever missed church because he was a deacon in his local church community. Love letters from George convinced me that his life was centered on him making me happy and that I would move in with him and Jenny as soon as we were married upon his return to the States.

As the documents appeared from the online bank showing that $400,000 and then $600,000 was deposited in my name, his story was verified. That is, until the bank restricted access. George asked me to transfer the money into a bank account here, and he would get it upon his return. I questioned him as to why he wanted me to do that, and he always gave me a good explanation. I asked how much would I take out at a time, and he said all of it. Once again, I questioned it because this was uncharted territory to me. He assured me he had done this many times. But of course, he didn't have an explanation as to why I was being restricted to total access. I received an email from the bank telling me when any amount over ten thousand tries to be withdrawn, certain rules have to be followed to make sure money laundering is not taking place. I asked myself how I got involved in this. The bank asked for several documents to be produced before they could release the funds. Of course, George told me it would certainly be taken care of, and he would contact a lawyer to deal with it. Finding out all this was in my name and I was responsible for coming up with the fees not only to the country but to the lawyer in a different country started to unnerve me. But good ole George continued to tell me that it was just a bump in the road and that any money I paid would be reimbursed and doubled for my trouble upon his return. The important thing to remember was to get access to the money since he had the company who employed him deposit the money in an account in my name. So diving into my IRAs and cashing them out, taking out all my savings, and even spending the money my son had loaned me to pay fees, I was able to produce what was needed to move forward. George produced a completion of job certificate from the company that hired him and all other documents needed, which I sent to the lawyer in London. Checking on the bank and the lawyer and even the company that employed him was my next move, and according to the internet, they all existed and were reputable as far as I could tell. He convinced me that the lawyer in London would handle everything to make a smooth transition. Of course, this is when I had to pay fees upfront for the lawyer's services as well as court costs. But I knew the money had been placed in my account, so it would all be returned to me. After one hundred thousand dollars later and word from the lawyer that he had taken care of everything and he only needed a final payment, I really began to question if this was authentic. The situation I found myself threw up a lot of red flags. But my love continued to support me and convince me everything would be fine and he would be home as soon as possible. Of course, the weeks started turning into months. He finally told me the job was taking longer than he expected, and he would come home, we would marry, and then I would go back with him to Dubai so that we would never be separated again. He would help me straighten out everything so that all my funds I had invested would be reimbursed. He even asked me to plan the wedding so everything would be set when he arrived.

When he asked me to ask my friends to borrow $40,000, I knew something wasn't right. But he made me feel as if all this was our problem and I had to solve it some way. So that's what I did. I asked my best friend for a loan, and thank goodness I did. She made me realize that this was not something someone who loved you would do. So with her encouragement, I decided to visit his office in Houston only a few miles away, just to find out if there were any employees there that could help us and if they even knew about us.

This is when I met the real G, who had had his identity stolen, was married and had a son, not a daughter, and was not off working in Dubai. I had been scammed once again. When I tried to get my money back and worked with the fraud departments of my local banks who had dispersed the money, I found out because I voluntarily gave the permission for banks to wire the money, no fraud had taken place, and I was simply out of all the money. My friend urged me over and over to tell my son what had happened, and I had too much pride to do so. I was so afraid of losing his love and respect.

This man had become so important to me. I nicknamed him my sugar because my son was always asking me if I was getting any sugar on the way to the mailbox each day. When I told George about this, he immediately told me that he would be and always be my sugar. I was so caught up in the fantasy of getting married to this wonderful man and had no idea that he was scamming me from the very beginning of our relationship. When we talked about marriage, we were going to make it happen as soon as possible. So I went out, shopped around, and set up a venue at a small Italian restaurant with a lighted outdoor area to hold the ceremony. They would also have a piano player that night, and we would have the reception inside. My wedding dress had arrived, and all plans were ready to make this miracle happen. My pastor would come to the location to do what was needed from him. Who would guess that all along, this person continued to court me through all technical means just to use me and obtain as much money from me as he could get and then toss me aside like a rotten tomato? This truly made this relationship like a love like no other. And yet once again, my bank account was emptied, including the money borrowed from my son. The truth was hard to accept, even though I had all the facts before me.

Just to make sure this was a scam, I went back on the dating site and set up a new account with a pseudonym and picture, and would you know, good ole George responded. He proceeded to send her the same emails he had sent me. The only difference was my pseudonym decided to fly to Dubai to meet him and join him. The day she arrived, he notified her that he had to make a quick trip to China and would not see her during the week she was there. I knew then he was used to communicating with other women and fooling them the way he fooled me. I had fallen hard for this man, but even with the information of being scammed by him, there was still a part of me in complete denial and wishing that this was not a scam but the real deal for me.

CHAPTER 13

Love in Question

As I struggled to get over my last conquest and what I now call fantasy love, I wondered if the next person who reached out to me would be sincere and, of course, real. I began wondering what was wrong with me since I seemed to turn toward instead of turning away from these so-called kind of men who enjoyed getting what they want from women. And how was I ever supposed to know the difference between true love and fantasy? Would I ever get to meet someone in person before they committed fraud or swindled me? Why did I always believe the best of people and never suspect the worse? Was I hiding my head in the sand or was I simply avoiding the truth standing right in front of me?

These and more were the questions that constantly took up space in my brain these days. So my next contact was from Corpus Christi, Texas. I checked out his phone line and address on the internet to give myself some reassurance that this person truly existed before I responded. In order to understand why I tend to respond or select the person that I might be attracted to, I will have to share some of their emails. Without them meeting the bare minimum criteria that I set for future possibilities, I would never take the time to respond. Knowing what to say to make sure the correct hook is placed to keep me interested requires a cunning, creative, manipulative, and yet supposedly responsible male adult. I am including the following emails so that as you read them there might be a chance that you have received one or more of them, and this could help you to have the courage to stop the relationship if you have not met the person face to face.

Meet Joe:

> I am simply online looking for the Love of my life...someone to make my heart skip a beat...shake my whole being... A fairy tale that lasts a life time. Someone to adore and cherish... I want to look at her face in the morning. I want to feel my heart...speak to "her" heart and know that our souls connect in the deepest, richest way, the way God intended.
>
> One thing about myself is that I share from my heart. I will not say things I don't mean, especially in a relationship but I also have had to learn how to be assertive and speak the truth in love—not be so scared and shy, worrying about what someone might think. It is always good to be up front and honest even if it is difficult. I am a fairly down to earth person and I hope you are beginning to see that.
>
> I won't lie to you, hide anything from you... I am an open book and believe in being honest with my partner... No surprises. That way everything is out in the open and nothing is hidden. If it was a nice sunny day I would love to get some wine and pack a lunch and go to the lake and have a quiet picnic, listening to some music, enjoying your company... I am very Romantic...lol
>
> To me, just the thought of waking up next to someone who loves me and who I love, is the perfect way to start any day...you can find quality time in doing most anything. It's been such a long time since I've been able to even think about planning my day with someone, that anything and everything would be wonderful. There's a

part of me that loves romance and I have learned that the one thing you cannot get back is time.

When it comes to my dislikes—deceit, disrespect, untrustworthy and infidelity are what I can talk about for now. I will let you know more in the course of time. If there's anything I haven't told you, then please don't hesitate to draw my attention and I shall whole-heartedly tell you. Stay safe and please keep in touch. Hope I haven't bored you so much…

Take Care
JB

Thank you for the compliments and indeed you said it all. I like discovering new things about the person I meet. I am a person who looks for the possibilities versus what cannot be achieved. Life is better going through with a special one instead of just any one. I respect the direct approach—that is saying what you mean and meaning what you say. I believe in smiling—even when things are not going as perfect as you had hoped. A smile can brighten someone's day—I like smiling—it is one of my trademarks…

I can boldly say my closest friend is my late wife…who lost her life to carcinoma cancer. She gave me much respect and also treated me as a darling hubby. I really do miss her in my everyday life and am still hoping if God will get me blessed by replacing such a significant being in my life once again. We were married for 33yrs. We had a son. He's 20yrs old and he is called R, pursuing his first degree at University of Cambridge in United kingdom UK. At least I'm grateful to

God all is not lost, for I still have my son to keep me company.

I have worked with so many companies—some construction companies in Brooklyn and some other states of the U.S. Some companies like A. Rahim Construction, Inc. Brooklyn, NY, U.S. That's a big company. I have been in Texas for the past six years since I started working on my own. I buy the land and build the real estate myself... I sell it out to individuals and don't deal in shareholding... I have got great customers that really love my hand in the work... Then I take investors from commercial sales to regular buyers and sellers. I did management in between commercial and regular customers. I am also a builder/contractor.

Yeah it varies from where I buy the land because I check properly on the land before I buy it. I am planning to build a commercial real estate and that is going to be outside the states but I have not planned exactly where. Time will actually tell. I enjoy the fact that you are a Christian. My faith is important to me, I am a practicing Christian and attend church weekly and like to be involved in the activities. I am convinced that if I walk in the Spirit I will NEVER go wrong. I consider myself fortunate to have been exposed to God and all the benefits of being a Christian.

I am constantly told that I'm good looking and both look and act far younger than my years (while still being responsible for the most part). I am considered intelligent, honest, capable of carrying on conversations on a variety of topics, kind, caring, giving, passionate, compassionate, a leader with a commanding presence, successful, possessing a quick sense of humor and so much more! You will find me a contradiction in terms. I can be intense yet laid back, intelligent yet do some of the most stupid things, outgoing yet shy, a leader yet not afraid to take directions and be a role player, funny yet serious, etc... Will write more...

Take Care,
Joe

Be thankful when you don't know something...
For it gives you the opportunity to learn.
Be thankful for the difficult times... During those times you grow.
Be thankful for your limitations... They give you opportunities for improvement.
Be thankful for each new challenge... Which will build your strength and character.
Be thankful for your mistakes... They will teach you valuable lessons.
It's easy to be thankful for the 'good' things... Yet, a life of rich fulfillment comes to those who are thankful for the setbacks.
Gratitude can turn a negative into a positive... Find a way to be thankful for your troubles and they can become your blessings!

Take Care,
JB

Oh, in a good relationship I envision honesty, passion, unconditional love and acceptance yet one needs to be able to be very honest and up front with the other person. Being able to share things in common, enjoy doing things together, goals, teamwork is very important. Being sensitive to the needs of the other person yet being also able to know how to disagree in the right way. If nothing else, agree to disagree, take it up later. And never go to bed angry! Respect, mercy, kindness, understanding things that come easy when you are in love and love the other person.

We have to make the best of it. I love life and enjoy waking up every morning knowing I have another day on this beautiful Earth. Now I have found someone to spend it with, to make her happy, and her to make me happy. It is such an awesome thing and what an adventure we are going to have. Some common interests would be good—while also having some differing interests also, to keep the relationship fresh. Mutual respect and admiration of each other is also important. But we don't have to have the same opinions on all subjects as long as we respect and value each other's unique contribution to the relationship.

Similar level of intelligence is helpful. Sexual attraction is important also. My ideal would be a true give and take relationship in the area of intimacy with my partner so we trust each other explicitly and can experience the true ecstasy of open, caring, sharing love without fear or judgment. Do you have Yahoo IM or Msn IM? We can spend time on there chatting. Let me know what you think... Take Care... Joe

Somewhere out there beneath the pale moonlight someone is thinking of you. Somewhere out there where dreams come true... goodnight and sweet dreams to you... I will reply to your message in the morning. What is your yahool ID? Sweet dreams...

Joe

A smile is a way of writing your thoughts on your face, telling others that they are accepted, liked and appreciated. So here's a big smile just for you. Every morning has a new beginning, a new blessing, a new hope. It's a perfect day because it's God's gift. Have a blessed, hopeful perfect day to begin with. I am ready, willing and able to dedicate myself fully and so whatever I share with you comes from my heart.

My condolence, my dear. May you take comfort in knowing an angel is watching over you. Sorry for your brother's loss. I am happy you still have your Dad alive and hopefully I will see him one day. My parents are deceased; I lost my Mom in 2005 and my Dad 2007. I am the only Child as well... Life has not been so easy for me... I love Classical and Country music a lot.

My experience about online dating is very much beginning. I have talked to some nice people on here but they all say the distance is too great. But I have heard some people actually got married from online dating. I hear it is the best. But I have suspended my account because of you. You are so special. I also play the Keyboard Piano, and it would be nice while I play and you sing one day... Thinking of you.

Food I like: broccoli, spinach, brussel sprouts, carrots, and corn. I am a very good cook. Talking about TV, I like American Idol, X factor, America's got Talent and the supernaturals. I also like Breaking news and Voice. I love Italian Restaurants... Can I have your yahoo ID for now? Thinking of you...you are very special. What else would you like to know about me?

Smiles…

Joe

Our passions, expectations, life experiences, and even our personalities all contribute to the level of happiness we experience in our lives. Some find happiness in their careers while others find ways to be happy in their marriages or other relationships.

No matter how you define happiness for yourself, there are certain universal and time-proven strategies to bring, and sustain, more happiness into your life. Spend Time with Your Friends. Although an abundant social and romantic life does not itself guarantee joy, it does have a huge impact on our happiness. Learn to spend time with your friends and make the friendships a priority in your life. Savor Every Moment. To be in the moment is to live in the moment. Too often we are thinking ahead or looking ahead to the next event or circumstance in our lives, not appreciating the "here and now." When we savor every moment, we are savoring the happiness in our lives.

Play to Your Strengths. One way to achieve flow is by understanding and identifying our strengths and core values, and then begin to use these every day. Once we are aware of our strengths and we begin to play to your strengths we can better incorporate them in all aspects of our lives.

Good Morning…

Joe

Life is too short to play games with other people's emotions, and too long to be alone. I feel people should like themselves before they can like someone else. One last note...no matter what you do in life try and smile, smile, smile! You will get there... God Bless you... Hugs...

Joe

You know what!? I'm so thankful that I've met you. I really enjoyed talking to you. I will never forget each little thing we talked about. I really hope to see you one day. You are such a nice person. You're just cute. I will really love to see you smiling. Can I be the real happiness in your life? I am thinking of you... Smiles...

Joe

Days go by with thoughts of you in my mind, and I've asked myself what is happening? My heart said I should follow it to where it leads me, 'cause it is always true to me. What is so special about you? Well, the reason is simple. I chose you because you are YOU!!! You make me feel special and wanted. I will honor, cherish, squeeze and hold you. You mean more to me than you realize. I am hoping that one day I can prove all of this to you! I want you for you!
Kisses and hugs...

Joe

You have overcome many obstacles within your life which have made you the wonderful person you are today. You should be very proud

271

that you have persevered all your experiences and with it you have lived, acknowledged, and learned and you have never intentionally done unto others as it has been done unto you for you know what it feels like and you have the strength to rise above it all. You are attractive, generous, honest, humorous, intelligent, kind, loveable, loving, passionate, and a wonderful woman. The person who will obtain the key within your heart in the future will be blessed to have the love in which you are capable of giving to someone. May God Bless you and always give you the strength for you to continue to grow and love. I just pray and hope that person to be your heart will be me. Love… Joe

Please have faith in us that we can make it through anything, together—forever and always. Kisses and Hugs…

Joe

You're always lighting up my heart with the things you do and say. I feel so happy just being with you this way. You will always be the love of my life, and please never give up; always have faith in yourself and you will gain the greatest gift of all, the gift of hope and love you righteously deserve. Every time I think of you my heart misses a beat. Thinking of you…

Love…
Joe

I just had to let you know that these last two days without so much as talking to you—has given me a lot of time to think about how I feel about you. I'm writing to let you know how I feel about you. I don't know how to tell you since we have not met face to face, so I am going to try to put my feelings in words. My feelings I just can't seem to tame. I am starting to care for you in a different way. I think of you every day! I love everything about you! I am pretty sure you get the point. I can't get you off my mind. Well, what I am trying to tell you is I am SPRUNG, and I am falling in love with you—yes, this is true! But I understand if you don't feel the same. Damn, I know this is sounding lame, but I have to let you know how I really feel. And this is no lie, I am for real.

How are your friends? I wish them a speedy recovery my dear. I hope to see your daughter any time soon and hope she is doing well now. I appreciate your care and loving ability. You continue to amaze me my dear one. It might be all the things I see on the surface, the things that everyone notices and admires about you, qualities, capabilities and a wonderful smile obviously connected to a warm and loving heart; these things set you apart from everyone else. But it may also be the big things…the person you really are that I hope to know more someday. And it might also be the little things God has blessed you with! If I ever figure out the magic that makes you so special, I'd probably find out that it's a combination of all these things. You are a rare combination of so many special things. You are really amazing.

Inside of me there is a place where my sweetest dreams reside, where my highest hopes are kept alive, where my deepest feelings are felt and where my favorite memories are safe and warm. I find that you're on my mind more often than any other thought. Sometimes I bring you there purposely just to make my day brighter. But more often, you surprise me and find your own ways into my thoughts. There are even times when I awaken, and I realize that you've been a part of my dreams. Then during the day, when my imagination is free to run, it takes me into your arms and allows me to linger there—knowing there's nothing I'd rather do. I know my thoughts are only reflecting the loving hopes of my heart because whenever they wander, they always take me to you.

Only the most special things in my world get to come inside my heart and stay. And now, I realize how deeply my life has been touched by you. There are no words to express the gratitude I feel in my heart that you came into my life, and how you make every day so special. You are my life, my heart, my soul. You are my best friend. A day without you in my life is like a day without sunshine, a day without food, or a day without air. You are the most wonderful thing that has ever happened to me. I could never imagine what it would be like if we were to lose each other. I don't even want to think about it. All I want to think of is you.

Love always...
JB

My feelings are growing stronger and stronger every day. You confide in me. That melts me inside. No one has ever in my life talked to me about their hurts and sorrows and I love that about you! We both have gone through so much,

274

and I feel like I relate to you on a much higher level than I have ever felt before. We have the same interests and the same likes. I know I am a person that needs gratification, and you seem to fulfill my needs in every way. I think that if we take our time and do everything right, this love could blossom into a fairytale romance. All I ask—and I know I have said it before—is that you be true to me and be true to yourself. I have put all my trust in you, and I have opened every fiber of my being to you and only you. Someone to hold, confide in, laugh with, cry with; someone I can watch football with, fish with, walk along the beach at night with. I want it. I deserve it, as do you. I sincerely hope that you feel the same as I do about you. I am honest, sincere, and true, and I have a lot of love to give if you are willing to be on the receiving end.

Your love…
JB

I am praying to God to review us. I pray every night and day that he sees the love I have for you. I feel like I can't breathe. You let me be me and make me feel so special. I know God has something good in store for us. He is not an evil God but a loving God. And when we are in each other's arms again, that love will be more amazing than what we have now.

Love always,
Joe

You mean more than anything in this world to me. Thank God I found you at last. You are my everything.

Love…
Joe

You are my knight in shining armor. I will never forget you. I miss you. I love every moment we share together and I love the small talks we share. I do hope one day, our friendship will grow into love. No matter whatever becomes of "us" I will always hold you in my heart.

No one in this world knows the feeling that I get when I talk to you. I am the understanding type. I just want to grab you and be in your arms forever and forever and never let go. I want to kiss your lips and never end—just keep going… hehehehehee.

Every time I think about you, it gives me more and more strength with which to carry on my life. It makes me happy to be alive knowing that you have come into my life and all I know is that I want to be with you!

My heart has already found its way to you. I want you and no one else. You mean everything to me. I think we should try and make this work. You have to know you're the one, and only one I want.

Not only are you perfect for me, you're the perfect friend and I hope we can and will be more. I could never ask for better than what we have. I am hoping you're feeling the same way because my heart is set on you, and only you, baby. Love Always, Joe

I started thinking today of all the ways you make my life complete, and I ran out of space when I tried to fit it on just one sheet. I love to imagine you smiling when reading this letter; I love to imagine you holding me even when we are not together. I love to imagine you and me forever. I love to imagine ways to always make our relationship better. What do you do on weekends?

Love always,
Joe

I am sitting in my office, in front of the monitor, with the keyboard in front of me. I feel you so near and so distant in the same moment. Every day I find something new in you, something that makes me feel different but sure in one thing—you are not only my friend, you are something more, something deeper.

After all these days and nights I know that I found a friend, but I am not sure if it is the real love, until we meet in person. But I know that I have found my first true love and I will keep it that way. I also know that I will give you all the love you need, or at least all the love you want me to give you. I know that I will love you in a way I cannot show and cannot explain to you.

I just want to be loved by you, at least as a friend. Let me know if you have changed your opinion about us. Let me know what has changed or if I am the one who does not understand things. I love you, my only sin! I love you as a friend and as a lover.

Love,
Joe

My beautiful Love, you are my sunrises and sunsets. You are my world. My love, my beautiful love, come to me and make me the happiest man in the world! If you're asking me if I love you this much, my beautiful, I do! Marry me, Beautiful... come spend eternity with me??

Love always,
Joe

The best gifts to give: to friend—loyalty; to enemy—forgiveness; to boss—service; to child—good example; to parents—devotion; to friends—love; to God—our lives; and to text mate—message. This message has no fat, no cholesterol and no additive. This is all natural except, with a lot of sugar. But it can never be as sweet as the one reading it. Smile!

Your Love,
Joe

I hope to grow old with you for the rest of my life—to celebrate good times with you and support each other through the bad times. We will not always have good times, but we will always love each other and work through our problems. We will have fun taking walks, and watching movies. I look forward to that day. Thinking and smiling…

Yours,
Joe

Honey, you have changed my life completely. You're the one who makes me handsome. You're the one who makes me strong. You're the one who makes me feel so important; you're everything to me. You show your love to me every day. I thank God that I have found a woman like you. Please forgive me for not giving you enough time to chat with me, but I promise I will make up for it once we are together.

All that I can offer you is a family. I can offer you a family that will stick together through the good and the bad. I can offer you a family that will support each other every day. Honey, that's all I can give… I hope that's what you want.

I really wish that you were near me. I wish that I could just call your name when I needed you and that you would be there. However, knowing that you love me so much is enough for now, and if I can be your husband and a father to your children, then I would wait forever to be with you. Ti amo tesoro mio. You're the only one that I want.

Trust me,
Joe

I miss you, I really do. God I'm blushing! There are no words that can possibly explain how I feel right now, because in fact, I've never felt this before…sounds so cliché doesn't it? But that's a fact that I can never hide just like the blush on my cheeks…always visible manifestations of the love I feel inside. Missing you…

Love,
Joe

Standing together side by side there is nothing in this world we can't conquer when it is just you and I. Love will lead you TO all your dreams. With hands and hearts together let's celebrate the joy of finding each other. We shall go to Paris for that, I PROMISE. If there is anything better than to be loved, it is loving. Let no one who loves be unhappy. Even love unturned has its rainbow. My love for you is like time, if you give it just one moment, it will last forever. It is not being in love that makes me happy. It's being in love with you that makes me happy… For an instant, love can transform the world… Remember, love is the link that holds two hearts together… While many a soul are unhappy with love, no one is ever happy without it… What do I get from Loving You? Loving You… How do I possibly put into words how much you mean to me? I know with all of my heart and every passing day that we were meant to be.

While you may not like everything your partner may say, freedom to be honest should be there in your relationship. Likewise, you need to be open and honest with your partner. A relationship based upon false truths is not likely to be successful, because both partners do not have the correct frame of reference in the relationship. In any organization with more than one person in it, there will be more than one opinion; work with your partner to see that both of you can compromise on different subjects. If someone is not willing to compromise, they are not willing to acknowledge your wants and desires. If they cannot acknowledge your wants, they are likely not emotionally developed enough for you to have your needs met... We all turn to our loved ones for support from time to time. When your loved one does not offer you their support it may be time to look at your relationship, as we all want to nurture those that we love. We want the best in life for those that we care about. If your partner is unwilling to listen to you, and to your problems, they are not meeting your needs when you need support.

Loving relationships have good qualities, such as support from your partner, a willingness to communicate, a desire to compromise, and open as well as honest communication. To love me is to accept me as I am. I do not want to be judged for the things I do. I want you to trust me. Do not do or say things because you think you are "honest," do them because of your love for me, and trust me even though you think I am wrong, just as we do not judge our children because they are our children and we love them. Please... Love is not always fireworks and shooting stars; sometimes it's a simple understanding and trust between two people. I love you more than any word can say. I love you more than every action I take. Love is not about finding the right person, but creating a right relationship. It's not about how much love you have in the beginning but how much love you build till the end. I love you. There is nothing else to do, run and I will run with you.

Love,
Joe

No matter what, there will never be another for me and I will always keep you safe. I love you…for all eternity.

Love always,
Joe

More than anything in this world I want to spend the rest of my life with you. You gave me room to grow, you opened the world that was closed for me, and let me breathe. You are extremely good… Whenever we fight, and let's face it we do, the only thought that's in my mind is how much I care to even argue with you. You are my friend, you are everything to me!

I realize that you only want me to see what you see in me, even if I don't believe that is possible. You have seen more in me than anyone in this world—including myself. I just want to thank you for hearing me out and listening to my problem. I love you.

Yours,
Joe

When we first started talking online, I never would have thought that our loving and caring relationship would've blossomed this far this fast! Don't get me wrong, Sweetheart. I love you and we deserve each other. I know deep down in my heart, Sweetheart, I LOVE YOU AND I'M IN LOVE WITH YOU! Waiting until we can be together finally, just be patient, Babe, and God will bring us together. Pray for me and my Son. We miss you.

Love forever and take care.
Joe

Honey, I have arrived already, but Internet was a Big problem. I am happy to have a Wifi here now; but it is late here. I will get a calling card and call in the morning. How are you my dear, are you tired, are you ok? The doctor said my son has bone marrow problem which can lead to a stroke. I have been very busy. I miss you and love you with all of my heart.

Your Love,
Joe

I am in the city of London and there is ongoing Olympics here, so it has made everything so expensive. I am in a hotel my dear. I will bring my son home when everything is alright. Each day that passes makes our love for each other grow stronger. Although I know it's hard for us to be apart, I know there is nothing that can keep us apart forever. Our desires will continue to stretch across any distance, over every mountain and ocean between us. Nothing can stand between us, and nothing will stop me from meeting you. You are my future and nothing can ever keep us from our destiny. I miss you more every day.

I love you…
Joe

I haven't heard a more touching song than this one from the Italian musical "Swept with the Wind." I haven't had a stronger feeling than this one I have now, that I want to face the eternity with you by my side. I want to wake up with you. I want to be there when you open your eyes. I want you to be the first thing that I see. I want to lay by your side. Baby I want to feel every beat of your heart and throughout the night I want to hold you tight. I want to wake up with you. All the love inside me has been sleeping—waiting till the right one came along. You can share the love that I've been keeping, Baby. You can put the music to my song. I want to reach out and know that you're there. And throughout the night I want to hold you tight and feel every beat of your heart.

Love Always,
Joe

You and I, under the moonlight, together until the stars don't shine any more. I miss you.

Love Always,
Joe

My love, I wish you were here with me. Missing you so much is breaking my heart into many pieces. Thinking of you makes me smile 'cause knowing that you love me so much means the world to me. Please, I really need you. When will you be online? Your love is what's keeping me strong. I am so depressed right now and your love is all that is keeping me strong. I love you so much. I can't wait to be with you physically one day. Forever that is.

Love always,
Joe

Hey, Honey…

I miss you. I'm just here thinking about you, like I always do. The thought of you in my arms right now sounds so good to me. I just want you to know how much I love you. I appreciate your love and care. I miss you every second of my life. Stay Blessed…

Love
Joe

If today, a smile should appear on your face, it's because at this very minute, I am thinking of you and I am smiling too… You are doing good and that makes me happy. So how is your neck and back my love? I miss you…and well, Honey we still need the funds, but I am trying my best to contact people who owe me… But if you can send it for God sake through someone my dear, I will really appreciate and God will bless you, because the health care plan here is different my love. Can we chat tonight? I would love to chat with you my love. Thinking of you makes my life complete. You are all the soulful love songs within my spirit, like an angel calling me…perfect for my soul! I love you so much.

Your Love,
Joe

Anything that we do as Christians that focuses our time on God brings Him glory and praise. When we look to His word for healing and guidance, we again are telling God that we need Him and we praise Him for His sovereign nature in all circumstances. In Hebrews 4:15–16 it says, for we do not have a high priest who is unable to sympathize with our weaknesses, but one who in every respect has been tempted as we are, yet without sin. Let us then with confidence draw near to the throne of grace, that we may receive mercy and find grace to help in time of need. This is a passage of love that speaks to all who are hurting. Jesus was tempted in every way so we can be completely firm in our belief in Him. Honey, write these verses on your hearts. We can have confidence in our Father in all circumstances. Stay in the word! It can heal the broken hearted. AMEN…

Love
Joe

Thank you for the message, and am so happy to hear from you. I really love and appreciate your care my love. You are so blessed and I thank God for you! You are wonderful… Yes there is still a little problem I am going through, but with the Lord all things are possible… He will make a way. I miss you and really want to be home and be with you my love. Please with her flight, she suggests Alitalia airlines. Check and let me know the price please. But honey do you mean there is no way you can send me some funds. Just anything from your heart, because I am spending a lot here and need some bucks in my pocket for miscellaneous expenditures. Please. Let me know what you can do. I love you and how has your weekend been? Thinking of you my love...

Love,
Joe

When you are sad, call on John 14. When you don't feel loved, call on Romans 8:38–39.

When you have sinned, call on 1 John 1:8–9. When you are facing danger, call on Psalm 91.

When people have failed you, call on Psalm 27. When God feels far from you, call on Psalm 139. When your faith needs encouraging, call on Hebrews 11. When you are scared, call on Psalm 23. When you are worried, call on Matthew 6:25–34. When you are hurt, call on Colossians 3:12–17. When you feel no one is on your side, call on Romans 8:31–39. When you are seeking rest, call on Matthew 11:25–30. When you are suffering, call on Romans 8:18–30.

When you feel you're failing, call on Psalm 121. When you pray, call on Matthew 6:9–13. When you need courage, call on Joshua 1. When you are in need, call on Philippians 4:19. When you are hated because of your faith, call on John 15. When you are losing hope, call on 2 Thessalonians 2:16–17. When you are seeking peace, call on John 14:27. When you want to do good works, call on John 15. When you want to live a happy life, call on Colossians 3:12–17. When you don't understand what God is doing, call on Isaiah 55:8–9. When you want to get along with others, call on Romans 12:9–21.

Ok my love, I miss you very much and not able to get wireless until tomorrow but my love just confirm the Ethiopian airline one way which is cheap. OK. I really need to come home. I miss you and so want her to come and take care of my son.

Love always,
Joe

Thank you my love and God Bless you so much, but let me know if the change is possible even if on the 10th to 12th. Any would be good enough for her to prepare. Will be on wireless later, so we can chat and I will call you. Love you… Joe

He gives power to the weak and strength to the powerless. Even youths will become weak and tired, and young men will fall in exhaustion. But those who trust in the Lord will find new strength. They will soar high on wings like eagles. They will run and not grow weary. They will walk and not faint. God bless you my love. Love always, Joe

I sit here pondering what life will be with you beside me. Sharing our thoughts and ideas towards what the future holds. You and I are hundreds of miles apart. Yet I feel as if you are here right beside me watching me as I write this letter. I feel as if I'm approaching home since Madam Dorinda will be arriving later today. My son is doing fine and we thank the Lord for his healing possibility and your care as well. Your spirit soars above me, watching over me like a protective angel. Your heart beats in unison with mine growing stronger and with fuller life with each passing moment. I know I have made the right choice in proclaiming my love for you. I have no fears and no regrets and I live for the day we are together for the first time. You have proven to me your love for me is stronger and greater than distances never reached. I love you. I am in love with you.

All my love,
Joe

Confused and do not know what to do... I have to give my son and Madam Dorinda some funds, so that I can come home asap. I am so confused. Can you do anything? I hate this; it seems that my request is all about money. Please let me know what you think and can do my love...

Your love,
Joe

Philemon 1:8–9 Accordingly, though I am bold enough in Christ to command you to do what is required, 9 yet for love's sake I prefer to appeal to you—I, Paul, an old man and now a prisoner also for Christ Jesus. Some people seem to be friends with everyone and other people seem to only have a few friends. No matter how many friends we may have, they will be important to us and will often give us confidence in life. When we know that another person or group of

people is a friend to us, we will be secure, confident, and thankful. Scripture also shows how we
should deal with friends and all people. Maybe
you are reading this because you do not have any
good friends. If this is true for you my heart goes
out to you. You need friends and sometimes we
need to learn how to become a friend before we
will have a new friend. Being a good friend will
often include being a good listener and being
someone that can be counted on and trusted. We
all will fail at times and it is comforting to know
that in Jesus we have a friend that sticks closer
than a brother. Jesus will never leave us or forsake
us in spite of knowing all of our sins and shortcomings. My encouragement to you all today is
that Jesus is the greatest friend you will ever need.
He is every bit as real as the neighbor next door.
We just don't see him face to face yet. But praise
God, one day we will.

Love,
Joe

Honey please let me know the little help
you can give because I really need it. Do you have
a good limit on your cards that are maxed out? I
could let a CC financial who owes me pay them
and so you can send me some... I really want to
be with you. Let me know what you think.

Love,
Joe

If I could give you one thing I would wish
for you, the ability to see yourself as others see

you, then you would realize what a truly special person you are. Love, Joe

Sometimes, life gets so busy that we could not find time to say "Thank you" to someone who has been so nice and wonderful. "Thank you!" and Good Night.

Love,
Joe

Okay my dear, We thank God… Could you send Dorinda some funds Please? I am still in a fix my dear. Just anything you can send her, because she really needs to take care of my son, Honey. Do your best for me… I am just sick and quite ill. Love, Joe

I miss you so much. Yes, I love you very much. We are meant for each other. I miss everything about you in every kind of way. Now that you are already part of my life I thank the Almighty for blessing me with such a very wonderful creature. You have changed a lot of me. You fired up my dry spirit and brought fresh water to my thirsty heart and soul. Your touch has ignited a certain passion in me that has never been there before. How I wish that you are here with me. That we are not separated by distance and constraints and necessities of life. But even though we are distance apart, in my heart, soul, and mind you are always here, alive, breathing, and touching my life. There's no word that can describe how much I love you since you have already conquered that whole essence of me. My son is not released yet. I know you believe that good things come to those who wait. I know you are asking why does the wait have to come with all these obstacles of hard and testing times? All I have right now are my dreams of you, so I will close now to dream of us, and wait for that precious tomorrow when I can wake up to my dream come true—YOU!! Stay strong, Baby, and I will always love you. Thank you for loving me.

Love Always,
Joe

Good to know you guys are doing so well. I miss you Honey. Ever since you walked into my life, I have been smiling. There hasn't been a day when I have gone to sleep with a frown on my face, and it's all because of you. Honey, I am glad that you came into my life. I have always wanted the love of my life to be understanding, loving, caring, faithful and most of all someone who would accept me for who I am. I love you with my whole heart. I have never trusted anyone the way I trust you. I always thought love was only in movies and songs till I met you, my love. To my surprise what you make me feel every day is the inspiration. I thank you with all my heart for being the most important part of my life, for being my wife, for with you my soul is everlasting and my love is eternal. I'm yours forever, not just for this lifetime but for whatever else follows. I love you. Thank you honey for everything. I pray to God every day to bless you with everything you deserve. I will love you until the end of time. Always and Forever Yours,

Love…
Joe

I know it is difficult for you, as it is for me. Life seems to be full of trials of this type which test our inner strength, and more importantly, our devotion and love for one another. After all, it is said that "True Love" is boundless and immeasurable and overcomes all forms of adversity. In truth, if it is genuine, it will grow stronger with each assault upon its existence. I have not heard from the Banker and the CC Financial yet... I cherish any thought of you, prize any memory of you that rises from the depths of my mind, and live for the day when our physical separation will no longer be. Until that moment arrives, I send to you across the miles, my tender love, my warm embrace, and my most passionate kiss. Will let you know when I hear from the Banker okay.

Love always...
Joe

Honey I miss you and the CC financial will call you. But please let me know as soon as he calls okay. I want you in my life. I love you more and more with each day passing and it eases me to know as tomorrow approaches, that I will love you more than yesterday and tomorrow will be more than today. My love for you cannot be measured by words alone as love does express my true feelings for you. I want you and always will and there is nothing that will ever change the way I feel about you... I love you!

Love always,
Joe

You and only you have given me so much hope and have made me realize how much I want you! You show the true meaning of how a woman should treat a man. God Bless you.

Love,
Joe

Okay my love, God is with us my love; just listen to Andrew and update me whatever goes ok? Love you. How is everyone?

Joe

You mean a lot to me. Your happiness and wellness also mean a lot to me. So, please get well soon. We may all get sick but it is difficult to see someone nice as you are suffering. Get well soon, darling! And Please, Everything will be alright. Let's believe in God for this move and everything will be fine... Yes I do trust Mr Andrew. All you have to do is follow whatever he tells you my love and make sure you tell me as well...and we will do better... I love you and I feel already Home... Happy to have you in my life! Thank you for your friendship and for being there when I need you. Whenever I am down, I can think of you and it seems to work. Thank you. May God Bless you and always give you the strength for you to continue to grow and love. Love you always and more...

Joe

John 14:27 "I am leaving you with a gift—peace of mind and heart. And the peace I give is a gift the world cannot give. So don't be troubled or afraid. I am so lucky to have you in my life. I adore and love you so much. Thank you for being an exceptional woman—you are one of a kind. Love you… I am sorry my love… Will talk more with you tonight. Andrew is calling so calm down and listen to what he is saying. I love you… Thank you for loving me despite my shortcomings and emotional roller coastering. Thank you for being an exceptional woman! love always… I want you to know how pleased I am to be a part of your life, how much it means to me to know I'll always be in love with you and only you! Keep praying us and we will do better.

Love you…
Joe

I miss you and I am sick now… Too much going on right now… I'm getting sick and just do not understand Andrew…too. Honey… I will be online early in the Morning okay.

Love you,
Joe

I know somewhere down the road things will change but for right now we have to be patient. No matter what we did wrong to one another, we've always made it through and that just goes to show my love for you. I just want you to know I love you and always will.

Yours truly,
Joe

Whenever life seems to drift you away from me, I can't help but cry. You've grown to be such a part of me that without you life is no more than a desperate sigh. They do say love comes and goes, and to that I disagree. So, here's my hand, take it and don't let go of me. Honey I am getting sick over all this. Andrew is not answering my calls… and I have not gotten the money and the Items you sent yet. I am worried…what are we going to do?

Love,
Joe

I know I have made a silly mistake by trusting Andrew… I was introduced to him by a friend since I needed help and thought I could trust him… I got only 2,500 from Him…nothing else—meaning he took everything and I am finding it hard to believe this happened to us. That is why I am getting sick and very shy to even correspond with you… I am sorry. I love you, I love you, I love you. Please forgive me, for I'm afraid I can never forgive myself. When did you send the 5,600?

Love,
Joe

Thoughts of you warm my heart like a moon lit summer night.

Love,
Joe

God's elect must be unshakable in these end times. There is nothing to shake about. God is on the throne, and you are HIS servant. God gives you the gifts you need to deal with anything, including the antichrist. Moreover, I am amazed at GOD'S trust that I am able to help you. I pray that GOD WILL SHOW favor on me, with this loan. and GOD WILL SHOW FAVOR with you. To love me, and be my helpmeet. I seek HIS WILL for my life. So, I go armed for battle, and knowing that I will seek GOD'S Unshakable ROCK. as my support. I will not be scared. well, at least I will try very hard to not show my fear. All things work together for good for those who Love GOD and are called according to HIS WILL.

Joe

I have had a rough time; sorry for not getting in touch. Nearly lost my son, But thank God for his miracles. His love endures forever…how is it going with you and I really miss you Thinking of you…

Love,
Joe…

A rainbow ahead of you… I wish you a day of happiness and perfection, little bite-size pieces of perfection that give you the funny feeling that the Lord is smiling on you, holding you so gently because you are someone special and rare. Good Morning…

Joe

"Never will I leave you; never will I forsake you." (Hebrews 13:5) "I will sprinkle clean water on you, and you will be clean; I will cleanse you from all your impurities and from all your idols." (Ezekiel 36:25)... A righteous man will be remembered forever. He will have no fear of bad news; his heart is steadfast, trusting in the LORD. His heart is secure, he will have no fear; in the end he will look in triumph on his foes. (Psalm 112:6–8) Commit your way to the LORD; trust in Him and He will do this: He will make your righteousness shine like the dawn, the justice of your cause like the noonday sun. (Psalm 37:5–6) Before they call I will answer; while they are still speaking I will hear. (Isaiah 65:24) Because God wanted to make the unchanging nature of His purpose very clear to the heirs of what was promised, He confirmed it with an oath...it is impossible for God to lie, we who have fled to take hold of the hope offered to us may be greatly encouraged. We have this hope as an anchor for the soul, firm and secure... (Hebrews 6:17–19) "Come now, let us reason together," says the LORD. "Though your sins are like scarlet, they shall be as white as snow; though they are red as crimson, they shall be like wool." (Isaiah 1:18) Surely God is my salvation; I will trust and not be afraid. The LORD, the LORD, is my strength and my song; He has become my salvation. (Isaiah 12:2) The LORD Almighty has sworn, "Surely, as I have planned, so it will be, and as I have purposed, so it will stand." (Isaiah 14:24) In that day they will say, "Surely this is our God; we trusted in Him, and He saved us. This is the LORD, we trusted in Him; let us rejoice and be glad in His salvation." (Isaiah 25:9) You will keep in perfect peace him whose mind is steadfast, because he trusts in you. Trust in the LORD forever, for the LORD, the LORD is the Rock eternal. (Isaiah 26:3–4) This is what the Sovereign LORD says: "See, I lay a stone in Zion, a tested stone, a precious corner-stone for a sure foundation; the one who trusts will never be dismayed." (Isaiah 28:16) He tends His flock like a shepherd: He gathers the lambs in His arms and carries them close to His heart; He gently leads those that have young. (Isaiah 40:11) But those who hope in the LORD will renew their strength. They will soar on wings like eagles; they will run and not grow weary, they will walk and not be faint. (Isaiah 40:31) "So do not fear, for I am with you; do not be dismayed, for I am your God. I will strengthen you and help you; I will uphold you with my righteous right hand." (Isaiah 41:10)

My son is able to speak today. The Lord is with us… Am so sorry for the financial inconvenience… Andrew has an answer someday, God is watching.

Yours…

Joe

How are you doing? I have been sick and admitted at the hospital myself…and that is why you have never heard from me my dear… How are you…well I am still in London and want my Banker to pay some money, but please do not use your account please…just open a new account here   http://payments.intuit.com/paymentnet-work-electronic-invoicing-online-bill-payment/

Please let me know when you are done… Will be with you soon… Son is now under surgery... We are doing fine now... God will make a way... Love and thinking of you...

Take care...
David

I made the Doctor write it for me. He is David because I'm sick on the bed. Yes my dear create account at http://www.paysimple.com And I will pay some money into it for you to pay some of the debt, do this ASAP... Love you. Good they closed all account; I will never forgive Andrew. Well if you're having problem with that bank, then try and open at Wellsfargo bank. Let me know what happens. Missing you.

Yes I am still in London my dear. Son nearly died, but I thank the lord for his mercies and loving kindness and his healing abilities... Well what is your bank? Thank you. Kisses & hugs.

My dear please... You have to work on opening the account I told you. Try it online. Wells Fargo prepaid and www.popmoney.com... Open this too please, do it online, your account is not accepting payment. Thank you honey...

Love,
Joe

Good... But will need the Login and Password asap to check on each transfer they wire ok... I love you and miss you.

Love
Joe

I know how you feel, but I am not giving the password to anyone. I also want to know the transfer, you think what Andrew did does not affect me? Can only continue this when I have the login and password. Thank you…

Yours,
Joe

No way, I think transfer per transaction at popmoney.com would take a limit of 4000 and yes am not giving the login to anyone. I promise… Did I tell you I'm flying to Ghana, because my friend Pastor got the Information and where we can find the Person you sent the packages to. What is the Name again? I wish your Dad speedy recovery my dear…

Love,
Joe

We have come a long way my dear and will also love to be with you honey. I need you. I want you and still love you. Right now am in London and flying to Ghana on Tuesday. Will fly back the following week hopefully when all is done here.

Love you…
Joe

Honey I will need your address in case I am flying there my dear… Okay…

I miss you.
Joe

Thank you so much my love. Yes I arrived in Ghana this morning and thank you for your message. I live and appreciate this so much. Payment will be made to pop money next week. Ok... Love and thinking of you... Keep me in prayers...

Love,
Joe

How are you my dear, I really miss you and things are not so easy down here in Ghana, honey am sorry, the transfer is taking Long because the Banker also want the login. It's because I promise never to give out. So I did not, but honey pen http://www.paysimple.com/ online and please do not use your existing account details please... Do this ASAP because I need money urgent for the Attorney here... The investigation is going on so well. We thank God. I do miss you and hope to be with you soon.

Yours...
Joe...

I am very sorry for how you're feeling... I am short of words. I feel very hurt... I'm not sure how you understood my last email... I said I did not give to them and so I told them I need no help from them... Well I have told a Financial Co to send you a cheque... That will be fine... Thank you for you help... God bless you... Bye... Joe

I am so Sorry B, I have not been too well. Being in Africa has been a hell for me... I was affected with a skin disease, But I thank God that am recovering… My Son is not too well too… Please am sending you a link open an account… do it as Stated. I will let my Banker send you some fund in there… Thank you!!! God bless you and check below: *http://www.nationalbankcard. com/*

How are you doing and hope the Lord is taking good care of you. I am sorry you have not heard from me all this while. I really care about you, but the means is a problem now; since Andrew has brought a lot of financial debt that Creditors are after me and all that; besides my son is so sick once again. I really care for you. Take care…

Joe

CONCENTRATE. Keep your eyes on the prize. Take charge of your choices and actions. You can't do everything at the same time. You can't please everybody. Losers run in all directions. In the game of life, WINNERS FOCUS THEIR ENERGIES. You're a winner; CONCENTRATE. Prioritize. Stay on track. Don't dwell on faults and failures; CORRECT YOUR MISTAKES AND MOVE ON. When the night is dark, FOCUS ON GOD'S LIGHT. When you find yourself in the valley, LIFT UP YOUR EYES TO THE HILLS. The Lord is your keeper. He is your light. SEEK DIVINE WISDOM. He will provide. He will guide. You have what it takes. CONCENTRATE AND WIN THE GAME!

Joe

YOUR FRIENDS SHAPE YOUR DESTINY. LAZY FRIENDS divert vision. FOCUSED FRIENDS direct vision. Some friends add to you; others take away. BE A FRIEND WHO ADDS. Release those who subtract. To win in life you need these friends: 1.MORAL GUIDES—those who help you do the right thing. 2.FAITH BUILDERS—those who believe in you and in your potential. 3.DREAM MAKERS—those who create opportunities and help you achieve your dreams. Do your friends celebrate when you win? Are they envious of your achievements? Remember: FRIENDSHIP IS NOT BY FORCE; it's by choice. RELEASE the dream killers. TREASURE the dream makers. MAY GOD BLESS YOU WITH TRUE FRIENDS!

Joe

To summarize, Joe lived in Corpus Christi, Texas. The address was verified along with the phone number, and once again, when I shared what had happened to me about previous scammers, he wanted to make it right so that I never was taken advantage of again. On his way to meet me, his son (who was suffering from leukemia) was in London and was rushed to the hospital. I told him he had to turn around and go to him. He could not let his son go through this all alone. So he did just that, called, webcammed, and reported on the Olympics, which were being held in London at the time. He spent all his money to help his son but needed a loan. I not only paid for the ticket for his caregiver to stay with his son and care for him. I gave him information on my credit cards in case he had an emergency. He gave this information to his banker, who chose to swindle me in more ways than one. I had fallen and hurt my back and was on pain medicine at the time. In three days, not only were computers and electronics charged to my credit cards, but cash deposits were made to pay off those cards, only to be returned ten days later for nonsufficient funds. So my credit cards were quickly run up to over one hundred thousand owed. Needless to say, all credit card accounts were closed and restricted. Joe called and informed me that he was swindled as well because he received only part of the money I had given to his banker. The banker was in New York, and the banks could not help me retrieve any of the money he had stolen.

One year almost passed before I heard from Joe once more. The following is part of the IM we had.

> J: Hello My Savior…
>
> B: I was really surprised to hear from you
>
> J: I really miss you more and more. I want to thank you for all you did for me and my Son. Unfortunately life has been unfair. He could not exist for long as Dr predicted… You are a very loving person to be remembered all the time.
>
> B: When did your son die? Were you alone with him when it happened? And was he able to know you were there with him?
>
> J: He died on the 6th March 2013. I tried to get to you on many occasions but to no avail.
>
> B: I can imagine the pain you must feel every time you think of it. I know it doesn't go away
>
> J: These are the feelings I am having for you as of this moment. Missing you
>
> B: I'll bet you even grew a beard while you were on all your travels. Did you tell me you ARE in Texas now? And you even remember our falling hearts.
>
> J: I am in VA
>
> B: You still have that romantic streak in you
>
> J: cannot be in TX now… I am doing hide and seek until am sort with the Bank…

B: So close to where I was for 3 months while I was in WV. Then I was 4 months in Louisiana with my daughter. I understand dear. You have to do what you have to do. I am still amazed you got ahold of me. I am even thinking I did see that number before and wondered who it was.

J: You are so special to me

B: I guess I am surprised you are able to have any feelings for anyone after losing someone so precious to you. That kind of pain goes so very deep. And I of course have put up a thick protective wall around me because I was so hurt.

J: I have to get going and will call you later tonight... Do you have plans?

B: No I will be here. So good luck in your travels. You can call and we can im some more if you like. Talk to you later. Take care and God Bless. You have me smiling again

J: God bless you too...and me too... Later

*****

That was the last communication I had with Joe. Of course after our text, I wanted to believe he truly existed and was not at fault for the financial destruction caused by his banker. But in order to move on with my life, I had to put him in a box and lay that box aside with it locked and the key to it thrown away.

CHAPTER 14

The Heart Tries to Heal

By now, I needed to take a trip home to West Virginia and clear out the cobwebs in my head. I needed to be surrounded by those I loved and trusted and maybe figure out how to fix the problem I had caused for myself. I had become such an easy target for those of the opposite sex to take advantage of. I knew for sure I no longer wanted to be a victim. I only wanted to be a survivor. The only way I knew how to make that happen was to go somewhere where I believed in myself again. After visiting all my friends and loved ones in West Virginia, I took a trip to Chicago to see my old classmate from high school. I ended up telling him everything I had gone through and asked him to help me seek divine intervention to get through all that was ahead for me. Not only did he help me to reach the inner peace I longed for inside, but he offered to extend his help and services emotionally, spiritually, mentally, socially, and financially. Would I expect anything less from him? He has always and will always be the one that had complete faith in me, in my actions, in my thoughts, and my will to serve God, and yet it took over forty years for us to find one another again. He stood by me. And I can honestly say that I never felt judged by him, no matter what.

My father was ninety-three years old. His health was failing. My two sisters spent a lot of time taking care of him as well as rushing him to emergency room time and time again. The last two years had been difficult for everyone. When I visited him during the summer, he requested my help to write a new will to ensure that his wife would be taken care of if something were to happen to him. They had been married well over thirty years, and he wanted to thank her for standing by him during that time. I not only prepared his will but made sure a witness was present as he had me write down his wishes. I then drove him to the bank to make sure everything was legal and notarized. It was good to get back to Almost Heaven, West Virginia, the beginning of all my roots. After visiting with previous coworkers and friends, my attitude was positive, and I seemed to have gained enough energy and endurance to face what was lying ahead for me.

After my trip to Chicago in the fall, I returned to West Virginia to attend a wedding for a member of my family and spent even more time with my father. He found the strength not only to attend the wedding of his grandchild but to attend her reception as well. She had a picture taken with all his family to commemorate the occasion. That was the last group picture he took, but one he was very proud of. I remember his staring at that picture and showing it to visitors who stopped in to see him. One month later, I received the call from my sisters to come home—the call that I knew would come one day. My father had been admitted to the hospital, and they weren't sure he was going to be able to return home. I knew that my father's time was getting short and I needed to be there. I also knew that if he thought his time was near, he would ask me to come be with him. You see, we had made this agreement ahead of time. I also made the same agreement with my sisters. If he did become able to return home, I knew I was needed to take care of him. I was assisting my daughter in her move from South Carolina to Louisiana at the time, so I dropped everything and traveled to West Virginia the next day to take care of my loving and ailing father. He had been released by the hospital by the time I arrived. My sister made arrangements for a hospital bed to be placed in his bedroom so that it was easier to take care of him. My brothers worked together to take up the carpet in the bedroom so that the wood flooring would be more sanitary for spills and accidents. Dad seemed to appreciate all the effort and knew that his family loved him because they were always there for him, no matter what.

It's kind of odd to witness unconditional love yet alone feel it. But that is exactly what I felt for my father. I didn't recognize it at first because I had never received it (except from my friend in Chicago). Let me be clear. I did not feel that kind of love from my mother or father or his new wife. Nor did I feel that kind of love from my children nor either husband. But I did recognize that kind of love. And it came from my heart for my father. Every action I took and every thought that I had were made in his best interest. Whether it included giving him a bath, wiping his behind, dressing him, massaging his body with healing cream or lotion, or bringing him something to eat, my only hope was that he could feel and receive that every action or decision made by me and given to him were given out of love. I never had to think twice, and I felt so honored to be able to spend the last two months of his life with him. There were times that he took his anger out on me and made me feel like I was not wanted. One time, he even told me to go back to Texas. I wasn't needed here with him. I knew he didn't mean it. But having his blood run through me, I tested him and said I would leave. He quickly made his wishes known that he was only missing me when I took a little break, and his anger came out toward me in the wrong way. Of course, he wanted me to stay.

I remember the day I arrived to help him, and his wife told me that she didn't need my help and she didn't want me there. So the only way I could respond was tell her that my dad wanted me there and he needed me. It was hard coming in that door each and every day knowing I was unwanted by her. As my sister-in-law and I prepared meals the night before for me to take to him, I could witness his strength and appetite improving. But make no mistake, there were days he wanted to eat nothing and drink nothing. And just about every time that happened, his condition declined.

Just as I was able to spend the last year of my mother's life with her, taking her for chemotherapy each week, I was able to spend the last two months of my father's life with him, getting to know him so much better than I previously had done. I am still in awe of the fact that not only did he fight in World War II, but he actually survived. He was part of the Eighty-Second Airborne, and he arrived in Europe in a glider. He loved telling stories about that time in his life. Since mom and my brother died, he had become very emotional about those events.

The war in Iraq touched him in ways we could not imagine. But making sure he survived each day, he sought help from the Veterans Administration and attended counseling every week to treat the PTSD he had developed. That is, until he became bedridden and did not have the strength to go anywhere but to the doctor. The support group there gave him the strength he needed to cope as the world we live in became more and more unstable.

We made arrangements for him to receive physical therapy two times a week to assist him in being able to walk again without falling. A nurse usually came once or twice a week also. We had access to a twenty-four-hour hotline to call the nurse when we were concerned about his health or other issues he would have. Even that service was something his wife did not want to accept. As I look back now, I wonder how much of her attitude was about being in denial of his present condition. Eventually, we had to make arrangements for meals on wheels to be delivered to him so that we could measure more accurately what he was eating.

Going to the bathroom was a major effort for him to accomplish. Some days, if he was unable to go, his whole day centered around the success of being able to have a bowel movement. If he did not have one, he became very cranky. Watching his medication and keeping note of what went in his body and what came out became very important to monitor for all his caregivers.

One thing about my father though was that when he was feeling okay, his outlook was always positive, and he still demanded a hug from any female who walked into the house. He would pride himself on all the relationships he had with women. His mind was sharp. And anyone could have long and hard conversations with him, and he would enjoy telling lots of stories about his past and his family. This man loved his family. He just had a little trouble showing it before my mother passed away. It took that to happen for him to realize how important his family was to him. He actually lived each day to be able to see and enjoy the company of his five children and their children now. I remember the last Christmas he was able to attend. He wasn't feeling well but knew in his heart that this might be his last one spent with the family, so he got dressed and agreed to come over to my sister-in-law's house for Christmas. That is where I stayed while visiting him and taking care of him. He was able to stay for two or three hours and enjoyed every minute of it. He also ate a pretty good meal that day. He loved my sister's potato salad.

My father died a couple weeks later after that Christmas. By taking care of him, my thoughts and worries dissipated from all the men in my life that I hadn't met in person, men who took my financial and emotional stability and slammed it into the ground. But I took those instabilities of mine and pushed them to the side, so nothing was priority to me but taking care of my father. His care and his stability mattered most to me. And when that day came that God chose to take him, I knew I would have no regrets. I was able to help him clear his conscience by forgiving others and accepting God as his savior before he left us. I was able to ask two preachers to visit him. He did not seem to connect to the first one, so we tried one that had gotten us through other family crises during past years. The pastor was able to spend the last couple days of his life with Dad and helped him to prepare for heaven. That was the greatest gift he could give to me and I could give to him. Yes, that tiny glimpse of unconditional love reassured me enough to know that I too could make it when facing the most difficult of circumstances.

The funeral was over, and it was time for me to go back home to Texas. I wasn't home very long before my daughter who, was expecting twins, requested my assistance in Louisiana. Her doctor was going to put her on bed rest to ensure that the twins would make it to full-term without a problem. Once more, I packed my bags, and off to Louisiana I went to be a caregiver. It was time for me to give that cherished and unknown unconditional love to my daughter and to the twins growing inside of her. She needed me. And in some odd way, after losing my father, I needed her too. Each day, I would pray that the two of us could get past all the hurt and the pain of the past. She was unable to attend Dad's funeral because of her high-risk pregnancy, but that didn't mean she didn't share the grief that I did.

In fact, she was never able to talk to me about her feelings concerning that. Even as my granddaughter and son-in-law watched the memorial dedication to my father on DVD, she chose not to participate. Sometimes, I felt like a robot doing my job, a job that was not satisfactory to her liking. But the last thing I ever wanted to do was to cause her stress and anguish, which could affect the outcome of the pregnancy, so I made myself endure many harsh words and criticism from her because I knew that in her own way, this was how she was dealing with the grief inside of her.

I also knew that because the two of us were unable to connect or communicate on an intimate level, the stress or anguish being developed between us would just get worse instead of better. What should have been the most wonderful time of our lives (spending time with her and her family, including a six-year-old granddaughter), the five months I spent there was less than perfect. It was very difficult for us to get past everything that had happened to her in the past, and she never hesitated to remind me of that.

I wanted both of our hearts to heal, and all I could do was pray to God each day that he would find a soft spot in her heart to help her release all the bitterness and anger toward me. I thought things would change once the twins were born, but in many ways, the relationship got worse. I had difficulty talking with her, and the pain that developed as a result of this grew stronger and stronger between the two of us. So when I found out that the in-laws were coming to visit, I decided this was a good time for me to go home and take a break. During the time I was there, I chose not to tell her of the medical problems I was having. I knew she needed me and depended upon my help. I also knew if she knew how much I needed to see my doctors, she would stop me from driving her daughter to and from school and other activities, which she was unable to do for herself. Each day, I prayed to God for more strength to help me get through one day at a time. I knew that once I was back in Texas, I would put priority on my health and try to get as much assistance from all my doctors as I could. Stress was contributing to her condition declining, and it was rapidly contributing to my condition deteriorating also.

After returning to Texas and talking to her on the phone, she confirmed my suspicions that things had not changed between us, so I felt it was better for both of us that I not return to Louisiana to assist her with the twins. She would be returning to work shortly and taking them to day care, so I thought the timing was right. But I was wrong once more. She resented me for not coming back to assist her with the new babies. And that resentment continued to grow. She resented it when I went back to my room between 9:00 to 10:00 p.m. each night when she needed help. She didn't accept or realize that if I didn't retire to my room at that time to debrief and take my medication, I would not be able to start the next day first thing in the morning and drive her daughter to school. She resented it when I talked on the phone to others when I could be helping her. She resented my using the house phone because she needed to talk to her husband when I was using the phone. She resented that I kept in touch with my ex-husband, whom she despised. She resented me talking to my sisters because she thought I was feeding them lots of untruths, which would turn them against her. She felt they did not go out of their way anymore to welcome her when she made visits back to West Virginia. She resented my talking to my friend in Chicago.

Resentment turned into anger and bitterness. I'm not sure that she will ever be able to forgive me for all that she is angry about. But I have to realize that my heart has to heal. If left in its present condition, it would dry up and become cold. If I couldn't get support and understanding from her, I needed to put some distance between us.

I love each one of my grandchildren and would give them or my children the shirt off my back. Any time I am with them, whether in person or on FaceTime, my heart begins to melt, and that is as close to healing as I can get. I know they are good for me because they are so innocent and untouched by judgment or criticism. So when I have a drop of depression set in, I call my grandchildren in hopes of Skyping, and watching them for a few minutes gives me a new lease on life.

CHAPTER 15

Believing in the Rescue

Memories of being scammed by Jerome, John, George, and Joe haunted me as I spent hours each day wondering what my future was going to be if none of these men ever came through to pay back the money I had loaned them. What if they were scamming me? I seemed to be thinking with my heart and not my head as denial of the circumstances affecting me continued to increase instead of going away. Admitting to myself that all these men simply used me was one of the hardest things I've ever had to do. Living in denial was a lot easier than accepting what I knew would probably ruin my life and my relationships with my children and family. Giving up on the prospect of having a secure and meaningful future threatened my very existence. How was I going to get out of this mess I was in without harming those I loved?

And then it happened. I remembered that one day I received an email from another person on datehookup.com. He sounded interesting enough, was very polite, and definitely sounded like God was a number one priority in his life. But he lived in Wyoming. Why would I ever want to correspond with someone that far away when I knew there was no chance of us ever being together? He seemed to be interested in me as a person. So I thought, why not? It was okay to have someone as a friend or pen pal just to unload or even share your thoughts and worries to, if nothing else. Lord knows I could use an honest friend. I responded to Roland by saying "Why would you want to even think about dating me if you live in Wyoming?"

Yet I knew from the past that reaching out to someone who is a short distance from you is no different from reaching out to someone who is a long distance from you. This person was more than special, but at the time, I wasn't sure why. This time, we only communicated by email and by phone. Every time we talked, it was as if we had known each other for years. I loved talking to him on the phone. He even asked me to sign up for Skype so we could see each other. Not being experienced enough, I thought you had to pay a subscription to use Skype to communicate. Now that I know differently, I wish I would have done that right away. By keeping in touch so often, it wasn't long before I was spoiled by receiving a phone call from him each and every day. This was truly a man of honor. It was as if our hearts melted the whole time we were talking. We had such a special connection. I felt as though I was back in high school and this wonderful boy was courting me. I felt so carefree and alive. For a moment, I even forgot that I had been scammed by the other suitors. Every time we talked, I felt as if this man would never hurt me, and if he did, it would not be intentional. He would only protect me. And I knew that I would do the same for him. What we shared with one another was entirely effortless. I had never felt safer. And I made sure he knew that if I ever hurt him, it would not be intentional either, only by an act of ignorance or accident.

After that first contact when he asked me how I was doing and if I noticed that he had winked at me on datehookup, well, it was a nice way to begin. He also told me to have a blessed Sunday and hoped to hear from me soon. I want to take time now to share this man with you. Meet my Roland.

> Hello BB… I hope you are really enjoying your day. Well I would like us to know each other better and probably we can just work everything out… I wouldn't mind relocating for the right relationship because no distance of place or lapse of time can lessen the friendship of those who are thoroughly persuaded of each other's worth.

Please let me know if you got this message. I want to know if I got the email right...

Hugs, Roland

Good evening Sweetheart... It's always a pleasure to read a message from you every morning and I enjoyed reading every bit of it. And thanks for taking all this time to write that long email about yourself. I am generally an optimistic person with a great sense of humor, fairly easy-going, and I don't think that I'm too critical about things, but I also believe that it takes two people contributing to a relationship to make it work. Our correspondence tells me we do share a lot in common and when enough attention is given something better might result. You have a lot of passion in your soul. I can tell by the way you write. It's wonderful. You sound very passionate, considerate and sweet. I like to think of the world as a big treasure map. The treasure can be found anywhere. That is how I view life. There just aren't that many people who know how to find the treasure. Life can be enjoyed in so many ways. Friends, traveling, culture are all links to the "treasure" of life.

Well my day has been really pretty good. I had a very busy day and am planning to go to the pool tomorrow, then on to shopping in the afternoon. I also call my kids on the weekend and check up on them. I think they are doing great and learning very hard. I really love my kids. They are really wonderful kids and I know you will like them when you meet them. I hope you had a blessed day and everyone is doing great there. I hope to hear from you soon. What are your plans for tomorrow?

Big hugs and kisses, Roland FOREVER AND FOR ALWAYS

Hi BB... Here is my profile. My picture is attached. I am an honest and good Christian who loves being surrounded by family and friends. I love working in the garden, cooking, playing golf and being around a couple of friends. I like to exercise 3–4 days a week. I enjoy watching action movies and romantic comedies. I like TV shows that make me laugh. I look for easy listening music on the radio. I love dogs. I like kids and they generally like me too. I live life as it comes to me every day and take my time to live in it. I am looking for a committed relationship, a soul mate and a companion—someone who will love me and love everything of me. Honesty is the most important quality in a mate. I'm also looking for dependability and a good sense of humor. I don't look at the outside so much as the inside. I want a woman who cares about others and is kind and loving, knows how to have fun, and is even tempered.

If you are a consistent, loyal, and a genuinely good person, we might enjoy knowing each other, and beyond that...who knows?

We continued to communicate as if it was not only the right thing to do, but because it seemed natural for both of us. We found ourselves being both intrigued as well as enamored with one another.

Hello BB... It is always a pleasure to read a message from you. How are you and everyone doing? I have been a little busy lately and am so sorry I did not reply to you earlier. I do understand and share your view as well. We sure did meet on the internet and no amount of talking on here will help in anyway more than meeting in person and getting to know each other to see if we have that physical connection and chemistry. I do believe we will go a long way to make our relationship work if we really are that interested in each other. I also knew distance would be a problem, but I would love to relocate if things would work out between us. Because despite the fact that I don't know much about you, I have the feeling that we both have a lot in common and we will get along just fine. I have been a widower and started dating three years after I lost my wife. I was involved with one lady for close to a year when things started falling apart. I later found out she was involved with another man that she had been dating for close to three years and was only using me. We had a terrible breakup. I do know how much it hurts to be in a relationship that you put in your all and later realize that everything you put into it was all a waste of time and attention. But that doesn't hold me down because I know there is someone out there that would love me for who I am and not for what I can give them. You are an independent woman and I am really proud of you. I want us to take things one step at a time, but I need to let you know that I am not on here for games and hope you are not either. We both deserve better than what we have been through. There are better days ahead. Hope you had a blessed day. I can't wait to hear from you soon.

Hugs, Roland

Good afternoon... How are you doing and how is your day going? I just had a break and decided to check up on my email. I am taking in a pineapple juice by myself. We had a storm over night and think we will have it again. How is yours there? Actually I lost my dog a few months ago so it's just me at my lonely home listening to music. What is your favorite music? I didn't know about your going to visit your Dad and family, but I think it's really nice to see them and as you said; it is also your Dad's birthday. Would we be communicating while you are there? Can I also call you on the phone sometime if you don't mind? I wish you all the best and hope to hear from you soon. Have a blessed day.

I care, Hugs... Roland

Good morning... How are you doing and how is your day going? I guess you really enjoy the raindrops on your skin. I wish I were there to accompany you to Walmart. I want to share every moment with you and share your life ideas with you. Just a little about my work—I do most of my work at home, but I do travel sometimes. I have been to most of the states and Canada, Australia and Ukraine. I like to get my hands dirty in the yard and like to go to the beach and relax listening to music. I do most of the fun things when my kids are back for vacation. I have really missed them very much after reading your message. Do you also like to travel and where have you been? I will end here and get back to work. I hope you have a blessed day and hope to hear from you soon.

Missing you, Hugs and kisses... Roland

Good Afternoon Sweetie... I am sorry for my late response. How is everything going, now that you have called everyone to check up on them? I have been worried after I read the message. All we need to do is to pray for them so everyone will be hailed in the name of Jesus. Well my work took me to all these countries, and it was just fun, but I didn't have much time to visit or look around in the countries. I am planing on going to vacation at Niagara Falls. Have you been there before? I wish you all the best and hope to hear from you soon. Hugs and kisses, Roland

Good Evening Sweetheart... Sorry for my late reply. I had an appointment so I was really busy. I'm just relaxing and taking some pineapple juice to take my stress away. I really missed you. How are you and everyone doing now? How is your weekend going? I hope you have already started going for shopping for Daddy's birthday.

Well I have been into this work for almost 30 years and I really enjoy it very much. I don't always travel outside the state very much, until it is very important or an emergency so I need to be there. I really loved to live here in Wyoming. Lusk is just a small town in the 1,479 population. But it is a very beautiful place to live and I am trying my best to invest and set up with an estate project here. I hope you will one day come over and see how beautiful this place is. Well I will end here and have a little rest. Do have a blessed weekend and I hope to hear from you soon. Hugs and kisses.

Take Care... Roland

Good morning... I hope you had a good sleep last night. Have you seen my profile and my picture now? Have a blessed day and hope to hear from you soon. I care, Hugs... Roland

I miss you Sweetheart. I'm just here thinking about you, like I always do now. I hope you're as happy as me; night is almost here again. The thought of you in my arms right now sounds so good to me. How was your day and hope you had a nice weather today. We are having storms here and they are keeping me indoors... I am missing you and hope to hear from you soon.

Hugs and Kisses, Roland

Good Morning Sweetheart... I am so glad everyone is doing well now. How are you doing this morning? Well I don't have grand kids; my children haven't married yet, so I would be going to the Niagara Falls with them. I think I would let them come around so we can go together. I have an appointment this afternoon, and am getting ready for it. How is your day starting today? Have a blessed day and hope to hear from you soon.

Hugs and kisses... Roland

Good Morning B... How are you and everyone doing? It's a beautiful morning here and the thought of you is still on my mind.

Well would I still be hearing from you while you are gone or hope you don't mind if I have your phone number? I am home now getting ready for work and will be going for an appointment this afternoon... I am in Electrical Engineering and also into buying and renewing dead companies. I hope you had a blessed weekend and hope to hear from you soon.

Hugs and kisses, Roland

Good Morning Sweetheart... It's a beautiful day again. How are you doing and how is your day starting up today? I will be with you till you get home safe. I will be right here waiting for you honey. Please take good care of yourself and drive safely. Have a lovely journey.

Wish you all the best. I care...

Hugs... Roland

Good Morning My Angel... How are you doing this blessed morning? I hope you slept well. I am so happy you are having lots of fun with your family and friends. Most of my family are gone, and I only have few left in Italy. My only best friend cheated on me with my ex girl friend and I only have business friends in my life now. My life has been really sad and I want to start over with a new family and friends now. I can't wait to have you back home so we can talk more and know each other better. Have a blessed day and hope to hear from you soon...

Hugs and kisses... Roland

Good Morning Sweetheart... Thanks for the eloquent mail. I was elated by when I received it and it definitely made my day start with such a bright outlook. You have a sweet and sexy voice. lol. I am glad you are doing great now and I know God will bring you back to Texas safely okay.

My birthday is 24/11 and yours? I wasn't able to come back home yesterday. I had almost two appointments and the last took me so long so I needed to wait. I love what I do very much because it keeps me busy and helps to take care of my kids. I promised their mom that I was going to take good care of them till they are able to take care of themselves. I love dogs very much, but lost mine a few months ago when I went away for a business trip. I will be shopping this weekend. I love to cook by myself and I always have something in the fridge if I have time when I come back home. I have always believed in Jesus, but in my childhood, I would never spend any time praying or reading scripture. I used to spend most of my day with bad company, even though God through Jesus has done so many great things in my life! I am a catholic and you? I will end here and hope to hear from you soon. Have a blessed day...

Hugs and Kisses, Roland

Hi Honey... It's the end of the day and I was thinking about you, as usual. I want you to know how much I sincerely love the times we have spent talking. It means so much to me. It truly seems like I've known you forever and I honestly can't imagine life without you now. Sometimes life hits you with unexpected things that take you totally by surprise. All I can say is you're the best surprise life has given me. I hope you had a blessed day. Hope to hear from you soon.

Missing you… Roland

Hi Sweetheart… How are you doing and how is your day going on? I hope your day has been the best so far… Just came back home from town and wanted to check up on you… I am always happy when I am reading your message. You really sound very honest and loyal. I know we are far apart, but I do know that someday will be the blessed day for you and I. We both have to work things together and make it happen.

I wish I were with someone that I can do things with—someone I can watch the sunset with, go on a carriage ride with through the park, cook your favorite meals for you, wipe away the days' stresses and issues, with just one hug or kiss, gently run my hand across your cheek and look into your eyes.

What matters most is our honesty and trust for this relationship to work out. If it is really love, we can see each other standing in our eyes, part of the abstinence that is worth dying for. If you long for that recognition that will not part by distance, in time our dream will be replied. Distance is just a test to see how far love can travel. Distance—it is a test of love. Many will fail, but for those who can withstand it—they have the answer for true love. All quality items must be tested to ensure promised high standards for the customers.

I would like to go the kitchen and find something to eat. Are you back from church? You can join me in the kitchen. Have a blessed weekend day and I hope to hear from you soon sweetie.

Big hugs and kisses, Roland

Good Morning Sweetheart… I am so happy to wake up this very morning with the thought of you still kept in my mind. You have really made me proud and I will never let you down. You are all I have now and I really thank you for making me feel this way. I never thought I was going to love again, but you have really made me feel like a real person again… Thank you for making me whom I am now. I know it may be easy to look around our world today and see the appearance of chaos, difficulty and strife. Yet, when we come from an open heart, we can also see our opportunity to love all things into balance, joy, harmony and peace. This planet does not need more visions of desperation, fear, doubt and hate—it requires an abundance of love, especially unconditional love, to heal and restore the beauty contained in every moment. This becomes the easier path once we take the first step and begin to share our love.

When we bring unconditional love back into our personal, professional, community and family lives, we begin the journey of restoring wholeness and happiness to our planetary adventure. Of course it takes determined effort on our part as the old ways of being are quick to return in our mind. However, this effort to love is rewarded with a new perspective on everything and all life benefits as a result. I wish you all the best and have a lovely journey… My greetings to everyone. Take good care of your self honey. Will miss you very much.

Big hugs and Kisses, Roland

Good Morning My Love… I am really really sorry for my late reply. I am doing pretty good and everything is going on great here, just missing you too and you always keep me dreaming of the day we will meet. I hope you are also doing good and feeling much better now. I have been worried since I didn't get home early to talk to you and let you know I am doing good but I am with you when you are all alone and I have never gone anywhere without you. You are always by my side. I love you so much and also thank you for making me whom I am and we have not even met each other yet.

Currently I have decided to travel to Dubai with my partner to look for (George) and see what we can do from there. Honey, please don't send any of these guys money even if they do tell you anything. Please try to keep your feelings and don't tell them you have given me any information about them. I think that will really help us if you don't tell them. We have gone through them and we have found a lot of differences about them. So please try hard to keep your feelings and don't send them anything honey. I do understand how much it feels to lose all these funds but I know God is going to make a way after we are done with all this. We will be leaving here early in the morning around 5.00am to JFK then from there to Dubai since we got a round trip flight. Honey I promise you I will make it up to you, because promises are not to be broken. I love you with all my life and am willing to spend the rest of my life with you till the end of time. I wanted to call you but thinking you are asleep and don't want to wake you up. Sweetheart I am glad you approved the letter with the debt consolidation company. I think it is a good idea with that. I will see what we can do with the payment when I am back from the trip. I am always there for you honey. You don't bother me with any of this. You were sent from heaven and I need to do everything just to make you happy. Well tell me about the Chase bank—have you heard from them? Honey I am having my cell phone with me so you can call me but I need to give you my partner's cell phone number too so you can catch me on his when mine is off.

I will go for now and get things ready. Please take good care of yourself while I am gone and promise you are going to be by my side. Promise me you won't turn your back on me. I love you Sweetheart. I am always by your side everywhere you go. Missing you so much. Love you more and hope to hear from you in the morning.

Love you, Roland

Hi Honey... I know you are not feeling much better at this point. I know you are so weak but I am not going to turn my back on you and never would I do that to you... I really love you and want you to know I am part of this and we are doing everything together. I want you to know I am forever going to stand at your back and work everything out till it is over. I promise you this. I am really sorry I haven't replied to any of your emails today and wish I were there to pamper you.

From the very first moment I saw you on the dating site, I knew that we were destined to be together. It has been so long since a woman has captured my attention so fully or made my heart beat. Your smile lights up my entire spirit. Your laughter fills me with joy, and your mere presence will warm any room. I have no doubt you are the woman Heaven has made especially for me.

I try to put these feelings into words, but fail miserably. This feeling of being both scared and at peace, of having both butterflies and a sense of calm, is a feeling that I have only dreamed about. As the days continue to pass, my love for you continues to grow. I never thought I had the capacity to love anybody as much as I love you right now. Yet, my love for you continues to mature, growing beyond the realm of my heart. It seems that you have become the fiber of my soul, the very reason for my existence. I could never forget you, not today, not ever, for you have entered my heart, where you will remain forever.

Please take everything easy and always know I am with you no matter what. I will call you tomorrow after church and please take good care of your self for me. Good night and sweet dreams,

Love you, Roland

*****

By this time, I probably should have questioned everything about him. But his kindness and willingness to be so patient and understanding simply made me want to know more about him.

Our expectations were both sincere and reasonable. When I looked up Lusk, Wyoming, on the web, I found out it was about the size of the town I grew up in. For some reason, that one fact started to draw me closer, and I wanted to know more. We became good friends, and the friendship seemed to become important to both of us. He never asked anything of me but my time and my honesty. It seemed to be so innocent. He called me faithfully no matter where I was or where he was. One time, I remember traveling to West Virginia, and he called me at the airport. The next day, he checked to see if I had arrived okay. From the time we met, God was the center of our lives. The more we talked, the closer we became while we started to develop special feelings for one another. He seemed so easy to talk to. I felt it necessary from the very beginning to be totally honest with him since that trait was so important to me also. That's what you do if you have a true friend. I knew eventually I would need to tell him about my past. I only hesitated because of the guilt and shame I felt for not being able to contribute to the relationship financially if we ever chose to make the relationship more than friends. It only seemed fair that he would need to know so he didn't get involved with someone who owed a lot of money and someone who had done such a poor job managing her finances. He told me not to worry and that he would make everything all right. I felt no judgment from him, only support. He showed no anger, just concern. He was more concerned about my health and stress level as the tears rolled out of my eyes while I confessed to him about my prior relationships. I told him he could ask me anything and I would answer him. I also told him he could walk away at any moment and I would understand. From the very beginning, he wanted to do all he could to relieve the pain I was feeling from dealing with all the phone calls and letters from credit card companies and collecting agents. He told me he would help me come to terms with my past so the two of us could have a chance at a future if we so desired.

We made plans to meet. He was going to fly to Houston, and we would spend the day together. We were both kind of excited about the meeting yet feeling a little nervous at the same time. And wouldn't you know? Right before this was scheduled to happen, he shared some news he had for me. I just finished telling him how the fraud department from one of the banks had called and drilled me about the money transfers I had previously conducted on my account. He questioned me as to why I was working with an agent from the bank when he had offered to get to the bottom of all this for me. I told him that it was a follow-up call to make sure I knew that the people I wired money to were actually giving it to someone else, someone who lived out of the country. It was his responsibility to follow up on attempted fraud.

Roland then told me that he had hired a private investigator, and together they would travel to Dubai to find George and to London to find Joe and then on to Ghana to find John. He apologized for not coming to Houston, but once he had put his plan in motion, he had to act on it immediately. He explained once more about how he felt it was necessary for me to put my past behind me if I were ever going to have a future with him. He wanted to clear all this up for me one way or another. I thanked him and told him I never expected him to take that kind of action, especially without talking to me or meeting me in person first. He explained he had decided this on his own and did not want to add any more stress to my already full docket.

I was so disappointed that our meeting was cancelled but was kind of touched by this act of heroism. I had really looked forward to meeting him and seeing if the same chemistry we had when we talked on the phone actually existed when we met in person. And we did have chemistry. I felt goose bumps every time I heard his voice. It was so easy to relax and go to dreamland. All evidence indicated he felt the same about me. I loved answering the phone when I knew it was going to be him. It was like a little girl being left in a candy store. He was so sweet to me. After he arrived in Dubai, we kept in touch by phone, email, and IMs as his search became very thorough. As he arrived and investigated the perpetrators in each country, he would let me know the status of the investigation on a daily basis. I continued to send him copies of all documents and emails he requested so that he would have something to prove to the authorities so he could elicit their assistance. His Dubai visit didn't last very long because the local authorities were able to prove that the name George had given to me did not exist and the person had not entered or left the country. And after following the documentation to London, he was able to show that the law firm used by George had really not been sustained, nor did they receive my communications. Along with United Kingdom Scambusters, authorities, in addition to the law firm, joined forces to discover the identity of George by tracing him through his email address and IP number. They sincerely wanted to claim justice for someone using the name of the law firm without permission. It turned out that he was actually a drug lord and made a living out of doing this to defenseless women.

In London, he was unable to find Joe or his son, Ronald, in the hospital. But he was able to track down the caregiver that I had provided an airline ticket for. She was from Ghana, so they assumed that she was a girlfriend of Joe. Accra was the next place he and the investigator traveled to.

First, Roland shared with me that he was able to visit his two children in the UK while he was there. He shared with them what was happening and was upfront with them concerning all the details. I admired the fact that he had such a good relationship with them that he was willing to tell them about this woman he had fallen in love with and desired to help clear up her past before he continued the relationship or planned a future with her. Oddly enough, they both supported his wishes and understood why he was doing what he was. That told me a lot about his character. I even proposed the question to him about what could drive him enough to commit this selfless act for someone he had never met. And he simply told me again that promises are meant to not be broken. He also said he had fallen madly and deeply in love with me. And he knew in his heart that he had to do all he could to help me. All these actions helped verify and prove to me that Roland was genuine in his feelings and his actions.

He and his partner hit the pavement running and quickly got the local authorities in Ghana to assist them. The police were able to have personal conversations with John by phone and otherwise to try to draw him out of hiding. I know this because John actually called me to ask me if I was working with the police or someone to find him. He did not like it that I shared information with someone else about him. I told him I was only trying to help him and that the person calling wanted to make sure he actually existed before he gave him money to ship the gold home. He said not to trust them because they were only after the gold, especially since it was all in my name. Then he proceeded to ask me for more money again to ship the gold home. Once Roland provided all the documentation to the judge that I sent him, the judge actually ruled in our favor that the gold held hostage by FedEx and immigration would legally be placed in my name to be shipped to me and not given back to Anglo Gold Company, who was claiming its possession. All this activity and business concluded in three months' time.

To prove that he was as authentic as a person could be, one day, I received a phone call from him telling me how hurt he was and how disappointed he was in me. I asked him why. He then told me that the scambusters had come to him that morning and told him that I was making contact with other men on the same dating site that he found me on. He thought we had sealed our relationship by now. So he told me he would make sure the gold was shipped to me and then he would step away from me as if we had never met.

I was in Chicago at the time, and the conversation we had was so short that he did not give me a chance to defend myself. I finally reached him by phone, and he answered. I then explained that yes, I did make a contact with a stranger who lived in Houston. But the reason I did that was to have someone physically to introduce to my son so I could get him ready to accept Roland as part of my life and to help him believe that you can meet someone in person from the internet dating site. It might have sounded manipulative or calculating, but I was getting a lot of pressure from my son asking what was causing me so much stress. I could hear and feel the disappointment and hurt in Roland's voice. That made me feel so badly. So I asked him if I completely went off the site and had no more contact with anyone on there, would that restore his faith in me and keep our relationship and love alive? He said yes, and he forgave me. This again showed me the kind of character he possessed. I had no doubt that we were meant to be together. He then sent his private investigator home because he was running low on funds, and after the court ruled in our favor, there was no need for the investigator to stay. He also had complete support and confidence of the local police department. The gold was in their hands at the time to test for authenticity. Keep in mind that up to this point, he had not asked for even one dollar from me.

The only thing needed was to ship the gold home, and we would be together forever. He told me that this would only take a week to arrange and that the gold was in possession of the police department as it was being tested for authenticity. Once the tests showed that the gold was actually authentic, he went to FedEx and found that DHL would be a safer way to transport the gold home. After that, he found that the shipping costs would take most of the money he had on him, which was a $20,000 traveler's check. Had I ever had someone go to these lengths to make sure my future was secure and all financial problems would be cleared? Never. I came to believe that Roland was indeed a man of his word. He was going to rescue me, and I could finally put this nightmare behind me. And then it happened.

Roland was out strolling the streets and became violently ill and had to be taken to the hospital. The doctor told him that he had to pay the money upfront before they could treat him or attempt to save his life. He was bleeding inside, and if they didn't operate, he would lose his life. And I would lose him. When I did not hear from him, I was really concerned. I had no idea what had happened to him, and it was very unusual for him not to call me or contact me or even let one day go by. I finally received a phone call from him and almost didn't answer the phone. It was a new number, and it belonged to his doctor. He sounded very weak but asked me to listen to what the doctor had to say. I found myself talking to his doctor so he could explain the situation for me to realize the seriousness of it all. I disliked this moment because I was having total flashbacks of what had happened to me before. I had to believe this was different. We had moved into this relationship with caution and a decelerated speed. This was the first time I felt nothing could go wrong. And I had to remember that Roland had never asked for a penny from me. I had to help him. I had to. He would not be there if it were not for me. And he had asked nothing in return of me prior to this. He had already proved his love for me, and I had no reason to question it. His traveler's check, along with everything else he had, was back in the hotel room (including his computer), and his phone battery had gone dead.

I had to work hard to get him the money he needed, and I had to send it to the doctor to make him believe he could trust Roland and myself. The doctor became our friend. Not only did he let me call him, but he would actually put the phone to Roland's ears so I could talk to him. He eventually allowed Roland to use his computer to keep in touch with me. The doctor even told me he was looking forward to coming to the States to attend our wedding and was envious of the kind of love we had for each other.

Roland was in grave condition. So after the operation and treatment, he had to have more money to get him released from the hospital. I sent him what he needed. His recovery was lengthy, but he was finally released from the hospital. The doctor had stood by his side and helped us tremendously. Upon his return to the hotel room, not only had the computer been stolen, but all his personal belongings (including the traveler's check) were gone also. This caused a lot of panic on his side and mine. Our goal became intense to get the gold shipped and released as well as to get him home. Our relationship had gone past the boyfriend and girlfriend stage. We had survived our first crisis together, and now we felt like we were married and simply doing what we could as a man and wife to ensure that each one was safe and sound.

I took a moment to read the last email I received from him.

It's always my pleasure to hear your voice everyday. It makes me feel a little better at least… How are you and Dad doing? I hope everything is okay and that you are doing great. I wish I didn't have to miss you. If only you could be with me always. I know I could never be any happier. But then again, I know that the day will come when I will be able to spend my every waking moment with you. I even miss you when I am sleeping!

I am sorry I have not written you all this while since I did not have access to a computer until now. I am locked up here in the library and quite worried since I have not heard from you and more also, it's election day here and voting which begun yesterday has crippled into the late hours of today as a result of some hitches here and there.

I have been indoors all day since it is quite scary and there is riot between the supporters of the opposition and the police but thank goodness the peace council which comprises of the Pastors, Muslim clerics and traditional priests have come to the aid and calmed passion down.

I miss you so much. I can't convince you how much I miss you. You know that I can't stay without you for one minute! I feel I'm going to die without you if you don't come to me one day.

Just a quick one here to let you know I am good and safe… Fill me in… I guess how Dad is doing—great—and so is everyone and the kids doing well—get back to me as I am sitting here with thoughts of you.

Adorably yours, Roland

Little did I know at the time that it could possibly be the last one I would receive.

Once again, another $100,000 was lost by me, and still no gold arrived. Even though Roland and I talked every day and tried to keep in contact, we found ourselves separated by both physical illness and financial difficulties. After months went by, I received a text from his private investigator and best friend wondering if we had been married yet and where we were living. When I let him know what was going on, he said he would help. He was shocked that Roland had fallen ill since he left him in such good condition. Getting Roland home had to be our priority. I had no idea at the time that this friend, who was like a brother to him, was going through turmoil and crisis of his own. Evidently, his wife was critically ill, and he had enough problems of his own on a personal level. He couldn't believe this was happening since Roland was in such good health before he left Ghana. He had to talk to him first because my story was so unbelievable he had to confirm the facts I had given him. But he stressed to me that I needed to do all I could to get Roland home. I gave him the information he needed to get in touch with Roland and did quite the same for Roland to get in touch with him.

No matter how we tried and no matter what we did, we seemed to run up against roadblock after roadblock to get the gold shipped. Meanwhile, expenses were piling up for Roland, and it was getting even more difficult for him to be released from Ghana. Even though his friend and investigator struggled to keep in touch with me, neither of them were privy to the fact that I was going through my own path of difficulties—my father's death, my daughter's bed rest, my new grandchildren, not to mention my own personal battle with my children and my newly claimed addiction.

I also became ill and was working on filing for bankruptcy. I was hospitalized twice in three weeks (five days each), and this made me focus my priorities on my health, then finances, and then past relationships. In order to move on, I had to put our relationship on hold and believe that if we were meant to be, God himself would make sure we would be together. To date, no gold has arrived. My phone number and email have been changed, which makes it difficult for anyone in my past to contact me without me wanting them to. But this is what I had to do to move forward.

Dear Roland,

I'm sitting here thinking of you and what you have brought to my life during the past year. It's hard to believe that we have been together for over one year now. And not once did I question that you would some day come home to me until now. And the only reason I question it is because I am so afraid that you gave your life for me and did not take care of yourself, and that is why you ended up in the hospital. When weeks went by and David said you were no longer conscious and had never regained consciousness since you were transported to the hospital, I could not imagine that your body would give out that quickly when you were so close to coming home. Someday I will be well enough to find out what happened. Someday I will be well enough to come there and get answers so I know for sure you did not die in vain. Even though I know you worked hard to make our dreams come true and to make sure the gold was shipped properly, I know if you were not able to do that, that something happened to you. I don't want to believe the Roland I fell in love with is gone from this earth, but I know after all the treatments and therapy I receive I will be able to face the truth more equipped and ready to face the future with or without you. So this is not a letter saying goodbye to you yet. This is not a letter to say hello again yet. This is a letter to tell you how deeply in love with you I still am and praying for God to grant our one wish of bringing us together. I do trust and believe in a higher power and have learned (if I didn't know before) to trust completely in his will. I will add more to this letter regularly until I am able to make it without you. So trust me. You still have a place in my heart, and at this point, I am not sure that place will ever go away.

My sweet love, Roland,

Today I decided to write you a letter so you would know (once you make it to Houston) that I continued to think about you and love you each and every day that we have been separated. I am so glad you decided to leave voicemails for me to listen to each day so that I could remember the love that we share with one another. That is particularly why I handwrote the letter I sent to you, because I knew that you would need something close to your heart to keep you going when you were fighting for your life in the hospital and we had no way of communicating to one another. I wanted to help you not give up on us, even if the letter had to be delivered by Paul Revere. When David told me I couldn't talk to you because you were not conscious, I was so scared. I was scared of losing you and never knowing if we would have a chance to make it. I kept asking David to tell you I loved you and I would wait on you. He said he was unable to talk to you and was waiting for word from the doctor. I just wanted to tell you in person what was happening to me and why I would be unable to communicate with you. After sending the $1,000 to pay the doctor and the $100 (all I had) in the letter, it was clear to my son that I had an addiction to you, and it was not called love, but a love addiction.

It was my last act I took before sobriety in June. So any time I would choose to consciously contact you, whether by phone, email, letter, text, etc., they say I have relapsed and have to start over again, that I have violated my sobriety. You see, I have been diagnosed as a love addict and I attend Love Addict Anonymous and Codependent Anonymous Meetings every week. I also attend Al Anon meetings because alcohol was a problem in my family growing up, which they say gives me the gene of developing some type of addiction. Just in case you didn't get my first letter, and I didn't keep a copy of it (sorry), the first few months were hard because I was all alone. I didn't know if you were alive or not, and each time I reached out to text or call, I wasn't able to get much information. David tried to keep me up to date, but when he found out that I was being monitored, every text, every phone call, and every email, he stopped texting me. He told me you had to have medication and the doctor be paid or you would not make it. So I wired my last 1,000 dollars to him and mailed your letter with my last 100 dollars cash. I sent the letter to David at his address but addressed to you inside the post office's special envelope. They said you would receive it in five days, and when I asked David, he told me he had gotten it. After one month went by, I had to try to contact William to find out if you were still alive. This was against all orders since I was forced to get new email addresses and new phone numbers. I was forbidden to give that information out to anyone but immediate family, therapists, and doctors. So I took a chance. But the contact ended up hurting my freedom and my progress. I had to believe if God gave us his blessing, that both of us would survive and once again He would find a way for us to be together. So with me in denial of admitting I was an addict and so much stress from everything, I ended up with my vertigo getting worse instead of better. I had to see the specialist and my family doctor each week and get tests run, etc.

All of this was in the same time fragment of me coming home from my daughter's and the news that the gold dust did not arrive and the risks I took sending money (causing me to be in financial jeopardy) was all too much. Everything was happening at the same time. So my son was very angry, and he said I would lose him as a son if I didn't tell him everything. So I did, and after forty-eight hours of his consulting with legal and counseling at his job site, he came up with a plan, and if I didn't agree to go along with it, I was out. So of course, I went along with everything he asked. He started researching places where he could send me for in house treatment and notified his sister that I would not be coming back to help her. By his count, he said that I had lost money to over seven people, but he got a little mixed up (because he counted William as one of my love contacts and also the banker from Joe, who caused all the havoc on my credit cards). So the total count was the following (and you already know all of this): Jerome in 2009, John in 2011, George, Joe (his banker Andrew), and you in 2012. My doctor said I had to do something about all the stress I was under because it was playing havoc with my body and that if I didn't, all the medicine and therapy in the world that he could offer would not help me, and I would have to go back to not being able to function. So after a couple falls and more trips to the doctors, I agreed to follow my son's plan. He actually found out that in house therapy would cost him around $50,000 a month. The two well-known centers were located in Arizona and Oklahoma. With that in mind, it would be more economical for him to find specialized therapists here in Houston. So after seeing doctors and therapists and turning all control of computer access, phone access, and finances over to my son, I eventually made enough progress that my therapist had a meeting with the family and was able to initiate a plan to start trusting me enough again that I could be depended (meaning I could drive myself) upon to attend meetings every day and therapy a minimum of twice a week. I also interviewed two different law firms to select one that would represent me and my situation in the best possible manner.

After selecting the firm and finding out my debt consolidation company was not approved by the federal government as a credit counseling institution, I terminated the contract and notified all creditors that I was in the process of filing bankruptcy. You wouldn't believe it, but after that, the phone calls from the collectors stopped. How wonderful. I was supposed to file in July, within a week of raising the 1,800 dollars needed to retain them. And then they notified me because of the disclosure of Dad's inheritance money, I would not be able to file till November 1. I had to take a credit counseling course before I filed and then take another one after I file. I have to send these documents of certification to the lawyers to present to the judge. My credit score is only 500, and they said it couldn't possibly go any lower, and my credit would be affected for seven years.

My life has changed quite a lot. The most important thing I want to share with you is that the therapy has been wonderful. I have dealt with a lot of demons in the past, and I have become closer to God for sure. They even had me write a letter to you and carry it on me so that I would not contact you again. I am to read it each and every time I get the urge and to prevent me from relapsing. So please know that the urge and need and longing to be with you and talk with you and contact you never goes away. But I hate to think if I follow through with any of that (which you know I did call you back once), I will go against everything that I have worked for. And I have promised not to have contact with anyone of my qualifiers, whom I have not met in person. So until we do that, I am at their mercy. I pray every day that you will find a way to work everything out and come home. Right now, I am struggling to meet the bills I have. I had to borrow from my son to pay the lawyer. My ex sent me the $2,000 to pay off the loan shark, and my son is paying for the therapy I receive. But my gas bill alone is 400 dollars a month because of my daily commute to downtown Houston. I have to allow four hours of the day to and from to only get one hour of treatment. On Wednesdays, I receive two hours of treatment. All other days are one hour each, except for Sunday, and that group is also two hours long. So now you know what I am doing and how I spend my day. My son tracks my every move, both on computer and phone. I am praying by November 1 that I can gain enough trust from family and therapists for my son to pull the parental controls off of me and my being able to function as an adult and a parent again.

You have to realize that we are only living out God's plan for us. We know not why we have had a hard journey during the first year of our relationship, but we can only hope that 2013 ends up better than it began. Only God knows how that will be. I do know that the hardest thing I have done is to pull away from you so that I can get my finances in order and my head in order. I guess somehow, all this year, I have been thinking "Get our finances in order" and that we would be married and be a couple. My groups and my therapists absolutely think I am crazy to have considered marrying someone I have not met in person. They tell me that even the smell or odor of a person can turn you off enough that you can't live with them. So I guess we will just have to surprise them when we finally do come together. I can't imagine it changing how I feel about you, but it seems that right now, I have to play by the rules to move forward. And the rules include me thinking with my head from now on and not my heart. My heart has always been my guide. However, after attending intense therapy four days straight from seven to eight o'clock each day, I now know that I have to stay in my adult and protect the wounded inner child. I have a lot of baggage, but I am hoping that now you will not see me as the emotional wreck that I was in the past and that I have dealt with most of the abuse that happened to me when I grew up and in my previous marriages. I feel safe now, and I even wrote a letter to myself from my deceased parents. That allowed me to deal with several triggers that caused me a lot of pain, but now I can handle responses to comments so much better. The pain has eased quite a lot.

I will go for now and write more later. Whether I ever give this to you or not will be determined in the future. For now, just know how much I love you and how much I care. It's so true that all of this has been a growth process. But it is a journey I needed to take. If or when you ever come to me, you will be happy with the news. Talk to you soon.

Love, B

Why does it feel so much better to be able to talk with you each night or day? I do it because you have become part of me, and knowing there is a chance of us spending the rest of our lives together means that I can be with you until we can. I told you once that your blood runs through my veins. If you talk to my therapists, they would say that I am living in a fantasy by even having you on my mind. I guess only time will tell. Meanwhile, if I can talk to you this way to keep my sanity, then let me live in that fantasy. I still believe in a fairy tale romance. They say that I become involved in online romances because I know that the men are unavailable to me, and that makes me a love avoidant. That somehow I know down deep that I will never be with those whom I fall in love with and that I use these relationships to fulfill a need to feel safe and loved.

Because my feelings are so strong for you, I feel that you should know some things about me that I haven't told you and things that have come out as part of my therapy. The four-day therapy session put me in a trance so that I could deal with the trauma and pain I had experienced as a child, which did affect the way I was feeling as an adult. It turns out that I experienced trauma at age four, eight, fourteen, eighteen, twenty-six, and thirty-four. With that much trauma, I chose to escape by becoming very active in working (starting at age nine) and being involved in many organizations and activities and, most of all, church. I can't forget the education either. I still yearn to learn something new every day. So as I confide in you about all of this, I am praying that you are just seeing another dimension of me and do not feel you need to judge me, criticize me, pity me, or walk away from me because of all the baggage I carry. My son believes in me and the process enough that he knows I will make healthier choices for my life in the future. Forgive me, my love, but as everyone keeps talking to me, sometimes I feel as if I am being brainwashed to believe that you are not real indeed. Each day that goes by, I miss you more and more. I pray for the day that you are able to show up at my door-step. But as time creeps by so slowly, I know the chances of that happening become less and less. I mean, how do you get enough money to pay off those you owe for staying there for over one year? And how do you ship the gold or even get it back to ship? We paid everything we were supposed to pay, shipping fees, etc., and still you are not able to ship it. I know none of this is your fault. We are both new to dealing with any of this, and you have had all the hard labor of it. And how do you stay healthy as time goes by? It's funny, but just as I was posing those questions to you, God put his hand on me and said, "Leave it to me, dear. I will take care of him." Here I am again, wanting to touch you and say good night to you as if you have been in my life forever. Someday, my love…

Someday. We must trust the process and allow God to do his magic. I love you so very much.

My sweet sweet love,

My willpower is wavering. It is so hard not to contact you and hear your reassuring and beautiful voice. I long for your company. I am praying to God that he help you in finding a way to come to me. I love you, sweet love.

My love,

My therapist told me last night that if I continue to listen to your voicemails and write to you and keep you in my heart, I will never get better. She said I am just putting a fancy spin on relapsing. I don't want to lose you, but she said that was the excuse I used every time I gave you (sent you) money. She praised me for not acting out and calling you, that I was simply living in denial and great disillusionment. So what do I do? I know now I have to talk to you one more time to see if there is truly any chance that you will come home to me. I love you so much.

CHAPTER 16

Reality Strikes

It finally happened. A package from Roland arrived, and the address it was sent from was Ghana, Africa. I was living in my son's house in the mother-in-law suite, so all packages came to the front door. What I was expecting was gold dust enough to pay all my bills off and also pay for shipping the gold home. I had made arrangements with a local gold and silver buyer to pay me $22,000 a pound, and I knew Roland had put five pounds in the collars of the shirts and had sewn up the opening with a zigzag stitch. I was supposed to call the agent, and she would meet me at her shop. What I ended up receiving was two shirts, which had been torn open at the collar and all the gold dust removed. I had to call Roland and tell him the package did not arrive as we had planned and the gold dust had been confiscated. When I reached him and told him what had happened, he was sure I made a mistake. He stayed very calm but was concerned about the situation at the same time. As the news started to sink in, he became devastated. He and I had just lost over $100,000, which belonged to the elders he had been dealing with. They were willing to let us keep one pound of every five pounds they sent to me. It would take no time at all for us to pay all our debts, including the shipping charges for the gold nuggets. Little did I know that this would be the last conversation we would have. He actually dropped the phone, and I heard nothing from him. I was devastated also. I knew at this moment that my chance for paying off all my debts had become slim to none. And things could only get worse for me at this point because I had no more money to access or to give Roland to ship the gold home.

Later that evening, my son came in to see me. He told me that he and his wife had suspected for some time that I was being dishonest with them. He said I had two choices. I either had to tell him everything that was going on with me or for the first time in thirty-eight years, I was in jeopardy of losing my son. I had twenty-four hours to come clean. He was so serious when he talked to me. I had never seen him so angry, hurt, and disappointed all at the same time.

Honesty is overrated when you know that the truth you reveal is going to hurt someone. It makes the delivery become very emotional because you are filled with an overwhelming sense of guilt and shame. This alone can be so powerful that it is hard to form the words you have to speak, let alone hear them come out of your mouth. But this is what I knew I had to do. Confessing my sins and actions of the last two years was very difficult for me, and I struggled. Tears fell from my eyes as I could hardly get the words out that they needed to hear. As I told my story to both my son and his wife, I came to realize how ridiculous it sounded and how gullible this person was who delivered the story in person.

As I spoke each syllable of each word, it was like I was having another out of body experience and I did not know this person who was sitting there talking. My son began to take notes as well as look up things on his computer while I was talking to him. I wasn't sure if he was taking everything I was saying seriously or even listening to me. Each time his wife wanted to say something to respond to something she had heard, he would stop her and tell her to let me finish my story first. When I was done talking, I was emotionally drained. I had done this once before during my visit to Chicago when I confessed everything to my friend the pastor. At that time, he stayed up very late and prayed and prayed and prayed for me to learn how to forgive myself. He asked that this heavy burden be lifted from my shoulders and set me free. That whatever was taken from me would be returned sevenfold as God would want. I remember him holding me in his arms as we prayed, and the peace and calmness that settled in my body from sharing this story with someone for the first time. I guess I had lived a secret life and never wanted to admit it.

This time, it was different. Telling my son and his wife hurt because I was seeing this large range of emotions come over both their faces. I was so ashamed and felt so much guilt from my actions while I was living under their roof. He even asked how I could give away the fifty thousand he loaned me to strangers without paying him back first. He trusted me, and I had broken that faith and trust.

I was very proud of my son. As angry as he was, he portrayed himself as the wounded parent and me as the wounded child. When I told him I thought I had done all this to seek out the unconditional love I had longed for, he questioned my motives. He asked, "Do you not think I have given you unconditional love?" I responded by saying no. I succeeded in wounding him again and even deeper than I had before. Yes, he was disappointed in my actions, but he informed me that we had to look at the solutions to our problems and not dwell on the past or in the past. He told me I would have to tell my daughter about what I had done. I agreed. He said he needed time to research and figure out what our next step would be.

In his presence, I managed to get up the courage to dial the number to speak to my daughter. As I heard her pick up the phone, I found I had difficulty making any sound and being able to speak to her. The guilt and shame I had built up inside of me was overwhelming by now. I knew she would be very, very angry and her response would be completely different from that of my son. I still kept trying, but the words would not come out of my mouth. So I had to hand the phone to my son so he could give her a small capsule of what I had just finished telling him. I remember him saying I had given money to about seven perpetrators and was continuing to keep in contact with all of them through emails and IMs. I could tell by the reaction on his face that she felt empathy for him but anger toward me. And the truth was that I deserved everything they were thinking and feeling about me. I had betrayed them.

CHAPTER 17

Picking Up the Pieces

Even though I was determined to find a way for my two children to forgive me for being dishonest with them, I knew that it could not happen until I figured out how I could be honest with myself. My actions had ended up affecting both families more than I had realized. My job now was to focus on my own health and recovery. As easy as that sounds, it's a very hard step to accomplish when you have been used to giving yourself to others and not making your own health and needs a priority. So how would I do that?

My first step was learning how to be honest with myself. I learned I could not be honest with my son while I was living under his roof and, at the same time, live in a fantasy world. I seemed to have justification for every action he questioned. I resented it when he or my daughter would ever question what I did. I truly believed that they would see how wrong they were after the man I was in love with came home to meet them and took care of all my financial woes. I did not realize that my actions would affect them and their spouses, their relationships, and their future.

The lyrics to the song "Addicted to Love" by Robert Palmer seems to say it all:

Your lights are on, but you're not home
Your mind is not your own.
Your heart sweats, your body shakes
Another kiss is what it takes.

AT FIRST CLICK

You can't sleep, you can't eat;
There's no doubt, you're in deep.
Your throat is tight, you can't breathe'
Another kiss is all you need.
You like to think that you're immune to the stuff...
Oh yeah, It's closer to the truth to say you can't get enough.
You know you're gonna have to face it;
You're addicted to love.
You see the signs, but you can't read;
You're runnin' at a different speed,
Your heart beats in double time.
Another kiss and you'll be mine, a one track mind;
You can't be saved,
Oblivion is all you crave.
If there's some left for you,
You don't mind if you do;
Your lights are on, but you're not home;
Your will is not your own.
Your heart sweats and teeth grind;
Another kiss and you'll be mine.
You're gonna have to face it
You're addicted to love. (Writer(s): Robert Allan Palmer...
Copyright: Bungalow Music)

Thank goodness, my son was able to talk to the employee assistance program assigned counselor at his place of employment. When he came home and told me that the counselor there had diagnosed my problem as process addiction, I was flabbergasted. What is process addiction? Of course, now the internet was my buddy, my library, my resource, my answer to every question. So what did I do next? I needed to find out what process addiction was. My own educational background included studying and understanding addiction, but I had no recall of process addiction.

After researching the internet, this is what I found: "A process addiction refers to compulsive behavior, such as compulsive gambling, sexual addiction, eating disorders and spending addictions."

As defined by faqs.org it is "a condition in which a person is dependent on some type of behavior, such as gambling, shopping, or sexual activity." This term is often used as a blanket for any behavioral addiction that does not involve an addictive chemical.

> What is a Process Addiction? Posted on October 19, 2012 by Process
>
> Process addictions are an often overlooked addiction. They are often overshadowed by substance addictions. This is unfortunate as the suffering, loss of life and family, and debilitating consequences are no less. Process addictions require psychological treatment to be overcome. Even though process addiction is often coupled with drug addiction, each addiction needs to be tackled in order for a full recovery to take place.
>
> The reasons that these addictions are often overlooked lie in a combination of shame, guilt and lack of understanding. It is somewhat easy to comprehend the chemical addiction of a person who abuses substances while the strong psychological compulsions of the process addict are often ignored. It is not as simple as "just stopping" or "willpower." There are real chemical and biological changes which occur in the brain of someone who has a process addiction. This addictive process is complex, and has several influencing factors. An individual's mental state, genetics, social status and past experiences all influence the addict and the timeline of their addiction. However, it is well known both for substance and process addictions that a person's reward center in their brain is stimulated causing release of chemicals into the body and brain which drive addictive behaviors. Put simply, this

chemical charge feels good. So the addict keeps chasing the "high" whether it is the up and down roller coaster of gambling or the highs and lows of cocaine addiction.

Most people enjoy this type of "natural high" in one way or another. Many people gamble for fun, or push their sports car on the freeway. Often we enjoy very large meals or go on a little spending spree when we get a nice bonus at work. This is how it can begin for the process addict however for unknown reasons some individuals keep doing the same "feel good behavior" over and over. This can have very damaging consequences. Obvious side effects of process addiction could be debt, bankruptcy, job and family disruptions—all of which were shining examples of what was happening to me.

Whatever the addiction or compulsion is, treatment is often necessary to completely abstain. Treatment methods vary but the most effective include identification and cessation of the behavior with a strong and long term commitment to keep it stopped. This long term commitment is the stumbling block. It can be difficult and include long term therapies, medications and other techniques. Treatment models and success vary but the most important step is to have a sincere desire to stop the behavior. Nothing can be completed without the crucial first step.

Habit versus Addiction... Posted on October 20, 2012 by Process

Addiction—Continued involvement with an activity, chemical or substance despite ongoing negative consequences.

Habit—Repeated action or behavior that may be unconscious

Compulsion—considerable discomfort is experienced if the behavior is not performed.

Process addictions are treatable conditions. This is an accepted fact in the mental health community. However some people still feel addiction is a moral problem, or a lack of willpower, or a lack of desire to stop. Addiction is a mental disease.

INTERNET ADDICTION: Posted on October 20, 2012 by Process

The internet is a very useful tool and it is almost impossible to work and function in today's society without some type of access to the internet. However, sometimes a person can develop a process addiction referred to as "Internet Addiction." This is defined as incontrollable, time-consuming and distressful internet use which results in difficulties with one's job, family or financial stability.

Now that I felt equipped with knowledge about process addiction, I began to question my past activities. Even though at the time, it did not cover what was really happening to me, I took my son's advice (as well as his counselor's). Using the names and numbers he gave me, I called two individual counselors who specialized in love addiction resulting from compulsive behavior. I then made an appointment for a consultation and was able to see both counselors the following week. Each professional was unique in her own way. The first one quickly diagnosed me with love addiction and directed me to cut off all internet usage, and make sure I never went to a restaurant or social activity alone. I was told to never be in a situation where I would be alone with a man. I would be very vulnerable to men if I chose to do so. The second one diagnosed me with codependent addiction. I decided that it was okay to be diagnosed with both conditions/diseases, because after looking them up, completing a survey and being interviewed by each, I felt I had characteristics of both, and I could live with that. I just wanted to get better. Down deep I wanted to be fixed so I could return to a normal life as soon as possible. I chose to go with the second therapist who wanted to see me once a week and wanted me to attend an in-depth therapy workshop on "Reclaiming Wholeness" as soon as possible. She also encouraged me to go to a SLAA (sex and love addict anonymous) meetings as well as CODA (codependent anonymous) meetings as much as I had time for. She felt that going to these meetings would help me to feel not so alone in my plight to get better. She made me realize that this was a disease that can't be fixed but must be treated and nourished for the rest of my life. What this meant was that I had to commit to God and myself and my family that I would do the work it took to get better. The process of recovery is just that...a process. And this process was going to take some time. Recovery does not happen overnight.

Everyone knows that pride will stand in the way of anyone admitting to any or all of the personal faults that we might have. Having the gene of stubbornness in your system probably doesn't help matters either. The first step I had to take is learning how to forgive myself. I had to realize that God has already forgiven all of us and that He is waiting to take our hand and help you go where you need to go and do what you need to do. The truth is that you feel very much alone in this process—until you ask for help. You become so humble that you are willing to accept help from a higher power. God is that higher power. As I share the twelve steps with you and my journey to get through them, I am hoping it will help you understand the process and maybe even create a path for anyone to move toward recovery within their own plight of addiction to change what is happening to them. I can tell you that you have to want to get better more than anything else you have ever wanted in your life. Even though it will seem like you are making sacrifices, you are not. You are really enhancing your life with every step that you take.

After you have found your therapist (the one that works for you), and you accept the fact that you need treatment, you will lay out a road map to recovery. That recovery includes lots and lots of therapy every single week which includes both individual and group therapy. And we can't forget the meetings you attend each week. Here you will meet others that have been or are going through what you are and you will find you are not alone. You are safe. You have support. Each step you take leads you to feeling more and more comfortable about the journey you are on.

Fortunately I lived in a large city that allowed me to scout out all kinds of available meetings within an hour's drive. When you attend your first support group (whether it be SLAA meetings or CODA meetings) you may question yourself as to why you are there and how you ever allowed this to happen to you. You will start to make sense of what is happening to you and why it is happening to you, but only after you find the meeting and the people attending that meeting that helps you to feel connected in some way. It might be a group that has similar problems as you do. It might be a group that is closer to your age group. It might be a group that is all women or all men. You have to find the right fit for you so you will feel comfortable enough to attend each week. I personally began by attending a meeting or therapy every day. That seemed to be the only way I could actually accept what was happening to me. I would listen to stories of others who were addicted and realize their stories were similar to mine in some way. The point was to reach a common ground. You will eventually be able to say the word addict and apply it to describing yourself. It won't be easy and it won't be quick, but it will happen. You will find yourself attending as many meetings as you can get to—every day if possible, because things have not made sense to you. Even working the 12 steps seems foreign to you and you want to give up on yourself many times. You know that your life is unmanageable (Step 1) but you haven't figured out why yet. So this is part of the first step. You attend as many 12 step meetings as you can till you can actually admit to yourself and others and God that you are powerless over your addiction and your life has become unmanageable. Sending thousands and thousands of dollars to men you met online and never met in person ends up affecting your whole life and those you love as well. Losing my savings, my home, and my retirement savings and income was not in my long term plan, but somehow described what I was about these days. Lying to family and friends—telling them I was not giving money away to men I met online and that the ones I was communicating with I had actually met before they left for another country, and they lived here in Texas—meant that my addiction was now involving the very ones I love. My physical health declined as the stress affected my vertigo spells and became intolerable at times. A strong and healthy amount of guilt and shame invaded my body as I tried to make my children understand what I had done and why I did it. Tremors and dizziness continued to become more evident of the consequences of that shame and guilt. I was spending hour upon hour crying to myself and talking to God, asking him why? I had no desire to date or be with someone that I would meet in a social gathering or at church, because I felt so committed and loyal to my online partners. If I was not a workaholic before I retired, I became engrained in keeping in continual contact with them. My focus was entirely upon the relationship I was building with them. I believed that I was following God's will and I believed I would receive the gold and/or the money that I loaned each perpetrator. If this did not happen, I would be ruined financially. I didn't want to experience that feeling of being unloved ever again. As my self-esteem and self-worth continued to decline, my need to be with someone online increased. I failed over and over to admit to myself what was really happening and fell deeper and deeper into denial. If someone questioned my actions, thoughts, or feelings, I became more and more defensive and usually ended or at least minimized those friendships or relationships so I would not have to face the truth. If you can only say this in your mind or your head, you don't quite believe it yet. You have to say it to God and to others. You have to be honest—not just with others, but with yourself as well.

It also becomes necessary for you to find a sponsor—preferably one who has gone through something similar that you have experienced—someone who is willing and has the time to help you work through the 12 steps of recovery. It must be someone you can trust and who will commit to see you through each and every step. If you are having trouble finding a specific support group, any 12 step program will help you. You just have to find the one that makes you comfortable and one that actually speaks to you and motivates you to return week after week.

So what are you going to do about it now? What you should have been doing all along—and that is working Step 2: Come to believe that a Power *greater* than ourselves could restore us to sanity. Believing in God is simply not enough. But reading His word, and following what He says and listening to Him as he answers your prayers—that is what takes courage. You have to follow His plan, not your own. Good things will begin to happen to you if you believe. And the amazing part of all this is you actually start to find some peace within your soul. The serenity prayer said over and over and over again—each time you started to waiver or slide, was the best help with getting through Step 2. The facts were if you really wanted to restore your sanity, you had to turn your life over to God. If not, you would remain forever in Step 1.

Steps 2 and 3 ask you to confront the question of what gives your life meaning. Without meaning in your life, your addiction will grow and thrive. Without meaning you cannot establish the priorities which help you to restore the balance, focus, and self-responsibility you seek. To make this easier you end up taking a spiritual inventory. This inventory involves your relationships with members of your family. You will not only review how God worked into your life while growing up, you will figure out what part God plays in your life here and now. This leads you to Step 3 to make a decision to turn our will and our lives over to the care of God as we understood God. Actually I thought I had done this all my life. But what I came to realize was that I took God for granted. I believed that He was always giving me the benefit of the doubt. That he would let nothing happen to me that wasn't part of his plan to bring me to him in the end (or should I say the beginning of life everlasting)? As you take a loss of reality inventory, you come to recognize how and why and when your life started taking negative turns in the road and how you made it easier on yourself to ignore all the red flags in front of you.

In fact, if you were told you had one year to live, what fantasy would you want to live out to be able to give you the life you wanted and never had, or the life you desired. That plan would give you a bird's eye view of the fantasy and nonreality you have been living in. We always seem to want what we don't have. And we think that life we don't have is one that has been forbidden to us. But that is not the case. That life is not reality.

Step 4 is that we make a searching and fearless moral inventory of ourselves. If you have never done this, this step was a definite eye opener. I found myself buying books that would give me aid in finding answers. I could not give up. But I had to be honest with myself. So I sat there making a list of everything about myself which caused me to feel fear. I found that fear began long ago in my life and had truly never left me. I was challenged to change my perception of fear. I learned as I went through my first divorce, I had the fear of being alone. My second divorce let me experience the fear of being threatened or unsafe. And now that fear has reinvented itself by realizing the fear of losing my children was greater than the fear of financial ruin. Taking this moral inventory opened my eyes and at the same time, opened new doors for me to discover how strong I could be if I was forced to start my life over again. Remembering all my losses and all the painful events from my previous life helped me learn from all that sadness. This meant that those feelings of unworthiness and self-hatred had to be turned into statements of self-affirmations which proved to help me face the world and all that it had with positive energy.

The hardest part of reflecting on step four was feeling alone while in a room with other people. I've learned that solitude can be inspiring as well as inspirational and tranquil. Nature and its contents invite inner peace and serenity.

Step 5 was admitting to God, to myself, and to another human being the exact nature of our wrongs. Going to support meetings helps to give you awareness and hope as well as support. But you don't get much from them if you don't give of yourself. And that means being not afraid to tell your story. To share your fears and your guilt and shame—is just a small part of what you do to help yourself begin the healing process. Positive expression of anger became another challenge for me. It was hard for me to demonstrate that feeling. Fear of being unsafe—or fear for safety was the word that poured back into the earth as I tried to reestablish friendship and harmony with myself and my higher power. And through that feeling of safety being restored, God was able to help me forgive myself. This was truly the hardest thing for me to do and took the longest to accomplish. Why did I even deserve to be forgiven after letting so many people down—especially God. He let me keep my inner child safe. I experienced this transformation in a "Reclaiming Wholeness" Workshop. Once again, it was necessary for me to give myself affirmations such as: I am lovable because I exist, I am accepted and feel part of His world, I am accepted and feel safe with others, I am accepted because I am me.

Step 6 was to be ready to have God remove all of these defects of character.

No one at your support meetings will judge you. It's as if you build character by attending these meetings. The only way to change how you feel about yourself and how you feel about others is to allow others to be responsible for their actions and you become responsible for yours. Self-affirmations play a large role in helping oneself become the person you want to respect. Forgiving yourself and placing yourself in God's hands—allowing Him to work His magic—is the only way you can achieve what you desire most. I am grateful for all that I am. I am enough, and I have enough. Good things come my way and I cherish each one.

Step 7 was humbly asking God to remove our shortcomings. Every day, in every way, I am getting better. I am strong with God's leadership and guidance. I am good enough. I am not right or wrong, I am just unique and different. It's kind of funny, but I find myself talking to God all the time now. Going down the highway, if I am not talking to Him, I am singing to Him. This is what He does for me. I want to serve Him. I want to follow Him. I am willing to turn over to Him all of my shortcomings. I am willing to work towards improving them and changing the outcome of all my actions. The following meditation has helped me enforce this.

> My God and Savior, I need you now because I am full of stress and anxiety. Reading your word brings comfort (Psalm 4:8): "I will lie down in peace and sleep for you alone. O Lord, keep me safe." I ask you to come and take my heavy burdens. I take each one and lay them at your feet. Please carry them for me so I don't have to. I receive your gift of peace and mind and heart. I know that you Lord will always keep me safe. I am not afraid because you are with me...always. In Jesus name I pray. Amen.

Step 8 was to make a list of all persons I had harmed and become willing to make amends to. This was difficult. I thought it was bad enough that I had been dishonest with my children and had hurt them, but as I took the moral inventory, I found that the list was longer than I had wanted it to be or even dreamed it would be. But as I compiled this list, I began to realize that compiling it was the easy part. I knew that the time would come when I would have to personally make amends to them. And of course, that meant that all pride had to be erased and removed from my character. Total honesty was hard but necessary. I learned that if you don't want others to judge you, don't judge yourself. Rome wasn't built in a day, so take your time to heal and process each step. Reward yourself with self-care and take thirty minutes a day for you. Trust the process. It's okay to take a day off now and then.

Step 9 was make direct amends to those I harmed wherever possible, except when to do so would injure them or others. I asked myself how this could be hard. I now know who I have hurt and all I need to do is to ask for forgiveness. Obviously I had to forgive myself first. Now that I have, letting go of all that guilt and shame is mind blowing. The effect on your body is astounding. And yet, the surprise was on me. Just because you ask for forgiveness, does not mean that the people you have hurt will forgive you. They have to take their time also to process what has happened. The pain was just as deep for them and disappointing. Some people I told even used the word "stunned." The memories they have of you hurting them may stay with them forever, but allowing them time to heal is just as important as the time it takes for you to heal. You have to be sure that your amends are sincere, however, so that there is no mistaking the sincerity behind your motives. And whether you choose to do it in an email, in person, on the phone, or by skyping, the important point here is that you choose to do it and follow through on completing the process. Because I was going through filing for bankruptcy process during this time, it forced me to make amends with those I hurt and had been dishonest with—one of whom was my exhusband. With all his faults, he chose this time in his life to show me that rare unconditional love I had longed for in our marriage. He continued to support me and not pass judgment upon me even though he had every right to. I had used him also.

Step 10 was to continue to take personal inventory, and when we were wrong promptly admitted it. Am I out of the woods? Not by a long shot. There are times, we want to slip and it takes a double dose of courage to follow through on this step. If you remain committed to the process, you will remain committed to the step. This step gets easier and easier as time goes by. The affirmation to remember here is: I am open to the spiritual healing of the amends process. Whatever the outcome of my attempt, I will take pride in trying to make the amend. I am open to the lessons that I can learn from making amends, and I am grateful for them.

Step 11 was sought through prayer and meditation to improve our conscious contact with a Power greater than ourselves, praying only for knowledge of God's will for us and the power to carry that out. Completing a ten day exercise helped me embrace this step. Those ten days were reflections and a simple prayer on the following topics: happiness, growth, and serenity, peace of mind, reality, achievement, intimacy, productivity, health, and spirituality. Not just one, but all of these components encouraged understanding of the twelve steps as well as understanding and acceptance of the process.

Once again, you have to believe in the process, and it will work for you.

I took this for granted. Yes, I believed because I was praying each day that my prayers would be answered. What I found out was that indeed they were—just not in the way I thought they would be or wanted them to be. Yet that was not my decision. It was God's.

Step 12 was having had a spiritual awakening as a result of these steps, we tried to carry this message other addicts, and to practice these principles in all areas of our lives. Wow, this last step was supposed to be hard. But what I found out was that by the time you get to this step, you are so ready to share your story with others—especially those who are hurting in the way you were. You WANT to help others and it becomes a legacy for you to leave to others. You can't find success with addiction by yourself. Only if you help others, do you reap the rewards. By witnessing to others, your appreciation of the program and the program's impact on your life deepens. By hearing the stories of new members, you are reminded of where you were when you started. Each day is a gift—one that you choose to accept, ignore, or embrace. It's your choice.

I'm choosing to also complete this step by writing this manuscript. It's not a requirement, but it is a vehicle to healing. When complete, it means I will own my actions and my journey.

CHAPTER 18

Starting Over
Slow but Sure

After seeing therapists and attending support groups for a few months, I began to realize that the only way I could begin to put things behind me was to let go of what happened to me, especially emotionally. There was a reason I had become so vulnerable. God has always been first in my life, but I was becoming more and more aware of the fact that I was asking him to guide and direct me to follow the plan I had outlined, not the plan that he had prepared. Without accepting his plan, without even knowing his plan for me, I continued each day to do what I thought he wanted, but it was really what I wanted or maybe even wished for. In order to accept help from him and others and in order to immerse myself in therapy and self-help theories, I realized that I must travel through the grieving process first to let go of the past before I could ever give everything I had to the recovery process. Because if the truth would be known, there was still a small part of me holding on to the fantasy of love and the future that I dreamed of having. I began to realize that the five stages of grief (denial, anger, bargaining, depression, and acceptance) could help me in that journey of letting go.

As I told my story to my son for the first time, even then, I was in *denial* that I had a problem. I didn't want to believe or admit that the person I was (who was educated and mature) could allow this to happen to her, not only once but five times. As I think back now, it even looks like an act that a desperate woman might have participated in. Each time I reached out or responded to an individual, I would think that he was the one for me. I was so determined to prove to my second husband that I could be loved totally and unconditionally by someone, even if he was unable to do it. I felt sorry for myself and played the victim role. That made me just vulnerable enough to be sucked in by the first guy that came along who told me the things I wanted to hear. Maybe it was good that they only took my money and life savings. Even though I was hurt and dumbfounded by all that happened, it felt like they took a piece of my heart as well. As I look back now, I also realize that I actually thought I needed a man to complete me, a man to make me whole. I believed I needed someone who would give me unconditional love and support. I kind of got mixed up in my head that I needed someone to do all this and allow me to feel true love. It's been quite a journey, and now I realize, however, that God is the only one that can make me feel whole and complete and supported. It is God I need.

As I struggled to cope with my feelings and my heavy disappointments, I felt alone for a while as I thought about all that had happened to me. Each person I fell in love with seemed to provide something that I needed, and they appeared to fulfill a great void in my life. Even though I told myself that I would set up roadblocks to never let falling in love with someone I had not met in person, I found it happening over and over again. I would fall in love first and then open myself up by being honest, allowing the individual to open the door to my heart, where I became most vulnerable. Doing that, I believed that I would not enter into the relationship with false pretenses when actually what happened was that I set myself up as another target willing to be taken advantage of just one more time. Because I spent time praying and talking with God each day, I thought I was carrying out his plan when in reality, I was carrying out my plan. As I look back over all the circumstances that led up to changing my life and admitting to myself that I might indeed be an addict, I never once got angry with any of these perpetrators. When I look back how not one but five different men continually raped me of every cent I had, not once did I get angry. I was unable to feel that emotion toward my previous husbands, my boss, or any of the people who attacked me personally or caused me heartache in my life. I directed all *anger* toward myself. I punished myself over and over. Guilt and shame continued to haunt me, but this time, I was strong. At least that is what I kept telling myself. I knew without a doubt God was on my side, but yes, I found it hard to forgive myself. And I couldn't forgive others until I could forgive myself. It took time for me to admit, participate, welcome, accept, and work through therapy and support groups that brought me to this moment.

I am able to see things in a different light, and I am finally able to feel and see the anger (which I refused to express or feel) have a place and value in my recovery. Each one, little by little, took advantage of my kindness, honesty, sincerity, and worthiness. Because of that, I have a right to be angry with them. Will I dwell on that anger? Will I ever get past it? I pray each day that God will help those who hurt me find their own heart and learn how to repent for what they have done. I can only pray for them to seek the truth and trust God as their savior.

I even *bargained* with God to make all of this go away and let me find the one true love I was meant to be with. This person would be the one who would find a way to pay all my debts and make everything all right. In return, I would become God's servant and do whatever he asked me to do this day and every day following, now and in the future. I prayed that I would never have to tell my children, friends, or family what had happened to me and that I would never bring them additional pain or heartache. I didn't want to face the disappointed look on their faces as they realized that their mother, who had been a strong role model for them all her life, had been dishonest with them. I didn't want to set a bad example for them. And I didn't want to lose their love. Pride stood in the way for me. When I finally realized the importance of honesty in any relationship, I realized that what I abhorred about all my perpetrators was exactly what I was doing to my children, my family, and my friends. Each time I allowed a person into my life and personal space that I had not met in person, I gave them a power and value that I did not give to my own children and family. God didn't want that, and he certainly didn't encourage it.

Everyone goes through a period of self-pity and *depression* at some time in their life. I have certainly experienced this after each of my two marriages ended up in divorce. This time, I stayed in denial for the longest time. I struggled, truly struggled, to get through the next few stages of grief. I never wanted to admit that any of these lovely gentlemen who reached out to me didn't exist as their profiles told me they did. I wanted to stay in that fantasy each time and never come out of it because that would mean I would lose the prize. I believed that if I fulfilled their request for money one last time, all of this would be over, and they would be on the next plane back to me. I believed that they would keep their word to me and I would receive in return all that I loaned them and more. Even as I write this, there are some feelings in my heart telling me that the last one who vowed to rescue me will walk in the door someday. I believed that we would start our lives together as man and wife. After receiving five marriage proposals and saying yes to each one, why didn't I realize that something was not right when I had met none of these guys in person? But there I was, continuing in the same path of destruction each and every time. I didn't want to admit what was really going on because then I would have to admit I am alone and unwanted, tainted, and not good enough for the normal person to select me as a soul mate to spend their future with. Then I would sink to a low and become depressed. I was spiraling out of control but was so far gone that I didn't even recognize the black hole I was living in. That black hole became my crutch, my comfort zone, and my escape from reality. That is what depression is, even when it is disguised as something else. I never wanted to go to that place again. I avoided every warning signal and red flag that appeared in front of me just to keep my fantasy going. This fantasy I was living in kept me happy because I knew any day now my life as it had been was going to change. And this change was going to be good for me and my family. I could finally show all of them that I deserved to have true happiness forever and always. I could finally live the life I always wanted to have.

But we all know the ending to this story. To live in that world was to live in a world of fantasy and denial. And it was time for me to live in a world of honesty and *acceptance*. That is the world of truth, ecstasy, faith, and empowerment. The first thing I had to realize is that my life had become unmanageable, and I needed to turn all of it over to God and accept his help to get me back on track. Whoa! What is happening here? I think I just referred myself to the first of the twelve steps of recovery: admit to yourself and others and God that you are powerless over love addiction and your life has become unmanageable!

And that, folks, is how it happened. Life's journey has been full of bumps and bruises and wrong turns. But it has also been full of mystery, surprises, pleasantries, and peace. Because of that, there are no right turns. There are only paths of discovery. Each of these paths became an adventure. And that adventure led to sorrow and disappointment, but it also led to experiences of love and fortune. I am so happy that God allowed me to take this journey and would not change any of it simply because I am a better person now.

To better accept the consequences of what has happened to me and to help move myself forward, I have written a letter to myself. This letter is one that will pull me back into the real world if there is ever even the slight chance of me slipping with my addiction and allowing myself to go backward instead of forward.

*****

Dear B,

I am writing to you as your adult and functional/rational part of your ego, just as I am writing to you, your child/irrational/emotional part of your ego. I am doing this so that you can read this letter or have some guidance as to where you should go, what you should think, how you should act, what you should do, and yes, maybe even what you should feel when you are tempted to act out your behaviors that are not acceptable for the adult part of your ego to have or before you are tempted just one second to give up your sobriety. You need to know firstly that when you dive into the child of yourself, you become very vulnerable to others. And there are several triggers that happen when you allow yourself to become that vulnerable. While I am acting as your adult and rational part of your ego, I feel responsible to help you travel back to me instead of away from me and keep you from hurting yourself and becoming a love addict once more.

First of all, I know you are hurting because you are not getting the attention and love from someone you were used to getting it from day after day after day. This contributed to your survival, and it also contributed to your liking yourself when you had doubts about your thoughts and actions. But you need to know—and please remember this—that you are loved, no matter what ego state you are in. God loves you just because you are you. And he gave his life for you to be here today. Not only has he forgiven you for everything you have done in the past, but he wants you to be happy and content. And the only way you can do that is to love yourself. Remember that your happiness does not depend on anyone else or their actions toward you. You must believe in yourself and your ability to survive and make good healthy choices about yourself. I want you to take it just one day at a time. No one says you have to plan ahead or even know how or what you will be doing next week, next month, next year, or even tomorrow. Remember what Ken continually told you to do. Look in the mirror each and every day and tell yourself that you are loved. And you are. I am not just saying that. You have so many people pulling for you and your ability to overcome this addiction. I know you want results quickly. But this takes time. And when you start shaking and thinking about even trying to contact one of your qualifiers, I want you to remember this: You got here today where you are with a lot of hard work and effort on your part alone and with the help of the twelve-step program, your sponsor, your therapists, your family, and most of all, God. Do you want to throw that away? Of course, you don't. You don't want to look back since June 22, 2013 (your first day of sobriety), with one ounce of regret. You only want to look forward.

So if you find yourself wanting to live in the red circle again, call your sponsor, go to a meeting, call a CODA member, call your family or friends, or do something that makes you feel good about yourself. You can take your dog Lucu for a walk, go swimming in Towne Lake, work out in the gym, read your Bible, go window shopping, drive to the beach or boardwalk, visit a friend in need, clean out your storage, plan a trip, work on finances, or anything else you can think of. And yes, don't forget to write in your journal about these feelings you have. You will be surprised that once you write them down, you will find yourself disbelieving that you are really wanting to go that direction. And that alone can help you walk away from those thoughts.

I want you to remember that even though you are thinking if harm should come to your qualifier and he doesn't make it, it is not and was not your fault. You did not ask him to go do what he did. He made that choice on his own. And now it is your turn to make choices on your own and do what is best for you. And that, my dear, is to think before you act and realize that you have no actual proof that any of these men are who they say they are, and it is time you put behind you any chances of wanting to find anything out about them. They are now in your past and part of your addiction. So please take my advice and talk to me before you act. This could save your life! Believe me.

Love, B

*****

Each time I even think of slipping, I pull this letter out of my purse and read it one more time. And each time that I read it, I become closer and closer to accepting the reality of what has happened to me.

CHAPTER 19

And Life Begins Once More

What does it mean to begin life once more? I asked myself this question over and over. My heart has been broken so many times. Is it even available for love in the future? How do I know if it's the real thing versus only part of an addiction or fantasy that I once wanted to complete in a fairy tale?

I do know this much. Moving forward is not an easy task, and it is very challenging.

Learning to forgive myself, trusting my feelings, and eventually trusting others will always be a big deal for me because of the emotional abuse I endured for many years in the past.

Do I hope and want true love? Of course, I do. I don't think a person ever gives up on that. But caution will always be a part of my vocabulary and a part of my actions. I remember once telling myself it is better to have loved and lost than never to have loved at all. I believed in this statement. No matter how hurt I was and no matter how manipulated I became, this was all part of my journey in life. Sometimes, you just have to learn to enjoy the ride and never count on the outcome you want, hope, or wish for because God may have planned a completely different scenario for you.

It was the day after Thanksgiving (Black Friday), and I asked my daughter if I could have a word with her privately. She agreed to sit down and talk with me. I shared with her the amount of despair I felt during my last hospitalization because I thought it might be my last day on earth. I didn't want to go to heaven without knowing that my son and daughter would be okay. I was fortunate enough to have my son beside me in the emergency room, and I took a moment and asked him to forgive me for all the grief and disappointment I had caused him but also for lying to him about my previous actions and happenings. Fortunately, he assured me that he had put everything behind us, and he was able to focus on living in the present and future. I was so grateful to hear that and was able to find peace in his response. I knew that with my time being uncertain, I needed to hear that from my daughter also.

Because of all the disappointment and grief she feels I caused her or brought into her life, she informed me that she could not find it in her heart to forgive me, and she did not want me to bring up the subject or have these kind of talks anymore on the topic of forgiveness. She informed me that she had lost all respect for me and could never put what I had done to her behind her. Even though I begged for forgiveness and admitted to all the wrongdoings I had done, her heart remained bitter and angry toward me. When she told me that she could never forgive me for the lies I told her or the fact that I had never put her first in my life, I began to feel that guilt and shame all over again. It took every ounce of courage I had not to be pulled back into that demon world of addiction and to realize once again that all of what she was saying was her perception of what has happened in her life. There was no breaking through the wall she had built up between us. That did disappoint me, to say the least. I had to tell myself all over again that she is an adult now, and I am not responsible for the way she feels. She is responsible for her feelings, and only she can change that perspective. Bitterness has taken over her life and our relationship. As she informed me that we would never have the relationship we once had and that her husband told her that she would not keep me from seeing my grandchildren, I couldn't help but feel sad. I did not want to lose my daughter, and I certainly did not want to lose access to my grandchildren. I have always felt the

Lord by my side, and I knew he would never allow me to suffer that much. But maybe the truth is I have already lost her.

Why can't I talk with her instead of wanting her to share my journey or read this manuscript?

Why do I text a response to receiving a picture from her instead of talking to her in person? Why have I not told her my story? Why am I talking to my ex?

How can I fix this so we can have a fresh start? Her response to this question was to stop talking to my ex-husband and remove him from my communication totally. I explained that forgiveness is found in many forms. And forgiving my ex gave me peace and allowed me to move forward and not stay in the past. Staying in touch tells her that she has never and will continue to never be a priority in my life. This, to her, seems to justify all her actions and feelings she shows toward me. All of these thoughts were words popping from her mouth to me. She said my ex told her he hoped she would die so he could piss on her grave. "What kind of mother could or would ever have a relationship with a man like that? You never protected me. We will never get back what we had because I will never forgive you. I am doing my part because I send you pictures of your grandchildren. I allow you time to visit. And the only reason I came here for Thanksgiving was you. You could act more grateful. You could be more grateful. I don't want to have a Christmas like this. I have to explain to people why you don't come and help me. I have no idea what to say because you think other people don't need to know what you have done." I simply told her if anyone has a problem and needs answers, just ask them to contact me and I will talk with them.

Does it hurt to know my daughter doesn't want anything to do with me? Of course, it hurts. I am very, very grateful to her and her husband for allowing me to see and spend time with the grandchildren. They give me such hope, joy, and peace within, not to mention love. Will not talking to my ex change anything? I really don't think so. I divorced him over thirteen years ago, and after that, I did not see my children any more than I had seen them (maybe even less) before I was divorced. I waited over a year to see him again, and it didn't make a difference. Both he and I have kept in touch, and we both have had major medical issues to deal with. Does talking to him make him or me a terrible person? I don't think so. I feel that when we talk, it is like going back forty-one years when we first met and became friends. We've formed a special bond and a touching friendship between us, one that accepts forgiveness and understands that it is best to put the past where it is—in the past. I will always have a feeling of love for him simply because we shared twenty-six years of marriage. I've tried to come to grips with all the negative feelings and only dwell on the positive feelings. After going through this experience, my ex became the only person who was always there for me, my new confidant, no judgment, no questions, just love and acceptance. If I had had this during our marriage, we would still be together. I trust him more now than I ever did. He gives without expecting anything in return.

It's time to start living the new normal. The journey begins once more to love myself by accomplishing my hardest goal ever—to forgive myself and move on while bringing hope to others through Christ so they can come to find and feel the peace I have found that lies within us. I know that someday, my children and I will reconnect according to God's plan, not mine.

Is there anything greater than love?

Gary M. Douglas wrote on May 6, 2013 the following:

> In a simple answer, there is. *Gratitude*. To have gratitude for someone means to have no judgment of them or you. With gratitude, you can be grateful for someone, whether or not they are being kind, happy, sad, angry, or anything else they're choosing. With love, there is always judgment. There are expectations of what you must be and do to show you love someone.

This statement spells it out clearly. We all want so badly to be loved, or at least that's what we think. The truth is that, we really want gratitude. Acquiring that may be the answer we all are looking for.

CHAPTER 20

A Second Chance

In 2013, I filed for bankruptcy. Time seemed to pass by slowly, but I am forever thankful to my son and to the government for giving me a new start. I know how important it is to meet someone in person, and if I am ever fortunate enough to have that happen, if I am lucky enough to find true love, I will grab it, cherish it, and hold on to it as if I found the greatest treasure on earth. God has been good to me. Mental and emotional trauma affected me in ways I didn't know was possible. Good health has become the top priority to me so that I can become all I can be physically, emotionally, mentally, socially, and spiritually. It wasn't easy listening to my son's advice that I might have to file for bankruptcy. That would be the all-time low, and I had already taken all the safety measures to protect myself. I had enlisted the services of Freedom Debt Consolidation Company (following my bank's advice) and was making regular monthly payments to them to pay all the negotiated balances left on all the credit cards.

After my son gave me a website that would link me to government-approved debt consolidation and credit companies, I found out the company that I had enlisted was not approved by the government and had a personal agenda of collecting fees for themselves rather than helping you reduce your balance in debt. In reality, they had kept me posted and had negotiated three major accounts down to less than a third of what I owed them. So I thought they were doing their job pretty well.

After talking to two attorneys and a credit counselor approved by the government, it was decided that my best action would be to file bankruptcy. My debts were too large to guarantee that they could be paid off with monthly payments, at least with my monthly income and my proposed life expectancy. In real life, as I was building up my debt by sending money I didn't have to men I had not met, I never once thought that I would be left with all this debt by myself. I had allowed each suitor to convince me that every debt would be paid off with the gold or money they sent to repay the loan upon their return to the States in two weeks.

Once again, that pride slipped in, and it was hard for me to admit that I needed to take this kind of action. I was always an independent woman and didn't need the help of someone financially and certainly never wanted to have a poor credit score. But now my score was low, as low as you could get. To quote the counselor and the lawyers, "The worst thing that happens to you if you file bankruptcy is that you will receive a low credit score." Noting that I already had achieved that, why would I feel bad about getting a chance to start life over? A second chance. This appeared to be my only solution because I did not receive enough monthly income to be able to pay off the credit cards and loans I had encountered. I felt so ignorant that I did not realize that I needed to pay the IRS a quarterly amount, a simple result of cashing in my IRAs, etc., so I was fined for that. I made sure that never happened again. I continued to make payments to the IRS to make sure that I no longer owed the federal government. My goal was to complete that task before the first of the year. Thankfully, I was able to reach that goal and actually not even include it on the day that I filed bankruptcy. Oddly enough, my ex-husband, who had been very supportive and understanding throughout this process, actually deposited enough money into my checking account in West Virginia to pay off the loan from a company called Plain Green which had very high interest rates. My advice to anyone would be to stay away from that loan company or anyone like them. I guess a another name for them would be loan shark. You receive the money immediately but have to repay it within two weeks or be charged an exorbitant amount of interest (higher than credit cards). Quickly, the payments and interest add up to at least five times the amount you borrowed.

My ex continued to show complete unconditional love toward me without judgment or condemnation, something that was missing during our entire twenty-six years of marriage, but something I longed for from him since the day I said "I do." After providing documents that were needed and proof of income, I started the process.

I have to admit that it was such a relief just to have the credit card collecting agencies begin to contact and call the law firm and not me anymore. If I had not accrued such good credit over the years, I could never have mounted up such a high dollar amount to owe. For almost two years, they were relentless and would call repeatedly every day and every night over and over. Even when I would agree to make a payment, one hour later, they would call and request even more. I became so paranoid I began to quit answering the phone.

The lawyer required a payment of 1,800 dollars before they could begin the process. Then they would file within the week. Just as everything else has bumps in the road, this one did too. They told me we couldn't file for several months since I had received some inheritance from my father (which was immediately handed over to the most recent scammer). After contacting them in November and letting them know I had just been released from the hospital, they said we would file after January 1. I met with them in two weeks, and bankruptcy was filed in the US Bankruptcy Court of Texas later that afternoon.

Nerves and concerns continue to build because I know not to count my chickens before they are hatched. As I patiently waited for this action to become official, I continually worked on my monthly budget as per the lawyer's request. I was to meet with representatives of all the creditors four to five weeks following the filing date. The whole case would be finished in ninety days' time. On that date, my ex called and told me he had received a discharge notice. I hadn't received mine yet, but when I picked up the mail, the notice was there for me and my son. It was finally over, even though I knew it would take seven to ten years to get my good credit reputation back.

That night, my son and I had a sit-down heart-to-heart talk. We listed our expectations from one another and our visions and goals for the future. He let me know that all he wanted was for me to become healthy financially, mentally, and physically. I told him that was what I wanted also. We agreed I would return to counseling so that I could gain more skills in talking with him and my daughter. I seemed to break down very easily and felt defensive when either of them talked to me, obviously still feeling guilt and shame. Besides I almost felt as if I was being attacked and would never be forgiven for the stunts I had pulled. Trust seemed to be the biggest issue. When I told my son I had already saved $8,000, he was pleased but wanted to scan my finances in case I needed assistance in making wiser choices for the future. He informed me he did not want any rent or money from me. He just wanted me to build security for the future and prepare for the day I would be moving out of his home and be on my own.

I realized I had not forgiven myself, and that was proving very hard to do. Sometimes, it is so hard to describe what you are feeling. But that does not mean the feeling does not exist. It hurts down to the very core of your being. When I am alone and no one else is around, I finally figured out as I write these words that I am not alone. God is here, and it is easier to talk to him than anyone else. Not only does he provide the unconditional love I am seeking, but he fails to judge my actions. He forgives me without question and continues to give me guidance, love, and hope for the future. Knowing all that does seem to comfort me. But the pain I am describing that is so deep, whether he recognizes it or not, is one that I am so familiar with. I have been known for having such a positive outlook and making upbeat comments to others. What others don't know is that I had to work at that. Being positive was not coming easy for me, even though that is the perception I wanted to give them. I wanted them to know all was okay. I was healing and doing all right.

The times I feel this pain deep in my heart ended up affecting every organ in my body. One day, I choked on the pills I was taking. I could not get my breath. I struggled so hard to make the one that was stuck to come out. I realized at that moment that not only do you fear death, but your life once again actually starts flashing before your eyes. I have always admired the way I welcomed death and that it would be my one chance to live an everlasting life serving my God. But in that moment, for some reason, I must not have been ready to leave this earth. Because gasping for breath and praying for God to give me more life became the priority. Priority. What does that mean? The one thing you most want to do or have happen. That is priority.

It took seven months to recover from all my physical health problems. Losing that independence I had discovered by getting better and moving to Texas was something that has deeply affected me. It comes close to killing me to ask for help. Why? Because when I do, I have to do it over and over. There are even times when I detect an attitude or resentment toward me as if I have become a burden to those around me. So even when I am weak, even when I know I am having a rough time, it's so difficult for me to feel like I am not a burden and imposing on someone else's time and effort. I guess I'm referring to the Lord knowing what I want at all times, so he is always there for me. It hurts and sometimes makes me feel forgotten when no one takes time or cares to check on me. Even though my son checked on me faithfully as soon as he got home from work each day while I was living with him, he also accused me of having a pity party each time he saw a sad look on my face. And yes, I have pride and sometimes fail to demonstrate how much I need and appreciate all their efforts and love that they show me each day. The day they told me I was a burden to them hurt like nothing else had ever hurt. I knew that those words would stick with me forever, especially coming from my children, and that I had to make plans to become independent again and start my life over without depending on someone else again. No one wants to feel like a burden. But if it happens to you, you never forget it. Your goal becomes one to carve out a life for yourself so that you can be true to yourself once again. You don't want to play the role of the child and your child play the role of a parent. You want to remove that disappointed look your child gives you each time you make a connection and prove to him/her that you can and will make it on your own once again.

As I took care of my father, I showed up every day and gave him all the care I could. And he knew, even when he told me to go home, that I would be back and I would be there for him, no matter what. I knew he was grateful for anything I did for him. Even though I was so grateful to have my children and their love and the grace of their allowing me to live with them, it was very hard knowing that my stay with them was a burden on them.

I'm not sure if this is grieving or a pity party. But as I spend more time alone, I realize how I was able to be taken advantage of by all the men on the dating sites. They gave me what I needed. I felt so empty inside and thought all I had to do was send them money after they asked for it. And for that moment, money became less and less important to me. Fulfilling my need to be loved became more important to me.

It's funny about pain. I remember when I took all those pills after my first marriage failed. That was the way to self-inflict pain, and yet I used them as a way to escape the pain.

My life can be anything I want it to be. The only problem is that my health seems to control what I am able to do and who I am able to do it with. The desperation that comes along with that pain is also indescribable. Of all the men I communicated with, the two I really fell for were George and Roland. I kept hoping that Roland would still find a way to come to my door. Then I could show him how very much I love him. We traveled through thick and thin, ups and downs, and over the meadow and back again. It was he that I spent so much time on the phone with and falling more in love each time we talked. He was my hero. And even though I received counseling for the codependent addiction I had, I still loved him and wanted to be with him. I would go back and play his voicemails just to hear his voice. I guess down deep, I believed in him and believed in us. I would drive by a house I looked at for us to live in and think of him. I would pass a car I was looking to buy for us, and I think of him. I would go to church and see the name Roland on the musical keyboard, and I think of him. I would crawl in bed each night and touch the pillow on the other half of the bed, and I think of him. He still had my heart. I had officially turned over the gold that was in my name to him, so I believed that he would show up one day with that gold and pay off all my debts, including my son's.

It was obvious to me I had a lot of recovering to still do. I had to turn to God to be the one who decides what happens to me next. I am someone who needs the company of the opposite sex to feel good about myself. That is what codependence is. Not that I need it to be happy. I thought I needed it to feel good about myself and fulfill the sexual urges and adoration that I deserved to experience.

They say it is textbook that you will do anything to make the pain stop. If that means doing something that is against all reason or doing something that would hurt you or possibly someone else, you end up doing it just to remove the pain. But what you find out is you never remove the pain. It is always there. You can only control how deep that pain is and change your perception about how to deal with it. You have to come up with healthy solutions not only to deal with all that pain but form a plan describing how to reach those solutions.

It has been years since I heard Roland's voice on the voicemail. They've all been removed. I stopped responding to any phone calls if I thought they were from him because I did not want to compromise my sobriety. I remember that last conversation with him. Absolutely no one understands how I felt about him and how I longed to be with him.

I attended therapy consistently and went to a twelve-step recovery meeting several times a week. I learned that twelve steps were the same with any addiction, but you had to stay faithful to the cause, meaning that you had to be constantly aware of those twelve steps and follow them. It doesn't mean that you won't slip every now and then, but with commitment and action, every person who attended those meetings became your support group. Whether it was love anonymous, codependent anonymous, alcoholics anonymous, or any other group anonymous, you received encouragement to keep working. I learned I will always be that addict, but I would be a recovering addict. The odd part is that I have no desire to be with a person or gentleman on the internet. The addiction, per se, was not a problem for me. The real challenge was getting rid of the shame and judgment you placed on yourself.

It wasn't that long ago that I felt like each day was a long day. And the day was hard because no one seemed to understand what I was going through. I thought it would help if I wrote my feelings down as opposed to holding them inside. I felt so alone. And it was such a familiar feeling. That feeling I got every time I reached out to search for my soul mate. And when someone reached back to me, I accepted what they called love too easily and too readily.

I went to that lonely place once more. I became so vulnerable but had no desire to act out and look for a soul mate because I was feeling the guilt and shame of not deserving to find that love that I thought existed just for me to enjoy. I have so much love to give. Living in my son's house made me appreciate everything they were doing for me. Of course, I appreciated all their support and their willingness to let me stay there until I straightened up all my affairs. I know they thought I was ungrateful for what they had done for me. I know they saw my actions as a betrayal to them. I interpreted that action as disappointment, judgment, and frustration toward me. I seemed to have no answers. And even though I would ask for something, I felt I didn't deserve it and I was still nothing but a burden to them. I didn't ask to get so sick that I was hospitalized. I didn't ask for a long recovery. But God chose to give that to me. I believe that God gave me extra time to recover so I could get over my addiction as well as spiritual and physical healing for my body. It seems like I will be paying for the actions I committed for the rest of my life. And the relationship I once had with my children is forever gone, forever in the past. I've been accused of living in the past and not the present or the future. And maybe I assume all the blame and the guilt along with the shame for all my actions. And even though I think God has forgiven me, I know I have to be patient and accept the fact that whatever happens, it is God's plan, not my plan, that determines the future and the timeline for my children's forgiveness.

I am tired of being ill. I am tired of not being able to do the things I need to do to live. But I am not tired of loving God and appreciating all the blessings he has bestowed upon me. The fact that is evident always is that God is beside me and walks and talks with me.

To learn it's not all about me, no matter how scared, how hurt, how disappointed, how frustrated, and how unloved, or lonely you feel, remember there is always someone else worse off than you. And it is your responsibility to reach out to others and share the wisdom you have acquired during this long journey. Someone is always by your side, and that someone else is God and others, others who need me, others who need God in their lives and haven't discovered a way to find him. The only way you can have freedom, the only way you can find peace, the only way you can find love and forgiveness is to put your life totally and completely into God's hands. This and this alone will most certainly help you start the long journey ahead.

Only in America can we be given a second chance to have a fresh start. Filing chapter 7 bankruptcy and ending up being a no-asset case made everything go fairly smooth for me. When I went to see the lawyer to give her my updated documents from banking statements, income changes, regular monthly bills, and the most recent credit card statements, I felt a little apprehensive. Can this really be happening to me? Will I truly never hear from any of these men again who I not only gave my heart to but gave my last penny and life savings to? Am I truly alone in this process of starting over again?

My son received another promotion in his job. I was so very proud of him. Yet I know in my heart how disappointed he is that his very own mother could be experiencing such undeniable emotional pain and suffering. Did I hate being a burden to him? Of course, I did because I caused him to worry. But I also know that down deep, he loves me and he is trying to do all he can to take care of me, provide for me, and protect me. That shouldn't be his job right now. He's got enough to be worried about. He is quite a role model to be around. Even when stress is at its highest point with him, he does his best not to let it affect our relationship. In fact, the only time I remember him getting angry with me was when he found out what I had done and again when I did not inform him of my deteriorating condition. And it wasn't about what I had done as much as it was about my lying to him and keeping him abreast of my actions and whereabouts while I lived under his roof. I have to believe that this was what put a wall up between my daughter and me also.

We all want to fix others, but we can't. That is the hardest lesson to learn. And that's what I had to learn for myself many years earlier. Today I am very proud of my son and daughter, not only of what they have become but of what they have done also. Tough love is hard, but it is necessary, whether it comes from the parent or the child.

Completing each step of the bankruptcy trial has certainly made me evaluate the situation I have been in and actually placed myself in. I blame no one but myself for being vulnerable to men who waited on the sidelines of the dating game to take advantage of a woman such as me. And only after attending the hearing for bankruptcy did I actually and finally face the consequences of all my actions. Only God can rescue me. Only God can be on my side. It was he who allowed me to forgive myself so I could go on living my life. As I waited those last ten months for Roland to appear and to experience the glory of giving myself to the only one I love, I finally realized that I was alone once again to face the world. My next challenge was to learn how to embrace the world and all it had to offer me. What is my passion? What is my vision? What are my desires? That is my next goal—to find it and to embrace it as I live life to the fullest. Do I have moments of doubt and confusion? Of course, I do. I am allowed to have those moments. I don't think I would appreciate the value and the goodness of having God in my life if I didn't experience both highs and lows in my life. And because of those highs and lows, I am able to keep growing. I want to discover the passion that lies deep within my soul. I want to feel the height of emotion once again someday. I want to give back and pay forward.

Moving forward and letting go. What does that mean? It's hard to do. But I think it means the final acceptance that none of these men were real, including Roland. It means that I have the opportunity to start over, to begin anew. Only I can do that. Only I can choose to complete the grieving process.

Filing for bankruptcy truly completed that process and allowed me to start over again. It's like graduating from college and getting my first teaching job with a salary of five thousand per year. My pension is more than that now, so if I was able to begin my life after

I graduated from college, I can do the same now. I have a chance to find myself again and to discover my real passion—reaching out to others. I can figure out how I want to do that.

Reading God's Word each morning and each night is the only way to bring that peace and serenity I have been longing for into my heart, my life, and my soul. In order to help others, I must first help myself. And doing that means allowing God to do his work, allowing God into my heart.

The process of filing for bankruptcy court is over, and it's time to begin again, time to start over. I remember when I graduated from college and received that first check for working in summer school. I had just gotten married and was beginning my life as it should be without my parents and family being responsible for my well-being. Now it was my responsibility to take care of myself, to manage my own affairs, to live within a budget, and to have a positive outlook toward the future and take advantage of any opportunity that came to me. This time in my life is relative to that moment I lived over fifty years ago. And as long as I maintain the same enthusiasm, the same drive, and the same character to approach the future that lies ahead, I know life will be good.

As I waited for my name to be called at the bankruptcy hearing at the US Federal Bankruptcy Court in Houston, Texas, I wondered why my lawyer wasn't sitting by my side to prepare me for the questions I would be asked in the hearing. And then I heard my name. I slowly turned and announced that my lawyer was not present yet and that I did not feel comfortable going into the hearing without her. The trustee said he would wait a little for her to show up. I called the law firm's office to make sure that someone was definitely going to be there for me. They assured me that my lawyer was on her way and had been tied up in another hearing. When the trustee announced my name one more time, I informed him that she was on her way, and he instructed us to come in immediately upon her arrival.

This was my first time in a hearing of this sort, and of course, I was feeling very anxious about it. The outcome of this hearing was going to determine the path of my future. The good part was that the trustee made me feel comfortable and made sure I did not feel intimidated by him or the circumstances. I answered all the questions asked to the best of my knowledge. The items that he did not have documentation for were to be provided to him within ten days, and we would reconvene at the end of those ten days. The entire hearing only took forty-five minutes, and I was informed that the order for discharge would be issued in twenty days. After that time, I would begin my life again. Only in America can a citizen be given this second chance for surviving. I will never be proud of the fact that I allowed five different men to scam me and talk me into giving them every cent I had. I would always be reminded that my entire retirement fund was distributed to people I had never met in person.

When I had my meeting with the creditors to file bankruptcy, the presiding judge was so supportive and understanding. As I gather the additional documentation to prove that this journey to bankruptcy began when I became romantically involved with men I had never met, I realized something that had not occurred or happened to me before. When the judge wanted me to prove to him or provide some kind of evidence that I indeed wired or gave away large sums of money to men who were conducting their business and relationship with me out of the country, I did not expect myself to react the way I did. Once more, telling my story to a complete stranger brought tears to my eyes and unsettled me quite extensively. But the act of actually going to the bank and requesting documentation that this act of mine actually took place seemed to offer some comfort and explanation at the same time to me. Finally, the thought of any one of these men arriving at my door seemed even less than possible now. In fact, after obtaining the documentation, it was as if the door to all these relationships was finally going to be closed. When I met with the lawyer to prepare for the reconvening of the meeting with the judge, I expected (and rightfully so) to be able to begin my life again, to have a fresh start, and put all of this behind me. There was finally a calmness and serenity that came over my whole being. And yet a feeling of jubilation exists that I was able to embrace the freedom the filing of bankruptcy allowed me to do. God bless America! This must be the only country in the world that allows its citizens to be forgiven of debts beyond our control and be given a second chance to live again without fear and continual taunting of those creditors that took a chance with you and ended up losing thousands of dollars because of your mistakes.

What I have realized is that I am a totally different person now. Not only because of my encounter with life and death but also with the fact that I now have nothing in savings for emergencies and have no assets to account for anything. I appreciate each breath I take and each moment I am given here on earth. Life is a gift, and you have to make the most of every second of it. I opened up a bank account to make monthly deposits to build my nest egg and give me hope for starting a new life.

Over seven years have passed, and I have put my former life in the past. My credit is good, and I am living on my own in Pennsylvania. I am blessed to have a good relationship with my daughter and look forward to living each day to the fullest. I continue to work on building up my energy and endurance so that I can face physical challenges ahead. When and if I decide to begin dating again, I will proceed with caution. I now know why you can be led astray when feeling vulnerable at the same time. I continue to have a good relationship with my ex-husband and continue to grow in faith each day.

The wedding dress that I purchased will be put away in a box in the back of the closet, never to be used but will serve as a reminder for me to remember that men such as those who scammed me no longer exist, not in my mind and not in this world because they will never have a chance to make me one of their victims again. That dress will never be worn. It is only a symbol of what can happen to you if you choose to fall in love with the idea of love without meeting that special someone in person.

It was time to move forward. Time to put this chapter in my life behind me. In order to move forward, I needed to get back to being involved in college classes, senior center activities, church activities, and life. I knew that if I could throw myself into something I am passionate about, I would begin to recover faster and more completely.

I struggle with health problems (COPD, asthma, vertigo, hypertension, and glaucoma) that prevent me from living the quality of life that I truly desire. I enjoy traveling and have taken several trips to enjoy what America has to offer. As soon as my health condition improves, I will never forget that *life is a journey. Enjoy it!* I have moved into a retirement community in Lancaster, Pennsylvania, near my daughter. Years have passed, and I am reminded again that every day is a gift, and the gift is knowing God.

This chapter ends with a grateful American citizen proud to be an American who has been given a second chance. My total loss in less than four years was over half a million dollars, enough to afford a comfortable retirement. But because of my ignorance and actions in this matter, I had nothing and had to start my life over again knowing I had thrown away my future. (Thank goodness for social security and monthly pension!) God provided a path for me, and that path led me to Lancaster, Pennsylvania. He gave me a new start and allowed me to humbly appreciate all that is provided to me. Each day is a gift, and I am hoping that the second chance given to me allows me the opportunity to grow, prosper, and share what I have learned from this total experience. I thank God for being a part of it and being there for me as long as I live. Without him, I would never have been able to see through all the smoke and mirrors of deceit and fraud. A clear mind along with a clear view finally allowed me the luxury of living my life as part of God's plan and realizing how much I have been blessed. It's a cruel world we live in—only if we let that world control us. If we put our lives in God's hands, that same world becomes uplifting, inspirational, hopeful, and inviting. It's up to us to embrace it.

Here are six steps to follow in order to keep your sanity and conscience intact. They've helped me, and hopefully they will help others.

1. Keep God as number one in your life by going to church, listening to outstanding sermons, and embracing the spiritual growth that takes place by just being there.
2. Pray the serenity prayer each and every day.

3. Surround yourself with other believers in God and welcome the nonbelievers so you can assume the role of sharing the word and leading them to Christ.
4. Participate in a Bible study each week to allow yourself the opportunity to grow in faith by studying his word and being challenged by followers of Christ.
5. Attend a twelve-step support and recovery group any time you feel you are getting weak or experience an urge to find a soulmate on the Internet.
6. Live each day like you are dying and rejoice about all the blessings you have received.

I know in time my children and their spouses will be able to forgive me and put this entire saga behind us. I'm not foolish enough to think they will ever forget because I myself will never forget the trials and tribulations of this experience. It is a project in progress, and with God's help someday, we will be a family again, respecting one another free of judgment and criticism, moving forward with nothing but a spirit of unity and love.

Until then, I am comforted when I read Psalm 27:14... *Wait patiently for the Lord. Be brave and courageous. Yes, wait patiently for the Lord.*

FEELINGS AND AFTERTHOUGHTS

Why is it when you love someone, they think they have the right to hurt you over and over again? I remember one night hurting so bad that I was willing to do anything to take away that hurt. You feel so alone. Your self-worth is zero. You can't find any reason to live because living means feeling the pain—pain that will not go away and is with you 24-7. You blame yourself for not being a better wife, a better mother, a better friend, a better coworker, a better person while trying to maintain the image of having it altogether when you are at work or when you are out among your friends and family.

I know that I am not the only senior who was taken advantage of in this manner. It is my hope that this story will help someone who longs for love but learns to wisely choose his/her course of action to find it before damage is done as it was to me. You might even recognize a few emails sent to you that were sent to me. I also learned that the heartbreak of working with local, state, and federal law enforcement to enlist their help in finding these perpetrators opened my eyes to the fact that we are alone in the world when seeking retribution and are left to our own resources to heal, as well as stay motivated to move forward with your life. Cyber scams and online fraud seem to be a way of life now, and we are the collateral damage.

B. F. Christman is the author of the new nonfiction novel *At First Click*. Being a retired educator and school counselor who spent a lifetime helping others, she was able to gain the insight needed to understand and cope with life's hardest challenges. She received her bachelor of science in family resources and master of arts degree in counseling psychology from West Virginia University. Enjoying traveling and experiencing new adventures, BF has traveled to over twelve different countries and almost forty different states in the USA. Growing up in the West Virginia Hills and moving to the Yellow Rose of Texas did not cut her any breaks when dealing with relationships of the opposite sex.

As a mother of two, grandmother of three, and one of six siblings, she possessed the background needed to face all trials and tribulations continually thrust at her. Hitting bottom and left with nothing to begin life's remaining journey, she experienced the importance of embracing God in her life to give her the clarity of becoming a survivor and not a victim.